FOREWORD BY CHEL

"*Real, vulnerable, relatable, pe*

HOPE *for* SECONDHAND SUFFERING™

TOOLS FOR THE HEART WHEN YOU CAN'T FIX YOUR LOVED ONE'S PAIN

CAMILLE BLOCK

Hardback ISBN: 978-1-963922-06-6
Paperback ISBN: 978-1-963922-00-4
Ebook: ISBN: 978-1-963922-05-9

Copy-edited by Jennifer Edwards, jedwardsediting.net
Cover Artist by Allison Teal Lewis, tealpatrickart.com
Photography by DebbieWaltonPhotography.com
Graphic Design Cover by Sharon Marta Creative
Select Design Elements, Maddie Spear

Dedication

To my brother, Kevin.

Words on paper will never convey the depth of my love for you and my empathy for your difficult life's journey. Yet still, you have lived it with more joy than many people who have been given everything. Your heart has been and forever will be entwined with mine as we have shared the two sides of deep suffering. And you have taught me some of life's greatest lessons and caused me to experience some of life's richest emotions.

Table of Contents

Acknowledgements

I'd like to acknowledge many people that are a part of my "village" of support. Without them, I wouldn't be who I am and would not have completed this book.

Bar none, without the full support of my college sweetheart husband, Jonathan, I would never have accomplished this book. He believed in me when I didn't. He saw something in me that I didn't. And because of his faith in me, his encouragement and support in every way, I was able to take this passion project and personal memoir to a full-fledged published book that I believe will add to an important cultural conversation and hopefully, help others. Fun fact – my husband heard about my brother through mutual friends long before we ever met. So, in a strange way, my brother played a role in our early connection.

My dad, Jere Yates, is a wonderful father and a huge part of my life. Ever since I began writing, right after my mom unexpectedly died at a young 73 years old, my dad has been one of my biggest cheerleaders for me to finish this book. I think he has read about five versions by now. In addition, my grown children hold my heart and their support for me, and their Uncle Kevin, means so much. Madeline, Abigail and Oliver have grown up honoring their uncle with regular visits, helping out when needed, praying for him with every crisis and each took a role in some sort of volunteer activity including visits to the facility with her high school group (Madeline), leading a successful musical fundraiser and singing and playing guitar for the residents (Abigail) or taking on various service functions out of his compassion for people like Kevin such as Special Olympics or The Ability Experience, his fraternity organization supporting those with special needs (Oliver). I also appreciate Madeline providing some social media coaching and a shout out to her husband and my son-in-law, Ingram, for his constant love and support to our family!

My brother Brian has always been there for Kevin when needed. Kevin adores him and enjoys watching Brian's daughter, Kevin's (and my) niece Avery, grow up. When Kevin had Covid and was isolated in a hospital for 20 days, Brian agreed to visit him daily and help "be his voice." It was not an easy environment wearing a complete hazmat-like suit daily. I also want to acknowledge my precious mom – now in her heavenly home until we meet again. She suffered greatly from Kevin's difficult life but always loved him deeply and taught me much about a mother's unconditional and strong love for her children, and grandchildren. We all miss her greatly.

My friend Karen Armstrong gets a special shout out for her always available compassionate care for Kevin and visits – especially when he was hospitalized for eight straight weeks when his life was on the line. Without her, my dad, brother and I could not have made it through those painful days and nights. And without my dear longtime friend Chelsea Cameron, I am sure this book would have never moved past its first draft. She saw something in my original writing and cheered me on to continue working on it for the last 10 years. She has been a huge encourager and a compassionate supporter of me and my brother Kevin over the years. She, her husband Kirk, and their entire family have modeled well how to give a purpose to their own secondhand suffering by hosting families with (often) terminally ill children to a life-giving annual family camp experience called Camp Firefly.

Thank you wholeheartedly to Kevin's incredible main doctor, Jonathan Nasseri, MD, who never tires of giving his best to Kevin, despite his very complicated health issues. He is a "difference maker" in my brother's life as he works with me to ensure quality of life is valued as a part of his health goals. And a huge thank you to the nurses of all levels and all shifts – your compassionate care, sacrificial work and love for my brother is forever esteemed.

I find it hard to find words for the dear angel-like caregivers who keep my brother alive and give him a reason to get up each day. These direct care staff members and nurses have the hardest job of performing those daily tasks associated with caring for a nonverbal quadriplegic person. While there are too many incredible souls to list, you know who you are. You mean the world to me and my brother, and you are doing a service that only someone with the heart of God would do.

I'm so very grateful for my dear friends in my prayer/life groups who constantly surround me with encouragement, prayers and beautiful friendships as we "do life" together. Many of you kept me from losing my mind during those those very dark days of the "Covid years" and supported my continued efforts to champion my brother's rights, even when nothing seemed to be working. You validated my advocacy, and you made me feel seen - something I learned is a huge help for secondhand sufferers.

One of the most fun surprises on this book journey was meeting and working with my cover artist, Allison Lewis. Beginning with a serendipitous encounter when we first "bumped into each other" at a conference, I have so enjoyed our relationship moving from working through a creative art process to now becoming great friends, sharing our lives together regularly. Allison went above and beyond to make this artistic cover something meaningful that captures the emotions expressed in this book. She is also an inspiring and talented artist worth following!

A special thank you to Brad Cummings for helping me define and cast a vision for the concept of secondhand suffering. And to Amy Downing, aka "The Creative Farm Girl," my friend/neighbor/writer who is always open to late evening questions about grammar, writing or just about anything. And I'm so thankful for Kristen Cummins who invested the time to read my manuscript twice over and help me through a significant obstacle in my final months of writing. And I'm grateful for my crazy, wild, fun friend Nancy Jones who brings out my inner joy through deep belly laughing (and sometimes snorting) more than anyone else – she has taught me much about living a life of joy, even when going through difficult trials.

I'm very grateful to have worked with a fabulous editor, Jennifer Edwards. Not only did she do a fantastic job with book editing, something completely new to me, but she also was an inspiring coach, encourager and became a friend along the way.

During the final stages of writing this book, I lost a dear friend. I'd like to honor Pam for her support of my advocacy efforts and my brother Kevin. She always had a very tender heart towards him, and she and her husband Vince have been an incredible support for us through all of our battles. I miss her so much, but our goodbye was not final.

I want to thank ALL of my endorsers – they each took time to read my unfinished manuscript, provide their feedback/endorsement and stand with me in this effort. Each of them is an incredible human being and a successful professional in their field of work. I am grateful beyond words for their support. And I'm so appreciative for Yvonne Noblitt for her support and "author coaching" as well as to Jessica Suggs for her invaluable help with marketing when I faced the daunting task of a book launch.

Finally, I'm grateful for a serendipitous introduction by author Steven Maddox to Jeremy Butrous at Radiant Publishing. Both saw something in the topic and my story and Jeremy was a divine surprise to get my project to the finish line as my publisher.

Foreword

Camille's three children and my own grew up together from the time they were all in kindergarten, and we have walked together as dear friends through countless seasons of life. I've had the privilege of experiencing her loyal love firsthand, and through her, I've had the blessing of getting to know her brother, Kevin. Camille and I would go together to visit Kevin where he lived, and she was pure sunshine entering the room when she saw him. On those days, as I watched Camille and Kevin, I could see how deeply she wanted him to feel known and seen, connected and loved despite not being able to use his voice. She so desperately wanted him to experience life to the fullest, to feel joy, to taste good food, to have meaningful relationships. She understood him in a way that no one else could and so was unwaveringly dedicated to being his voice when he couldn't use his own. Camille and Kevin have a powerful, unspoken bond like I have never seen before. They are an example of a relationship based truly on the core of two people's spirits and not on anything superficial. Nothing made Camille happier than seeing that giant smile light up Kevin's face or hearing his big belly laugh of glee as she raced him around the courtyard in his wheelchair. Those are the moments that were so healing, both to Kevin's heart and to Camille's.

The apostle Paul, in 1 Corinthians 12:26, compares true community to a body, saying that "If one part suffers, every part suffers with it; if one part is honored, every part rejoices with it." Empathy and love are inextricable from one another, and though this interconnectedness can be the source of so much of life's deepest meaning, it can also be the source of its deepest pain. Any parent of a sick child, any friend of someone with chronic pain, or, in Camille's case, any sibling of someone with a physical disability knows the challenge of watching your loved one struggle and not being able to take it away for them. "Secondhand sufferers" is a term I learned from Camille as we walked together through so many seasons of her brother's hardships, the loss of our mothers, my family's Camp Firefly, our own children's challenges, and more.

How do we care for our loved ones' hearts in the midst of their struggles and take care of our own simultaneously? How do we deal with feelings of guilt for living in a healthy body while others don't have that same privilege? How do we have an abiding relationship with God and keep gratitude as our anchor when pain and anger are sometimes all we feel? Each one of us will face these questions at some point in our lives, and when they come, they often come in shouts, not whispers. Camille so gracefully walks us through each of these moments in Hope for Secondhand Suffering ™ in a way that is not only extremely comforting but also highly applicable and practical. The book felt very therapeutic as Camille's heart is postured not just to tell her story but to minister to people. It's real, vulnerable, relatable, hope-filled, and perspective-changing, with beautiful bits of advice and spiritual insights throughout. After reading it, you will surely, as I did, feel refreshed and filled with gratitude for God's loyal love even through our struggles—especially through our struggles.

Over thirty years ago, my husband and I founded Camp Firefly: a camp for families with a child battling cancer or other serious illnesses. The goal is to give them a week of deep peace, joy, and refreshed relationships. Over the years, the importance of caring for secondhand sufferers has become increasingly highlighted in our minds and hearts. This book is the resource I wish I'd had during the hardest moments of my own secondhand suffering as well as the book I will now be giving to everyone I know walking through similar experiences. I am so excited for you to read and be encouraged.

—Chelsea & Kirk Cameron,
TV & Movie Actors | Speakers | Camp Firefly Founders

Endorsements

It has been a pleasure to know Camille Block and her remarkable family. Throughout the years, I've witnessed her unwavering dedication in advocating for her brother and championing the voices of those often overlooked. Camille's strength in sharing the profound bond she shares with her brother is both inspiring and courageous.

Her perspective as a sibling offers a unique insight that deserves sincere recognition within professional circles. Camille's narrative not only unveils her personal journey but will also resonate with other siblings facing similar circumstances.

—LORI ANDERSON,
President and CEO Momentum
www.momentum4all.org

This book, like a few others, identifies one of the more pervasive emotionally and spiritually confusing conundrums—the dangers of secondhand suffering. Pain and suffering reach far beyond just the direct victims.

If you have ever struggled with the unanswerable "whys" and "where is God?" in the complex mess of life, Camille's book will offer you hope and tangible help for navigating through life's more painful hallways.

—BRAD CUMMINGS,
Co-author and Movie Producer of The Shack,
General Editor, The Founders' Bible

As the son of a physician, I chose to follow in my father's footsteps to pursue a medical path for my career. As a sibling growing up with a handicapped brother, I could never understand why my brother couldn't do certain things, and so his life was highly influential on my fascination with the brain. What began as a blind journey turned into a life trying to understand and improve the human condition through a career in neuroscience and neurosurgery because of lessons I learned from my special needs brother.

Camille's book on this unique concept of secondhand suffering is the emotional guide that would have helped me navigate some of my journey had it been available. It is a masterpiece of empathy, resilience, and advocacy, offering invaluable insights and strategies that only someone who has lived this experience can provide. The topics covered are an important work in an arena that is difficult and underserved. For me, this book resonates deeply as it tackles a tornado of emotions, including guilt, sadness, and the pursuit of hope, while also intersecting with my professional role as a physician serving brain-injured patients.

I have had the privilege of knowing Camille's family and brother, Kevin, for over two decades and attest to Camille's expertise on this important topic. If you are emotionally gripped by the suffering of a loved one and desire a place to feel understood and gain tools to champion them, I wholeheartedly endorse this book.

—IAN I. T. ARMSTRONG, M.D.,
American Board of Neurological Surgery,
LTC USARMY Reserves,
Senior Medical Consultant, Army Futures Command

Though I have walked this journey alongside Camille, my friend of twenty years, and I knew many of these stories, reading the weighty copy you hold in your hands was like reading it anew. The ineffable power of presence permeates this book. It is not just the presence of Camille in her brother's life: an ever-loving big sister who doubles as a fiercely courageous advocate. Just as poignant is the presence of Kevin in Camille's life: a joy-filled little brother who radiates a delectable joy amidst adversities of pain and suffering that words fail to adequately portray. Camille also highlights the ineffable presence of God, who meets her in the midst of the pain and confusion as she identifies her own struggles with "Secondhand Suffering."

As a Marriage and Family Therapist who specializes in grief and loss, I am blessed to get to sit in these deep moments with others, with first and secondhand sufferers, to hold the tension for them in the moments when their own hope muscles fatigue and their eyes can cry no more. As an academic in Trauma, I am grateful for a resource to share with those who cry out for help with these deeper questions of life and loss, of sickness and despair. The irony of holding in tension the indescribable beauty of the Creator of the Universe, who can and does heal, with the "already/

not yet" of overwhelming pain and agony, is not easily explained. And yet, Camille addresses this mystery with an emergent faith despite ongoing opposing evidences.

In this clarion call, Camille sends forth flares in the dark night skies to all who find themselves burdened with their own or their loved one's harrowing pain and suffering. These flares disrupt the darkness, lighting the path forward, which metamorphizes answers from an "either/or" classification into a "both/and" solution. She deposits seeds of hope and faith into the deep soils of pain and sorrow, into the places where intimacy with the Lord amidst life's deepest sufferings invites His healing presence into hurting hearts.

—Kristen Cummins, EdD, Traumatology,
Licensed Marriage and Family Therapist,
Board-Certified Professional Christian Counselor

Why do bad things happen to good people? Why does God allow suffering? In Hope for Secondhand Suffering™, Camille asks the tough questions some refuse to even consider. Through powerful and poignant stories of her relationship with her disabled brother, she shares her personal faith journey of contending with such questions and navigating from helplessness to hope. With an inability to help heal her brother, she learned how to heal from her own secondhand suffering and find her God-given purpose. This is a universal struggle in a fallen world where we struggle to understand God's purpose in our hardships. I highly recommend this book to anyone who struggles with such difficult existential questions and to anyone who deeply cares for others in pain. I especially recommend this book for Christian mental health professionals to help guide their patients (and themselves!) through the treacherous waters of secondhand suffering.

—Shannae Anderson, Ph.D.,
Clinical Psychologist and Professor, Liberty University,
Director of Psychology, American Association of Christian Counselors,
Former Professor, Fuller Theological Seminary,
Speaker

We all experience pain, loss, and complicated circumstances that leave us with a choice. Do we escape the pain we feel, or do we navigate it in such a way that we are better because of it? The latter requires tools, equipping, and learning.

Camille has done a masterful job of unpacking the difficult and often ignored topic of suffering, not only directly but perhaps just as painful, indirectly, as we watch, love, and support those in direct suffering. The pages in this book offer insights and help for all of us, personally experienced by Camille, as we search for and lay hold of hope in the most trying of circumstances, ultimately discovering that hope is at the feet of the God of all hope (Romans 15:13).

—Reggie Mercado,
Senior Pastor, The Fountain Church, Moorpark, CA,
Author of The Wildlife,
Former Youth Pastor, The Church On The Way with Pastor Jack Hayford

Over twenty years ago in my senior year of college at Pepperdine University in Malibu, California, I had the honor of getting to know Kevin Yates, Camille's brother, through a Service Leadership course taught by Camille's father, Dr. Jere Yates (one of the founders of the business school at Pepperdine University and still my favorite professor to date). Throughout a career in business spanning private equity, venture capital, and real estate – and on the personal front, as a husband, father, and follower of Christ – Kevin's story and that of his loving family, serve as daily inspiration for me on so many levels, even still to this day.

Camille's book really does a wonderful job in helping explore the universally human struggle to understand certain "whys" presented in life happen, the complex human emotions that come with that struggle, and the potential opportunity for growth (spiritual or otherwise) stemming thereof.

—Shaun Limbers,
Entrepreneur and Professor
CEO, McIntyre Investment,
Faculty, Baylor University Department of Entrepreneurship

Hope for Secondhand Suffering™ is truly a masterpiece, one that has my highest endorsement. Camille has done an incredible job of bringing honesty to the pain of secondhand suffering, yet at the same time so much hope, healing and joy. This is one book that I am not only delighted to endorse but one that will take a special place in my book collection as a source of truth, love and understanding. It is one that, as a father of a precious daughter with cerebral palsy, I will be reading and referencing over and over again. Thank you Camille for sowing your life, your pain and your time into helping others find life and hope in their trials.

—CHRIS GORE
Author: The Perfect Gift - Seeing the Child not the Condition
Former Director of Healing, Bethel Church, Redding, CA
Chrisgore.org

"When we are no longer able to change a situation, we are challenged to change ourselves."

—Viktor Frankl

Note from the Author

This book is the birth of something that took many years of labor. It started out as a story about my severely disabled brother and was called "Why?" It was raw and rough. It evolved into something I later named "Locked into Hope," referring to my brother being locked in, but somehow, I still clung to hope. Yet, halfway through the process, I realized I had learned a lot about many things that could help others. And did anyone really care about my story unless it could benefit them? Maybe my ten closest friends and family, perhaps. Thinking about how my story could possibly benefit others gave me a surge of energy, which spurred me on to give this quasi-memoir a final push to birth a multifaceted book – one that connects to the hearts of others who need real hope and encouragement for an often unseen but deep sadness.

To be honest, I never intended this to be a spiritual book. It is purposed for anyone who identifies with this idea of secondhand suffering, and I didn't want to limit the readers to a certain subset of people. Yet, to be true to my story, my best hope for others involved a faith journey. In fact, there are three stories in one ahead of you—my memoir as it relates to my brother, lessons learned to help you practically, and my spiritual journey explained with raw honesty for people of all backgrounds, without pressure to take on my personal conclusions. These mini-sections within each chapter become intertwined as the book progresses—something I couldn't avoid as my spiritual journey grew from a compartmentalized afterthought to the key to unlocking authentic hope for secondhand suffering.

I invite you to come along with me for the journey and allow these words to sink in as you think about your own life. Many of the quotes throughout are meant to be pondered as they connect to the heart of each section. And consider taking a pause after each chapter as you reflect and engage the "Tools for the Heart." My hope is that as you read my story, you will allow the musings of your own mind and heart to become unlocked, and you stay postured to walk through your own transformation toward hope, gathering helpful tools along the way. I hope you will join me to the end.

CHAPTER ONE

Admitting That Life Isn't Fair (for starters)

"There is always inequality in life.
Some men are killed in a war and some men are wounded
and some men never leave the country.
Life is unfair."

—JOHN F. KENNEDY

Sitting crisscrossed on the floor, I was mesmerized by the woman on TV holding the round, magic mirror against her face, looking side to side into my family room, "seeing" all the different children. *Why did she never see me?* She saw Ricky and Julie and Greg and Suzie and Stacy and Tommy and Peter and Kathy. But she never saw Camille. For those who didn't grow up in the 60s or 70s, I'm referring to a popular young children's TV show called *Romper Room*. It was my favorite show at the time because I always hoped I would be seen through the magic mirror, too. This show caused me great frustration and sadness because I was invisible to the lady with the magic mirror. I wanted to be seen and called by name. Sure, my name may be uncommon, but if the mirror was truly magic, it didn't seem like a difficult request.

A similar feeling came over me when I was dragged along on errands with my mom. One day, while waiting in a store, I excitedly stumbled upon a turnstile filled with little blue license plates. With great anticipation, I spun that thing around furiously, searching to find the name "Camille." My heart sank when it wasn't there. In fact, it was never there, no matter how many times I searched over the years. (I still find myself sneaking a peak and making a spin when I see those turnstiles to this day . . . just in case.) It didn't seem fair that my friends and brother all found their names. My only consolation was my friend Adrienne had the same problem.

We all come to realize life is unfair at some point in time. For some, it begins earlier than for others. It can be as simple as their name not being on a license plate, or maybe it's a random tragedy like a family member being struck by lightning or a child getting a rare birth defect. But we all eventually get to the conclusion that life being fair is not part of its DNA. JFK's quote above about the random unfairness of war captures the depth of how difficult the discrepancies can be. Can you imagine losing a child in war? Perhaps you can because you have, and if so, I'm truly sorry.

There is something inside of us that cries out at injustice. We seem to have expectations wired into our being that say, "Everything should be fair, just, right, and good." And when that expectation is disrupted, we experience the tension. Not being seen by the *Romper Room* lady is one thing, but as we age, our level of exposure to what is unfair grows, and the tension increases. Pain, suffering, and stress follow, but these feelings of injustice can also bring maturity, strength, and perspective.

Details of how my brother Kevin got Cerebral Palsy are sketchy for me. What I remember growing up was a phrase I memorized to make it easier. People would ask me, "How did your brother get like this?" I would simply and rather mechanically say, "He was two weeks late, and when he came out of the birth canal, the umbilical cord got wrapped around his neck, and he couldn't breathe and breathed in and/or swallowed a lot of meconium (fetal stool) mixed with amniotic fluid, which caused him to be deprived of oxygen for a time and killed certain brain cells." I never questioned this nor really understood it. I just accepted it and repeated it when asked. Children do that, I guess. Today, this is referred to as Meconium Aspiration Syndrome (MAS).

Indeed, the cord was wrapped around Kevin's neck, but we are not sure if it was wrapped so tightly that it caused the "accident" of losing oxygen or if Kevin had swallowed the meconium/amniotic fluid at the wrong time during the birth process or if something else happened during the pregnancy. Either way, most doctors seemed to agree that he lost oxygen to the brain. And somehow that affected his motor cortex in his brain—the part that "controls the planning, control and execution of voluntary movements."[2]

I remember shortly after Kevin's birth, my parents had some of their church friends over to the house for a night of praying because they thought he was going to die. They prayed he wouldn't die, and he didn't. But no one knew the severity of the damage that resulted from his brain injury. Sometimes, I wondered if my mom secretly wished God would have just taken him to spare him the life he would live without any control over his body. She never said that . . . but sometimes I sensed that she wondered about it. I think my mom ended up suffering more than anyone, although I didn't realize it back then. As a mom myself, I freaked out when my son got Lyme disease and other health issues. I cannot compare what my mom must have dealt with over Kevin's precious life being so severely robbed short of what she had expected, but I have a better idea now.

I wondered if my mom secretly wished God would have just taken him to spare him the life he would live without any control over his body.

At first, my parents didn't know the extent of the damage Kevin would have. How could they when he was just a newborn? But they started noticing he was not progressing like I had when I was his age. Kevin was three and a half years younger than I, and with each developmental stage of a "normal" baby, they became increasingly aware that he was not progressing according to plan. At three months of age, Kevin began having seizures. My parents took him to Children's

Hospital in Los Angeles, where they were informed of the horrifying news. Kevin had a severe form of Cerebral Palsy (CP) called Spastic Quadriplegic Cerebral Palsy. According to the Centers for Disease Control and Prevention, "*Cerebral* means having to do with the brain. *Palsy* means weakness or problems with using the muscles. CP is caused by abnormal brain development or damage to the developing brain that affects a person's ability to control his or her muscles."[3] There are many forms of CP, which can vary from mild to severe. The four types of CP include Spastic, Dyskinetic, Ataxic, and Mixed.[4]

In my brother's case, his spasticity is considered the most severe. What this meant to me was that Kevin could not walk, control his movements, talk, communicate, sit up on his own, stand, use any real muscle strength, control his need to go to the bathroom, or really anything. Throughout my life, I saw others with CP who could walk, talk some (even if it sounded funny), and communicate with others. I didn't understand why Kevin couldn't do these basic things when his eyes cried out that he was *fully* in there—feeling all the emotions, such as love, laughter, sadness, frustration, and longing to be rescued from his prison. His eyes didn't lie. I remember thinking that if he was going to have CP, couldn't he at least have the kind that wasn't so severe? Why couldn't he at least talk like others with CP? Or just walk funny? Why so severe?

Apparently, kids must have an innate sense of what is fair and what is not because I knew at a very young age that Kevin's life certainly was anything but fair. He did nothing to deserve to live life in this manner. No doubt someone you love didn't deserve their lot either. Wrestling through this tension of carrying an inner sense of justice with our present reality can be a heavy burden—or if we intentionally block out the difficult emotions, the burden may appear lighter, at least for a time. While I don't have the answers about why Kevin was randomly affected by this birth accident, I believe I am better off facing it head-on by allowing my feelings of anger, confusion, sadness, guilt, and beyond to surface than simply reframing his reality with sugary platitudes that cover up and avoid going to those deep places in my soul.

My guess is that you have wrestled with these complex emotions like I have. I'm curious if you've come to grips with and accepted that life isn't fair. If so, how have you dealt with this reality? Do you have workarounds for the pain, coping mechanisms, or comforting routines that help? Do you sometimes want to hide your head under the covers and dull the difficult realities by binge-watching a mindless TV streaming series, or do you face it head-on, like in a scene out of Braveheart? Maybe you live somewhere in between, and that's okay. Some of us are wired more emotionally than others and seem from the outside to be carrying a heavier weight, while others may look like they have just "checked out." I know some people who are resentful, bitter, and angry as their lives have been severely damaged by relentless disruption, and others who are profoundly stoic and stuck because it hurts too much to let themselves feel. Secondhand suffering looks different for all of us, and much depends on the details of our situation. Yet, we connect on the common bond of that (possibly) unspoken feeling of injustice that accompanies the pain—for our loved one or maybe for us as well.

As we peel back these prickly layers of complexity to this type of suffering, like a metaphorical artichoke, I pray we will find nuggets of "meat" to chew on that will eventually lead to the heart of the matter—a place of new insights and hope, offering a deeper satisfaction than seems currently possible.

INSIGHTS FOR THE HEART

Gaining a New Perspective

*"Life isn't about waiting for the storm to pass.
It's about learning how to dance in the rain."*

—Vivian Greene

Living life with sweet Kevin allowed me to come to terms with some of life's inconsistencies as a kid. For a girl raised on Brady Bunch and Happy Days sitcoms, discovering the shocking lesson that there are not always happy endings was a hard reality. Escaping into the world of thirty-minute resolutions to life's everyday drama was an entertaining alternative to thinking about what my brother was doing that day without us. The sobering news for him, we were told, was that "there is no cure."

There is something to be said for accepting this fact of "lack of fairness" in life as a young child. While life may not be fair, I had to learn the value of a different perspective that stems from circumstances. For example, when my friends were upset because of a broken arm, or they didn't make the cheerleading squad, I looked at things differently. At least their arm would heal. And who had time to cry over not making the cheerleading squad? They had legs and arms that could move, unlike Kevin. If I argued with a friend or family member, I was thankful that at least I could talk. If I got a bad grade on a test, at least I could attend school. When there were prettier, more popular girls and kids smarter than me, I tried to remind myself that Kevin would give anything to have the opportunities I had no matter how I looked, faired in popularity, or scored on tests. Kevin's life offered me a bigger perspective and a reality check. Perhaps it also served as a coping mechanism and a safeguard to keep me from being dragged into the drama of life that so many kids are pulled into.

Holding strong expectations plays a big role in how we handle the injustices in life. For a much lighter example, think about seeing a movie. If the reviews are amazing and your friends rave about it, your expectations are high. With this mindset, it is more likely you will be disappointed rather than impressed, given how high your expectations are about enjoying the movie. I'm not saying we should have low expectations about life, but I do think having a sober grasp of life's "unfairness" can help us manage our reactions to life's circumstances. A different example is when my dad taught me to drive. He told me to expect there to be bad drivers out there, so I should drive defensively.

This has helped me control my temper when a bad driver cuts me off or does something dangerously dumb. Expectations play into our reactions. Life isn't fair, but if one doesn't ever expect it to be, then there is a greater gratitude for when things go well. And when things don't go well, there is a perspective that they could be worse. What *is* fair anyway? We are all given a different hand of cards we don't often control. Yet, we can either play our hand wisely or quit because we don't like our cards. The choice is ours.

> *"I have seen something else under the sun:*
> *The race is not to the swift or the battle to the strong,*
> *nor does food come to the wise or wealth to the brilliant*
> *or favor to the learned; but time and chance*
> *happen to them all."*
>
> —Ecclesiastes 9:11 (NIV)

When you learn the lesson that life isn't fair and gain a new perspective on the role of our expectations and how we perceive our circumstances, it takes away an excuse to give up. It also provides a foundation of wisdom, a sense of empowerment, and a counterforce to an attitude of entitlement, something destructive that leads to bitterness in our thinking that slowly eats away at us like a cancer. Accepting that life isn't fair may be our entry point to experience healing from the grip that secondhand suffering can have on us. Continually striving for fairness is exhausting and insatiable and unwinnable. Yet it's in the surrender of control that we can begin the greater journey.

When I think deeply about this issue of fairness, I wonder why we even assume that there is this thing called fairness when apparently it doesn't seem to exist. Where do we get this innate sense that there *should* be fairness? There seems to be a universal acceptance that certain things in life are unfair. These clues helped me discover how we are internally wired for justice, equality, and a meaningful and purposeful life. And when that doesn't happen, we can experience something called cognitive dissonance, meaning a "psychological conflict resulting from incongruous beliefs and attitudes held simultaneously."[5] Somehow, at a young age, I knew life *should* be fair, but it wasn't. Most kids realize this, but usually, at least in America, perhaps, it's more about their sibling not sharing a toy, not about him or her being unable to walk, talk, or move.

Accepting that Kevin's situation wasn't fair became necessary for me to surrender my right to make it fair. Then, I had to find ways to accept his situation, control what I could, and find tools to gain new perspectives to protect my heart and still allow for a pursuit of hope through action. I held all this at a subconscious level for so long. A different way of saying some of this can be summarized in a small portion of "The Serenity Prayer":

God, grant me the serenity
To accept the things I cannot change;
Courage to change the things I can;
And wisdom to know the difference.[6]

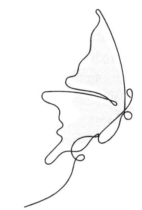

SPIRITUAL REFLECTIONS

An Inherited Faith

"When your mother asks, 'Do you want a piece of advice?'
it's a mere formality. It doesn't matter if you answer yes or no.
You're going to get it anyway."

—ERMA BOMBECK

I remember studying philosophy in college and reading what Karl Marx said about religion: "Religion is the opiate of the masses."[7] We were asked to debate this quote in class. While Marx had an entire political agenda around his observation, at face value, it is an interesting concept to discuss. Is religion simply a tool made by man to placate the people that there is something more than life on earth with all its troubles? Or is there actually something beyond this world that makes all the troubles of life lead to something beyond just the here and now? Or maybe religion is something entirely different. Perhaps the options of organized religion are really a distraction from a good and all-loving God who many believe created people for His purposes and calls to us at an inner level with an ongoing whisper that may take a lifetime to discover. To me, these questions were fascinating.

At some point, we all are wired for a spiritual journey. Some of us cut it off early on due to some terribly bad experience done in the name of religion. Others pursue something with many beautiful rituals but never connect the reason beyond the traditions and find it empty. Others may agree with Marx—it's just a silly crutch to get through life with some fairy tale, man-made hope offered on a dessert plate. My faith journey is my own; you have yours, or maybe you buried it, ignored it, or haven't started. I can only speak for myself when I say that the journey and struggle to faith is worth it. It's the only thing that has girded me up with the greatest perspective to give me hope as a secondhand sufferer. Perhaps my spiritual pursuit and transformation will spur you on in some way to seek and find that which speaks to you from your own soul.

My spiritual starting point as a young child was similar to others who were raised going to church every week. Doing religion, church, or praying was more of a ritual and a cultural habit. My parents made sure we went to church weekly, and their parents did the same with them. There was a loose belief in God and honoring the Bible attached to showing up at church, but it seemed it was more of a tradition and a way to check the box of being "a good person." Certainly, there is nothing wrong with being a good person, of course. But as I grew, I recall having some questions about weightier topics, which I think most kids do, but I never quite found all the answers in Sunday School.

I remember being in the back seat of the goldish brown Oldsmobile driving back from church, heading to lunch at Love's BBQ in the valley. Yes, this is the same "valley" that the song-turned-cult classic called "Valley Girl" by Frank Zappa was made about, and it was the same region where my brother lived (San Fernando Valley). Love's BBQ was my dad's favorite place to eat, and my mom loved the BBQ beans that tasted like candy, so it was a hit. But it also meant a long day ahead of us. Brian was not a fan of any of it—well, except the food, I guess—as all these activities ate up his "playing with friends" time. And me? I carried too much guilt to give a full-out revolt to see Kevin. We owed him a visit. We didn't see him enough. Who was I to think anything selfish about my wants when he just sat there bored all day in a wheelchair, wondering when his family would visit him again? But while I wanted to be with him when I saw him, the anticipation of our visit seemed more dreadful to me than exciting. Why? Perhaps because the encounter was never satisfying. It brought pain, guilt, and suffering. But it was a duty.

> *Who was I to think anything selfish about my wants when he just sat there bored all day in a wheelchair, wondering when his family would visit him again?*

I remember this one time when Kevin was on my mind as we drove to his place after stuffing ourselves with lunch, and I asked my mom and dad, "Why didn't God heal Kevin?" My mom quickly glared at my dad as if he should have the perfect answer, like, "Hurry up and come up with something, Jere." Much to her dismay, he responded with the most profound yet unexpected answer: "I don't know." In retrospect, this was a brilliant response.

My mom, apparently wanting to "level up" his weak answer, said something that had a strong imprint on the next couple of decades of my life. She confidently explained, "Well, Camille, I don't believe God gets involved in the lives of people, exactly. He just created the world and then let it spin. He doesn't intervene in our lives; we are basically on our own, except we can go to heaven one day when we die. So, God didn't heal Kevin because He doesn't really get that involved in the details of our lives."

And that was it. My mom seemed to have it figured out, and my dad pleaded ignorance. God was out there somewhere, and I had Him to thank for making the world, birds and trees, oceans, people, and my dinner. But I never held out a lot of hope for Him to do a bunch of stuff for me. My mom had taken away her expectations for God to heal him, it seemed, and this solved another problem. We didn't have to blame God, and we could still go to church and smile as we dressed our Sunday best without holding any hard feelings against God. Since He was distant and more of a philosophical theory than an actual person, there was no need to connect to Him on a personal level either.

Looking back to those early years, I guess my beginning faith foundation was that I was a church-going Deist by inheritance. Little did I know then how unsatisfying this would be to me later in life. The ramifications were feeling distant and unconnected to the Creator and my purpose.

TOOLS FOR THE HEART

*Accepting that life isn't fair is often the entry point to healing
from secondhand suffering. We can pivot from focusing
on life's unfairness to embracing a new perspective.
Through our unique insights and lessons learned,
we can make a difference with things in our control,
surrendering anything outside our control*

Questions to Ponder:

1. When did you first realize that life isn't fair? How old were you, and was there any trauma attached to it for you personally? (Or was it just that the *Romper Room* lady also missed your name?)
2. How did this early sense of injustice affect or change your perspective about life?
3. What were your first recollections of the role of God (or lack of it) in your family life?
4. What are some things that are out of your control that you need to surrender?

Practical Steps:

Memorize "The Serenity Prayer" or write it on a 3" x 5" card to keep with you when you need the reminder that although life isn't fair, hope is still ahead.

The Serenity Prayer

God, grant me the serenity
To accept the things I cannot change;
Courage to change the things I can;
And wisdom to know the difference.

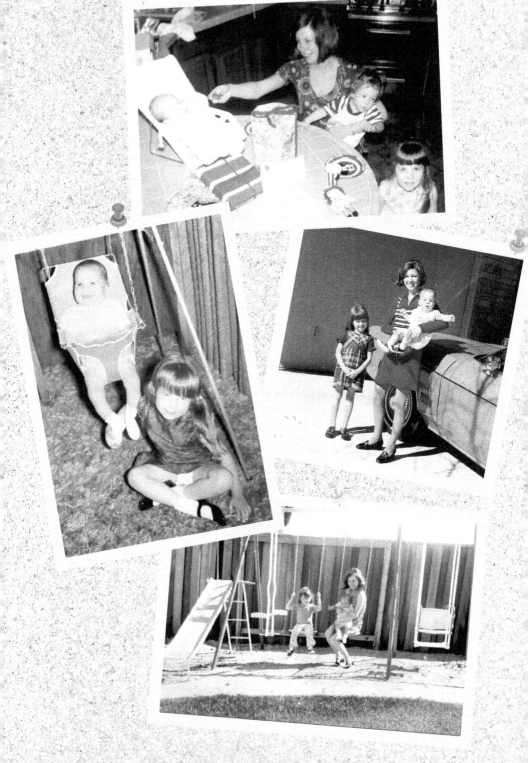

CHAPTER TWO

Trusting Your Gut and Giving It a Voice

"Don't let the noise of other people's opinions drown out your inner voice."

—STEVE JOBS

At his core, Kevin's disposition has always been joyful.** He seems to feel deeply, whether joy or sadness. Kevin could not ever talk, walk, or control any bodily movement except his eyes and his smile, as far as we knew. When he was a baby, he was easy to move because we could just carry him or put him in the car on my dad's lap (before car seat laws) or buckle him up with a seatbelt in the passenger seat when he was older. My parents were under extreme stress. Before he was three-and-a-half, he lived with us full-time. My mom had Kevin and me to take care of until my youngest brother, Brian, was born two years after Kevin. So, taking care of three kids five and under, with one of them fully disabled, one an infant, and me starting school, couldn't have been easy. As the oldest, I remember a lot of my time was spent alone, mostly because I could fend for myself. I was the easy one, I suppose.

I remember, as a very young child, walking across the street and sitting in the living room of an older woman named Meryl, who was an artist. She would paint beautiful landscape paintings on her canvas that was propped up on easels while I would sit and watch her for hours. She inspired me, and it was her influence that made me tell everyone that I wanted to be an artist when I grew up. My dream of one day being an artist was fairly short-lived. I still can't even draw a stick figure, but as a child, watching Meryl paint was something I really enjoyed. It helped me escape into a world of colors and imagination. It was peaceful and inspiring, and something in me longed for the ability to escape into a creative realm. Her life seemed so peaceful as I watched her create beautiful pictures. And I think she liked my company, plus I was clearly looking for something to do while my mom was always busy.

Taking care of Kevin was a lot of work because he wasn't developmentally able to do the things other kids could at each stage. I remember hearing that the doctors did not know what kind of damage would surface with Kevin. We would just have to wait and see, they said. And as we waited, we saw. Kevin couldn't gulp down a bottle quite like I had done. He wasn't making attempts to talk. He couldn't sit up on his own. He never tried to crawl. His arms didn't move like a "normal" kid. Neither did his legs. He cried a lot for no apparent reason. He seemed to get pneumonia often. And interestingly, the doctors told my parents that Kevin was mentally retarded. In those days, it wasn't taboo to say phrases like that. Now, at least, we say "special needs" or "cognitively challenged." The doctors said it with so much authority. It seemed to have the flavor of: "You shouldn't worry too much about Kevin and how you choose to raise him because he really can't understand anything anyway and doesn't have the capacity to know what he is missing." To some degree, I believe my mom needed to hear this to justify what was to come, even though I know she knew, deep down, that this wasn't completely true. Yet, she clung to the doctors' opinions on this—no matter how unfounded and unsubstantiated scientifically they were—because it partially medicated her from the reality of her guilt and Kevin's plight.

One day, my parents told me that they knew Kevin would never be "normal," and they didn't want me to feel like an only child. It was then they announced they were going to have another baby. Brian was such an easy and happy baby, and it seemed upspoken that he became the "healthy brother/son replacement" for Kevin's lack of development.

Once the decision was made to place Kevin in a home for disabled children with cerebral palsy, I had no choice as a six-year-old but to accept it. After all, the experts told them that most marriages end in divorce when they try to manage the stress of a fully disabled child at home, and it affects the well-being of the other children. Who was I to argue that? The day Kevin drove away with my dad was the day that left a forever imprint of sadness on me and in me. I learned later it was one of the hardest days of my dad's life.

As Brian grew older, I remember my mom unwittingly telling him, "If your brother Kevin had not been handicapped, you would not be here because we weren't going to have any more kids." Hmm . . . while her intentions were only to be truthful and encourage my brother to be extra thankful for Kevin, I realize now as a mother how damaging these words are to speak to your son. She might as well have said, "You better be glad your brother is severely disabled, or you might not be here." That had to be a tough message to handle for a child, no matter how well-meaning my mom was. In fairness to her, however, I know her motive was to encourage my brother not to complain when he had to give up his Sunday afternoon to see him. Honestly, I could see myself doing something similar without thinking if I was ridden with guilt, deeply grieving my son leaving my home, and didn't want to hear complaining from a healthy child. I know my mom never meant to hurt Brian; what mom hasn't slipped into pulling the guilt card every once in a while to get their kids to do something? Still, in retrospect, I'm sure it must have affected him, if even at a subconscious level.

As the years went by and the visits with Kevin grew further apart, I remember the time when we heard the horrendous news. Kevin had gone down a playground slide with a caregiver—on the employee's lap—when one of his legs got caught, and his leg completely broke in an agonizingly painful injury. He was sent to the hospital, where they determined he needed a cast, and for some reason, the doctor got overly ambitious. He informed my parents that "while the hip didn't go out of place exactly, *it may in the future,* so we might as well do hip surgery to overcorrect it now to prevent a future problem of his hip coming out of the joint."

Oh, how I wish my parents had pursued another opinion. If only they had learned the art of trusting their gut feeling, which was uneasy about the surgery. Since nothing is wrong *yet,* why put him through unnecessary pain over something that may or may not happen? If I had been there in my adult form, I would have said, "Mom and Dad! Trust your instinct, and get more opinions! Don't put Kevin through more pain than necessary." But, of course, I wasn't there, and hindsight is 20/20. Unfortunately, they went with the original doctor's suggestion because he was "the expert." He did a full hip surgery on one hip.

> *If I had been there in my adult form, I would have said, "Mom and Dad! Trust your instinct, and get more opinions!"*

The reason why this choice was so horrifying for me was that to recover, the surgeon had to put him in a *full body cast,* including both legs in casts *held three feet in the air, attached by a metal bar between them.* He would live in this ridiculously torturous prison for at least eight weeks.

When I saw Kevin like this, my heart sank. No one should have to experience this torture, let alone a kid who already couldn't do anything for himself. He was miserable and devastated, and he let me know it. If there was one thing that Kevin *could* do, it was to communicate his feelings with his eyes and emotions. He was *not* happy. My dad admitted this was one of the lowest points with his son as he remembered Kevin's glare at him when he came out of surgery. "If looks could kill" became a new reality. It was as if Kevin was saying, "Why did you let them do this to me?" When my eyes met his piercing stare of sheer horror, I wanted to rip off those casts and yell, "Why are you doing this to a kid who can't even walk? How is this going to help him?" It was just one more scene in his play when I wanted to tear up the script. Even now, forty-plus years later, I can barely recall this scene without cringing and re-living his suffering.

After watching this gut-wrenching time in Kevin's life, a seed was planted in me that gut feelings are often right and doctors are not gods. Of course, I am grateful for doctors, their brilliant minds, years of training, and their expertise in helping their patients. But I've seen people put too much faith in one person's opinion because of a degree without realizing that healthcare can often be more of an art than an exact science. No one doctor has a monopoly on truth, and the good ones admit this. And people without these medical degrees tend to doubt their own commonsense intuition and assume they must be wrong. Watching this scene of Kevin in the body cast was one of countless times to come that instilled in me the need to question and challenge the doctors' opinions. After Kevin suffered in this torturous position for eight weeks, doing nothing but lying flat on his back, it appeared to be all for nothing. As Kevin grew, the one leg stopped growing anyway. His deformity with his hip got worse, not better. His legs grew to two different heights (by about six inches at least), and all hope was lost for him to ever be able to stand or walk, even in a standing walker, mostly due to this unnecessary procedure.

A different life-altering decision for my brother planted another seed that grew into the fruit of my skepticism of the experts—inserting a feeding tube. As a child, Kevin suffered many bouts of pneumonia and had frequent stays in the hospital to treat it. But this one time, in his late twenties, he looked really sick. He was having such trouble breathing, and he looked scared. I was told he almost died. While in the hospital, the doctors decided that it was time to end the battle with pneumonia. They convinced my parents to let them surgically insert a G-tube into his stomach so he would only be fed a liquid diet straight into his stomach from then on. They said it was the only way to dramatically reduce his risk of pneumonia because, according to them, when he ate and drank, he was having continual issues with aspiration.

The problem with the doctors' so-called logic was this: they did not take into account that Kevin had only one real joy in his life, and that was food and drink. Kevin *loved* to eat. When someone began making food for him, he would light up, smile, make expressive noises, and wiggle whatever body part he could in excitement to let us know how happy he was to eat. He would squirm restlessly and tighten up spastically in excitement. Kevin's joy about eating orally may have been disproportionate to most people since it is not typical to react so exuberantly when anticipating a meal. Kevin's reaction to a simple meal was similar to another kid's reaction to being told he was going to Disneyland. Eating was the highlight of his day. Each meal got the same reaction of eager anticipation and a true sensory pleasure for a guy who doesn't get many. Taking this away from him did not seem right; another gut check inside of me. This time, though, I was much older. Instinctively, I knew there was more to life than just the number of years he lived. And who says this doctor was right? Maybe there was some other issue causing the pneumonia or contributing to it. And what are the risks of a G-tube?

Back then, doctors didn't talk about quality-of-life vs. quantity-of-life like we do now. Even if the GI doctor was right about the G-tube, was it worth saving Kevin from the risk of pneumonia if it meant he would be forced to give up one of the few things in life he truly enjoyed? Were there other workarounds? When pressed, the doctors admitted that he was at risk for pneumonia just by swallowing his own saliva. Many years later, we learned that G-tubes can and do *cause* aspiration pneumonia at least as much or *more* often than simply eating and drinking.

To me, the decision to put a G-tube down Kevin's throat and take away his oral feeding seemed easy. My thoughts were "NOOOOOO!" But no one was asking the sister. From that day forward, Kevin was fed by a G-tube as his main source of nutrition. Several bottles of Ensure, or worse—cartons of what essentially was corn syrup—were poured into his stomach as his "new normal." I never could get on board with this decision, even though I understand why my parents felt it best at the time. But Kevin didn't understand why he could no longer eat and drink. His roommates would all meet for three meals a day while he was off in a corner in his wheelchair in front of a TV or his bed, listening to the mealtime chatter and smelling the aromas from the kitchen. The sadness in his eyes caused me to feel a deep and familiar pain inside. I imagined what he must be feeling to have had that simple pleasure of life taken away, and it hurt!—a strange feeling for someone who hadn't even been a mother yet. Every time I would eat a meal, my thoughts would go to my brother being banned from the activity I was enjoying, which brought about guilt and affected any enjoyment I was having.

While hindsight may be 20/20, sometimes simply trusting our initial instinct about a decision may prove to be a powerful tool in getting the decision right. As a fan of Malcolm Gladwell's books, I resonate with his insight when he said in his book *Blink: The Power of Thinking Without Thinking*, "There can be as much value in the blink of an eye as in months of rational analysis."[8]

One of my first victories for Kevin as an advocate came after he had an agonizing eight-week hospital/skilled nursing stay where he suffered ongoing, chronic, unrelenting pain. This was years after he had only been on a feeding tube, and his health was worse. Through this experience, we stumbled onto a new doctor who seemed to care about Kevin's quality of life and not just about him staying alive. This new doctor had a palliative care focus and served a large group of disabled individuals in his spare time. He agreed to let Kevin have a new swallow test to possibly let him taste and enjoy food again. This doctor offered a glimmer of hope for my brother I hadn't felt in years. And this experience emboldened me to find a way to restore his joy of eating, even if just a small amount.

The people overseeing Kevin's care doubted he would ever pass a swallow test since he had been on a G-tube for so long without eating or drinking. But I knew that he could do it. Don't ask me how, I just knew. This was my moment to fight for Kevin. I had cracked the door of hope, and I knew I had to attend the exam while they did this test.

Good thing I did! The technician gave Kevin something to swallow that had a solution on it so it would show up on the X-ray. It was a chalky substance, and Kevin grimaced after his tongue tasted it. The technician proclaimed, "See, he can't swallow." But knowing Kevin's entire quality of life was at stake, and that this technician was making a wrong conclusion without exploring the issue, I went into action. Something wasn't right. I said, "Please, don't stop. Allow me to ask some questions." I asked what the solution was going into his mouth and asked to taste it. It was Barium, and it was disgusting! I said, "No wonder Kevin doesn't swallow this stuff!" Kevin was spitting it out, not because he couldn't swallow, but because he thought it tasted gross.

Realizing Kevin must swallow this stuff to get his freedom, I went into full-on sister mode and explained to Kevin that if he could show them he could swallow it, he could eat food again, like pumpkin pie and ice cream. I begged him to do it for me. I took my time to explain the situation and pleaded with him to swallow it, even though it tasted bad. I knew he understood me, and he opened his mouth and began to swallow multiple bites in a row to defy everyone's expectations and *pass* the swallow test! I was so proud of him.

What I learned was that the battles continue despite overcoming this obstacle. Even when he "passed" the swallow test, everyone was worried about liability (the root of many of Kevin's battles). Our new doctor worried Kevin was still at risk and would not sign off on regular feedings from the staff, but he did allow the family to feed him, at least at first. The staff, as much as they wanted to honor the family's wishes, was at the mercy of the doctor's medical recommendation due to their liability concerns with their licensing. So, I took the short-term win of family-only allowed feedings, and whenever I visited Kevin, he would light up when I'd say, "Kevin, do you want some chocolate pudding?" or pumpkin pie or apple sauce . . . He would open his mouth like a little bird, laughing at how his sister fought the naysayers and found a way to bring back a little delight to his palate. I would tell him, "Kevin, stop laughing, or you will end up aspirating and then get me in trouble!" He would only laugh harder. He has a truly rebellious side.

As Kevin has aged, he has battled several more serious rounds of pneumonia and skin infections—most of these hospitalized him for weeks. The battles continue, and the journey is long for him—yet he lives life to the fullest and rebounds each time, though it is getting tougher on his body. Sadly, a few years after he was approved for family-only feedings, he was hospitalized with another severe bout of aspiration pneumonia—so severe that he was almost put on a ventilator, and they feared for his life. Sadly, I was not there to advocate and speak to Kevin before his swallow test, and the doctors wouldn't sign off on his feedings. The slight possibility that his sickness had come from these random and rare feedings (I was only seeing him around once or twice a month then) held more weight than the family's cry for "quality of life" for him. Liability is powerful in decisions like this. No one will risk the blame. This time, I felt hopeless.

For a period of time, I had to surrender the fight to convince others of what I believed to be Kevin's rights—to enjoy small amounts of food rather than live "safely" on a G-tube. Enjoying my own freedom to eat eroded when I knew Kevin was being denied his cherished pleasure. Perhaps that has happened to you when someone you love can't enjoy something you can. Of course, I never wanted Kevin to be in danger, but I listened to my gut about what was best for him and questioned the conclusions of these doctors, nurses, and government licensing rules. Eventually, my advocacy followed my instincts, and once I learned his occasional oral gratification was very likely *not* the cause of his last pneumonia, I picked up the battle to regain my brother's simple pleasure.

> *Of course, I never wanted Kevin to be in danger, but I listened to my gut about what was best for him and questioned the conclusions of these doctors, nurses, and government licensing rules.*

With each battle, I sharpened my critical thinking skills and became more courageous to trust my gut, concluding that living to avoid risk alone should never override the joy of meaningful life experiences.

Through persistence, I raised the oral gratification feeding issue again, and this time, re-negotiated with his doctor a way to get Kevin back his food. The truth was that even *without* any food or drink orally, Kevin continued to have incidents of aspiration pneumonia, and it became apparent to multiple GI doctors that it was resulting from issues with his G-tube formula feedings, such as reflux, inflammation, and constipation—not his minimal bites of pureed food. At the time of this writing, Kevin regularly gets simple, small meals that bring him much joy—especially his morning banana or his chocolate pudding. He doesn't like oatmeal, though.

INSIGHTS FOR THE HEART

Advocacy: Honey & Vinegar

*"Unless someone like you cares a whole awful lot,
nothing is going to get better. It's not."*

—Dr. Seuss, The Lorax

As a sibling, I had no authority to make decisions for my brother. Looking back, I see how much easier it is to simply trust an expert. The emotional toll of making these decisions is heavy. Yet, there is power in learning to trust your gut, ask the hard questions, challenge the status quo, and persevere to advocate for those we love. Most of the time, it works better with honey. Every once in a while, vinegar is necessary.

Advocating for my brother and others unleashed something within me that had been bottled up, probably due to having to sit by and watch Kevin's life be so affected by critical decisions pushed by those in authority. While my mom and dad didn't challenge the doctors like I would have liked, my mom had raw advocacy skills in other areas. I'm fairly sure if she hadn't been so wounded by Kevin's disability and culturally programmed to trust others more than herself, she probably would have done things differently. Because my mother was emotionally crippled by my brother's disability, her advocacy skills tended to kick in on the simple things instead of the big stuff—those things that she lacked control over kept her paralyzed. So, she naturally focused on those things she could control, like making sure his fingernails were clipped, his face was washed, or he had lotion on his dry hands. It seemed she made herself numb so she wouldn't feel the pain of being unable to fix her suffering son.

In my parents' generation, doctors were the almighty authority source. They were never questioned. While I have tremendous respect for doctors, my generation and the ones that follow have come to understand that there are a myriad of medical opinions out there, and no one doctor has all the answers. Most doctors would agree, I think. While they may be MDs, they are not "M Deities," as my friend says. We have learned to search out second, third, and fourth opinions. We have discovered that the body is a holistic unit, and there is value in an integrative approach to health. What we ingest into our body matters to our health. Pharma drugs typically only treat symptoms, not root causes, resulting in a possible lifelong dependence on drugs to manage symptoms instead of promoting health. Discovering answers to health issues takes longer than a ten to fifteen-minute appointment, the allotted time doctors have with patients if they bill insurance. More and more people are realizing that uncovering root causes is the secret to long-term healing.

Healthcare opinions can be more of an art rather than a science. Because of so many medical experiences with my brother, I have learned to question the so-called experts and give credence to my own ability to think, question, research, and seek out the truth using logic, reason, and even exploring medical opinions and journal articles to serve as a medical conservator to my brother.

> *"Trust instinct to the end,*
> *even though you can give no reason."*
>
> —Ralph Waldo Emerson

When the doctor said that Kevin was mentally retarded and couldn't understand anything, I knew this was not true. In my gut, I just knew. We saw Kevin smile at us when we visited. He cried when we left. He laughed when my brother Brian and I fought. He squealed with delight when it was mealtime. He looked intently into our eyes when we spoke to him. His look is always piercing, as if a laser beam of supernatural light is penetrating straight from his heart to ours. My parents' doctor for Kevin got this one wrong. I often wonder what we could have done differently if the doctor had told us that Kevin did *not* have cognitive brain damage. He was, in fact, perfectly normal mentally, but he only had damage in his motor cortex—the part of the brain that controlled voluntary movements. Would we have been able to teach him to read? Could he have been a candidate for one of those computers that reads your thoughts and writes them out? Would they have invested in discovering a way for him to communicate? Would they have kept him home longer? Would he be walking today because they would have made a greater effort to mainstream him like so many people with special needs kids do now? Would he have had a speech therapist working with him regularly to speak? Perhaps much could have changed for Kevin had we not believed the falsehood that Kevin's brain didn't work.

I do not blame my parents; it was the culture of the day to accept the experts' opinions and to "stay in your own lane." And I don't blame the doctors either, as I'm sure they believed what they said. I do believe my mom and dad played the best hand they could with the cards they were dealt. Without the internet, they were not empowered like today to do their own research or find alternative views.

A few years ago, I met a man in his 50s, fully wheelchair-bound, with severe cerebral palsy, who had a mother with her own opinions that ran counter-cultural to mainstream medical opinions, even in the 60s. This gentleman can speak, but with great difficulty, and to those he meets for the first time, his spoken words can be indiscernible. When I initially met him, I was surprised to learn he had written a book.

My ignorance humbled me as I learned this man was an intelligent go-getter. He had two college degrees, was a computer programmer, and spent twelve years of his life typing an autobiography *using only his left pinky finger.* He credits his mom with *not* believing the doctors who told her she should place him somewhere that could care for him. Instead, she chose to believe in the capabilities of her son and raise him at home. How did she have the courage to go against the culture? She dedicated her life to teaching him to read, speak, think, and learn. Having never been institutionalized and allowed to pursue his education and dreams, this man was given a life no one thought was possible.

*"I try to take what voice I have
and I give it to those who don't have one at all."*[9]

—W. Eugene Smith

An old American proverb refers to people with the quality of persistence, relentlessness, pursuit, or advocacy as being the "squeaky wheel" because if a wheel squeaks, apparently, a mechanic will give it oil to shut it up. In essence, the "squeaking" works. The wheel gets the attention it needs.

I guess this could describe an advocate, defined as "one who pleads the cause of another."[10] But while the phrase "squeaky wheel" has a negative connotation, an advocate connotes that the motive is a worthy cause and is "other-focused," a much more positive approach. As a secondhand sufferer, I have learned to embrace advocacy to function and heal. Perhaps you, too, have found ways to advocate for the one you love (or perhaps the cause they represent). We have all seen it: the mother who lost a child to a drunk driver becomes an advocate for saving other kids from the same fate (M.A.D.D.); the father of an autistic child who pours himself into discovering what caused the sudden change in behavior and then starts a fund to uncover the cure; the teen sibling of a special needs brother who stands up to the bullies trying to intimidate his brother; the daughter who constantly asks questions of the direct care staff at her mother's assisted living home to make sure her mom is eating enough and getting her proper medicine and daily activities; the friend who is determined to spend all the time she can with her terminally-ill friend, bringing joy to a dire circumstance; the spouse who challenges the oncologist who says there is no way to cure cancer other than chemo and instead pursues integrative ways to find innovative healing treatments to go after the root cause; the mom who speaks at the school board meetings when her third grader is exposed to something age inappropriate outside of approved curriculum.

These people are all advocates. And perhaps none of their advocacy actions will change the situation completely, but they do help and can give meaning and purpose to life when we stand in the gap for another to be their voice. To be an advocate is to do for others what you would want them to do for you. However, advocacy without diplomacy and honor may not work. While "the squeaky wheel may get the oil" a time or two, "you catch more flies with honey rather than vinegar" over the long haul. The Golden Rule still applies: treat others as you want others to treat you. In my case, I am dependent on others to help my brother. If I am rude, demanding, irritating, or lack self-control and grace, I may feel a momentary release of stress by venting raw emotional frustration, but it will likely produce a longer-term negative result with my brother's caregivers and overseers. Other times, I take the time to build relationships with Kevin's care team, and at times, I let things go and show them grace for the difficulty of their jobs, lack of enough staff, and the reality that living in an institution regulated by public health departments comes with unavoidable drawbacks.

I've learned the hard way as I have taken on many complex and emotionally charged battles for my brother. In general, when people are upset about something or gripped by fear, anxiety, or anger, it is not always easy to remain peaceful, loving, respectful, patient, and kind. In fact, it takes intentionally being self-aware of these triggers of emotion to guard our tongues and remain steady and effective as an advocate. I have not always been successful at this, especially in those times when I knew with all my heart that Kevin's rights were being violated during the "COVID years" with so much confusion and overregulation. Sometimes passionate advocacy coupled with wisdom is needed—when honey turns to vinegar. This kicked in for me when Kevin was hospitalized with COVID-19, and I took on the hospital that was denying him life-saving treatment while giving him a drug without our permission that was harming him. My unrelenting drive to save his life took me all the way up to the Chief Medical Officer of the hospital, and I was able to diplomatically yet fiercely get Kevin what he needed. Even though he recovered in forty-eight hours, he still was required to stay for twenty days and then quarantine for another ten when he went back to his home. This was an extremely difficult time for Kevin; the isolation took its toll. Thankfully, I was educated on what was happening and what Kevin needed, and I was well versed on the details of the COVID outbreak so I could have intelligent conversations with the doctors, aiding in my credibility. In this situation, it took a combination of honey (respect, kindness, and wisdom) and vinegar (unrelenting boldness, annoying tenacity, firing a doctor, and not giving up) to save my brother.

Almost always, we need to decide which battles to fight and which we should let go of out of pure emotional bandwidth. Some are winnable, some are not, and some don't rank as important as others. The wisdom is knowing the difference. Our gut, heart, instinct, conscience, etc., often tell us when something is not right, and it is then that we are in the right position to "squeak," hopefully with honey, and advocate for what is right for our loved ones.

SPIRITUAL REFLECTIONS

Keeping God in a Sunday Box

"We can't box God in, but we can box ourselves out. If God isn't living up to our expectations, maybe it's time to change our expectations of Him."[11]

My advocacy for my brother—and my kids and friends—grew bolder with time. This may have stemmed from my early inherited beliefs that God was distant and wasn't just going to swoop in for a rescue. My mom epitomized the saying, "God helps those who help themselves." While I actually agree with some of the underlying principles behind this statement, I was surprised to find out later this wasn't a Bible verse. And with this belief comes a heavy burden to be always in a state of alert to control and protect circumstances as much as possible. While I promised myself I would never be a "control freak" like I thought my mom was, I no doubt struggled with this tendency, especially when I became a mom. My mom felt that since God had failed to cause her labor to be on time and He is a good God, He must not intervene in human affairs. She blamed herself deep down for not demanding that the doctor deliver her baby on her due date, as she assumed those two extra weeks of being late were what caused his cord to get in the wrong position. Since God wouldn't take care of things, she would need to be in charge. And that she did with just about everyone else in her life from then on.

While I am a huge fan of being an advocate, I believe my original motive for advocacy was born out of distrust of God. Just as my mom modeled, I thought I must act alone. Though subconscious at the time, I see this in hindsight. My spiritual life was disconnected from my emotional life. At this stage of my faith journey, God was in a separate compartment—all by Himself. My spiritual life was in a box and only something I opened up on Sundays when I was expected to go to church. The rest of the week, God stayed in His Sunday box. Don't get me wrong, I had some wonderfully loving Sunday School teachers, family friends, and church memories. I memorized the Twenty-third Psalm and enjoyed the warmth of a loving God through my teachers and family friends. But my two worlds didn't usually overlap in the same week. And this was the same for my parents, it seemed. They had two sets of friends—church friends and community friends. The wine came out for one, and it stayed locked up for the other. I don't judge this, but it always seemed odd that there wasn't a lot of integration.

My Sunday box stayed on a shelf during the week as God did not seem relevant to our everyday lives. To me, God was more of an old man with big powers written about in an old book. I liked knowing He was there, though, and generally thought He was someone I needed to respect. But looking back, He was distant and historical more than anything. I never questioned His goodness at this point, but I subconsciously questioned His usefulness.

TOOLS FOR THE HEART

Trust your instincts, and don't be afraid to be counter-cultural by challenging the status quo, even if it goes against the world's "wisdom." Become an advocate for those without a voice, especially those you love, but do so winsomely, as much as possible. An additional benefit of advocacy is that when we are empowered to make a difference, it alleviates a small bit of our secondhand suffering.

Questions to Ponder:

1. Do you feel the compulsion to control things in the present due to being out of control in the past? What do you try to control, and how has this worked for you? Any ideas on how to let some of it go?

2. Do you doubt yourself at times and struggle to stand up for what you think is right when the "experts" are giving you another opinion? What can you do to gain more confidence in your gut instinct?

3. Have you experienced the role of being an advocate and the thrill of making a difference in someone's life? If so, what is your proudest moment? Have you experienced success with the honey or vinegar approach—or both?

4. Do you believe God can intervene in human affairs, or is He somewhere off in the distance, just letting things happen as they will? What has your experience been with God in this way?

Practical Steps:

Consider giving your inner voice more credence by paying attention to your gut feeling when it comes to decision-making, whether for you or your loved one. For instance, if you feel unsettled or uncomfortable with something an authority figure is recommending, take time to pause, ask critical questions, seek out alternative opinions if needed, and muster up the courage to challenge the status quo.

Get inspired by reading a biography of healthy advocates. A few of my heroes include:

- Queen Esther (Holy Bible, Esther 1–10): Queen Esther was strategic and wise in her advocacy to the king and saved millions of her people from extermination.
- *The Hiding Place* by Corrie Ten Boom: The story of a Dutch watchmaker who risked her life by helping Jews and underground workers escape from the Nazis and survived the death camp to tell about it.
- *A Stroke of Insight, A Brain Scientist's Personal Journey* by Jill Taylor: The story of how a mother helped her adult daughter recover full use of her brain over an eight-year period following a devastating stroke.
- "The Persistent Widow" (Bible, Luke 18): The short story of a woman who has little power in the world's eyes, but she refuses to give up on getting justice.

"And who knows but that you have come to your royal position for such a time as this?"

—ESTHER 4:14 (NIV)

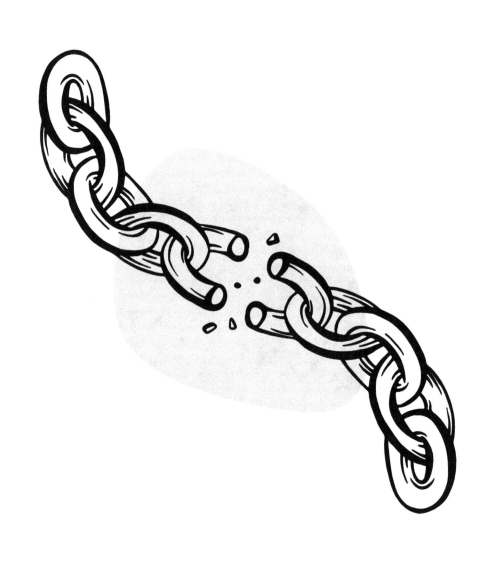

CHAPTER THREE

Breaking Up with Guilt and Fear

"Guilt: the gift that keeps on giving."

—ERMA BOMBECK

Years ago, a woman I know wrote a book for parents of children with special needs. A few days before the book went to press, the author, Janet, and I literally bumped into each other as we entered a local coffee store. When I learned of her book topic, I shared that I was the sibling of a special needs brother, and she asked for my perspective on one of my biggest struggles. Without hesitation, I blurted out "guilt." She thought it was providential that we ran into each other a day before her book was to be printed and was able to add it in time to a relevant section. Below is a portion of my quote in her book:

"The Big Sister"
(Excerpt from *Until I See: Peaceful Paths to Parenting Children with Special Needs* by Melonie Janet Mangum, used with permission)

> While it may not seem logical, guilt is a very big by-product for the sibling of a disabled individual. Ask any of us.
> As the older sister of a severely disabled brother with cerebral palsy, I have grown up feeling helpless, guilty, and in a constant state of searching for answers to the deepest mysteries of life. With no authority to be a decision-maker

*in my brother's life, I had no choice but to be a frustrated
observer as my parents called all the shots for life decisions
for my sweet yet helpless brother.*

*Kevin is without the ability to control ANY of his
motor functions except his beautiful eyes and smile.
Standing by as a protective big sister, watching him grow
up and being unable to "fix him," I am in a constant state
of discontentment and restlessness. Not a day goes by
without a deep, dull ache in my soul because I am able to
live a "normal" life while my own flesh-and-blood brother
is locked into a body that does not work.*[12]

While there are so many types of secondhand suffering, being
a parent to a special needs child ranks as one of the most common;
siblings to those children/adults are equally common, although
sometimes more hidden. Growing up with a severely disabled sibling
takes its toll on one's thought life. And unlike a parent, they have no
decision-making power for anything. They inherit the unintended
consequences that tend to go under the radar for parents to even see.
For me, I was forced to grow up a bit faster, think a bit deeper, and
feel the weight of guilt perhaps a bit more than my peers. In my brief
research on this, I discovered a book called *The Normal One*, written
by Jeanne Safer, Ph.D., the sister of a difficult sibling. She writes about
the struggles of being "the normal one" in a family where her brother
suffered from severe mental and social instability. In her research,
she discovered something she coined as "the Caliban Syndrome,"
which she derived from the relationship between Miranda and Caliban
in Shakespeare's "The Tempest." Often, the siblings of very difficult,
high-maintenance, disabled, or dysfunctional people experience four
common characteristics:

1. Premature maturity
2. Compulsion to achieve

3. Survivor guilt
4. Fear of contagion (dread of magically catching the disability)

Safer describes the "normal ones" as:

> Cheerful caretakers, mature before their time, they are supposed to consider themselves lucky to be normal. They feel tormented by the compulsion to compensate for their parents' disappointments by having no problems and making no demands, and they are often unaware of the massive external and internal pressure to pretend that nothing is amiss.[13]

While Dr. Safer's sibling situation was nothing like mine, I do think she has done some valuable work in examining the effects of disabled and/or difficult siblings on the "normal" siblings. My parents' decision to place Kevin in a home early on may have been an unconscious preemptive attack to prevent my brother and I from suffering from a crippling dose of the Caliban Syndrome. There is no doubt I have carried all four of the above characteristics Dr. Safer lists. Recently, I read an old yearbook entry from a friend in high school. She was very popular and won just about every award for her beauty, personality, and grades. I found it interesting that she wrote in my yearbook: "Camille, deep down I always know you are right about things we talk about. It bugs me because I don't want you to be right, but deep down I know you are." I don't recall what I said or did that was "right," but I do remember always feeling like a misfit with kids my own age. Some people call it an "old soul," others call it "a nerd," and perhaps others say, "mature for her age." I don't think I was necessarily more mature in the traditional sense, but I do think my insights, feelings, and perspectives were unique due to watching my beloved little brother be placed in an institution while I struggled with guilt over living a "normal" life. Don't get me wrong—I was still a normal teenager who rebelled against my parents, slammed doors, pouted in my room while listening to records my mother ended up breaking in half (ACDC . . . Rush), and made my share of juvenile, stupid mistakes with half a frontal lobe. Yet, there was something deeper in me that disdained the shallow, silly, flighty conversations and actions of middle school and high school kids. I carried a deep, inner sadness that left normal teenaged attempts at "fun" not fulfilling at all. I may not have been more mature, but I certainly seemed to have a depth inside me that grounded me and made me feel different from others my age. Or maybe I was just odd.

As a first-born, I could attribute my desire to excel and achieve to my birth order. However, it makes sense that a sibling of a disabled child also feels the need to excel . . . perhaps subconsciously to make up for what the other sibling can't do. Or maybe it's to please the parents who are grieving over the loss of ability for their other child. It seems intuitive in hindsight, but often the drive to succeed was nothing I was conscious of at the time. Striving for that A, feeling defeated over B-pluses, running for student government positions, having to make the Varsity cheerleading squad just to prove that I could, trying to please my parents to get that pat on the back, impressing teachers and future bosses to make them think I was the best student and employee. Admittedly, I was a bit obsessed with achievement for most of my early life. Deep down, I think I was searching for a way to feel special and unique—a form of achievement in and of itself. I never realized this subconscious performing or competitive drive could be due to my connection to Kevin.

Guilt, however, was the elephant in the room that none of us ever acknowledged. A question that ran constantly through my head, and I have heard from others with similar struggles, was, "Why him . . . why not me?" After all, we have the same set of parents. We were born in close proximity by around three years, and there didn't seem to be any apparent reason for Kevin's birth accident. It could have been me. But it wasn't. Why did I deserve a full life, and my innocent brother is sentenced to a wheelchair, diapers, a locked-in body, and a mute voice for the rest of his? The guilt ate me up inside. I remember friends asking me, "Do you have brothers and sisters? How many?" I remember thinking it would be easier just to say, "Yeah, I have one brother." Yet, I could never do it. I was always honest and said, "I have two brothers: one is at home, and the other has cerebral palsy and doesn't live with us anymore." I didn't just want to say "two brothers" without giving more detail. I'm not sure why, other than I wanted everyone to know who he was and for him to have others care about him. Usually, people shrugged and didn't really know what to say, so we would move on and play on the monkey bars.

Occasionally, there were very special people who took the time to show real concern. They would ask more questions, ask me how it made me feel, or suggest they visit him with me sometime. These people usually turned into good friends, or they were people who had experienced their own hardships and had learned the art of true empathy and compassion. They knew how to engage with someone dealing with heartache. That was rare but so meaningful to me (and still is).

What began when I was a child continues as an adult to this day. My thought life was and still is consumed with voices that taunt me: "Why are you having fun when your brother is stuck in a wheelchair?" "What gives you the right to enjoy chewing your steak dinner when your brother has no options other than a puree of institutional food?" "How dare you toss and turn in your sleep to get comfortable when Kevin can't move unless someone lifts him and turns him!" Another haunting thought came to me whenever I had an itch and went to scratch it for relief. I couldn't comprehend what it must be like for Kevin to have an itch and not be able to tell anyone or scratch it. If I went on a date, a jog, or a walk on the beach, I would feel guilty and not allow myself to feel any happiness. It's like I purposely sabotaged anything good in my life unless Kevin was able to experience the same thing. It seemed that no matter how good my life was, I would always have a way to diffuse the joy with self-induced guilt that would compare my life to my brother's—almost as a way of punishment. The minute I would catch myself experiencing happiness, laughter, or even contentment, guilt would wash over me and chip away at my joy. I would not allow myself to feel joy to any full measure . . . it was consistently cut short with guilt and haunting lies, half-truths in retrospect.

During the end of this book writing process, I discovered that my guilt complex went even deeper than the "why him and not me?" questions. Through some inner healing work with a trainer, I unlocked something deep down—I felt like a misfit of sorts in that most of my childhood, I had often felt like an outsider, one who never quite fit in and was overlooked. Whether it was not being a part of the "cool groups" in high school, being picked second to last for kickball teams by my peers in fourth grade (yes, there was someone worse than I, apparently), or not being invited to a friend's birthday party in second grade, I never felt good enough to be chosen, and as a result, I was attracting that kind of label (or giving off that "vibe" to others). Turns out this feeling of never measuring up to peers may have been a subconscious way to counter the guilt I had when my parents "chose me" (and Brian) over Kevin when they placed him in an institution. Tucked away in the corner of my heart, I had been carrying guilt that I was the reason my brother was sent away so that my parents could give their "normal children" the attention and focus they needed.

> *I believed deep down that Kevin sacrificed his life with his family for me.*

In other words, I believed deep down that Kevin sacrificed his life with his family for me. This realization was an even heavier form of guilt than the guilt of him being disabled. And somehow, I had subconsciously taken on Kevin's abandonment and not being chosen and put myself in situations where I wasn't chosen, or felt left out, like some sort of self-punishment. These thoughts and feelings of guilt—some conscious and others unconscious—have followed me my entire life and are a wrestling match to this day, although I'm slowly healing.

The final item of the "Caliban Syndrome" is a little harder to detect in my life, although I do believe it was there in a bizarre form. Did I often think about inheriting cerebral palsy myself? Yes and no. I knew intellectually that I could not "catch" the disease per se because it was only brought on by an accident. It was not contagious. Yet, I did often worry about "slipping in a bathtub" as I would stand up or fool around while taking a bath because my mom would warn me that falling could give me cerebral palsy. I think this is one reason I was risk-averse with physical acts. I think my mom, out of her own fear that something dreadful would happen to Brian and me would intentionally plant fear for us to take risks. I never wanted to ski beyond a bunny hill or advance much past snow plowing for fear of falling head over heels. I've never wanted to fly in a small plane or helicopter for fear of crashing, and I've refused to consider scuba diving for fear of suffocating. But more than that, I grew up worrying that somehow I was destined to have a baby with cerebral palsy—even though there was no logical reason to think this way. But it entertained my thought life often. Maybe God would give me a child with CP or another disability because He knows I can understand it. Where did I get that theology?

Interestingly, I also developed panic attacks as a child. I didn't have a name for it, though. I do not know if there is any connection to Kevin, but I guess I will leave that to the psychotherapists to debate. To my best recollection, they began when I was around four years old. The first time I remember it happening was right after my parents got me a new swing set for our backyard. We had just moved to California a couple of years earlier so my dad could start his work at Pepperdine University as one of the early professors in the late 1960s and early 1970s. He had just finished his Ph.D. at Boston University (where I came on the scene) and had taught college for a couple of years in Arkansas before being recruited to Pepperdine. We bought a brand-new tract home in a new community called Westlake Village, about twenty-five minutes from Malibu. I remember there were hardly any trees, and our backyard was all dirt except for this new swing set. Kevin would have been about one year old when we got it. I think my parents were worried I wasn't getting much attention due to Kevin's profound needs. Maybe they wanted to give me something to enjoy while they were busy managing Kevin, the new job, and home.

One day, in the backyard, my dad began pushing me on the swing. I got fairly high and remember feeling out of control and experiencing a really funny and new feeling of fear—the kind when your tummy drops out of your body on a roller coaster—and . . . I freaked out. I began screaming, "Dad, STOP!!!" Much to my horror (and his complete lack of understanding of the complex emotions I was feeling), he didn't stop on my first command. Or my second or third. Perhaps he just couldn't stop me instantly like I wanted, and I remember feeling an intense panic coming over me as I realized, "I can't stop this swing," and I felt that my "tummy was tickling me," and I needed to get OFF! So, feeling completely out of my element and suddenly allergic to speed, heights, and lack of control, I jumped off to save my four-year-old self. My dad most likely thought nothing of it at the time because it probably happened in a split second. But to me, it seemed an eternity, and I remember the emotions vividly to this day. This "tickling in my tummy" would haunt me for the rest of my life in the form of panic attacks whenever there was a feeling of being out of control or intense pressure or fear—often, but not always, it was combined with speed or heights.

A panic attack is "an abrupt surge of intense fear or intense discomfort that reaches a peak within minutes."[14] It happened again when I was a little older, and my parents' friends took me to a carnival where there was a Merry-Go-Round. Benign enough, right? Goodness no. To my complete dismay and embarrassment, I humbly admit that once I got on that thing and it began spinning, I screamed and screamed and screamed (including shedding tears) to get off! I remember the absolute horror of my parents' friends begging the Merry-Go-Round "boss" to stop and let me get off. They did, and with it came my new life with phobias of speeds as slow as Merry-Go-Rounds—as well as the panic that comes with being out of control of myself.

It wasn't until I was a full-blown adult that I even realized there was a word for what was happening to me when I was overcome with this irrational fear. Knowing other people experienced panic attacks gave me some consolation that I wasn't completely crazy. I guess a diagnosis is often the first step to a cure.

While I've had much improvement over the years, the same feeling carried with me as I got older and occasionally happened when I began driving on freeways—especially in the fast lane—because of the feeling of being trapped by speed. I sometimes feel it when a plane is going at high speed during takeoff or has a lot of turbulence. (I can't stand turbulence!) Not a great thing when all my grown kids now live in three different states, and I travel often. But, like all of us, I am in process! The consequences of guilt and fear have been crippling in my life, even as I look super normal to most.

All four characteristics of the Caliban Syndrome manifest differently for each of us. I've shared mine with great vulnerability as I hope that by doing so, your heart will be unlocked from areas that have been closed off. It is only when we shed light on these hidden wounds that may have hindered our ability to thrive that we can find freedom to hope again.

INSIGHTS FOR THE HEART

Our Blessings Are Non-transferable

"An unpeaceful mind cannot operate normally."

—WATCHMAN NEE

It is interesting to me to hear different stories from other siblings of special needs individuals who feel suffering differently than I have. In my case, I didn't lack attention. In other families, it was different. In the book Being the Other One, author Kate Strohm, whose sister has cerebral palsy, shares her childhood struggle with anxiety that lasted decades later:

> I began to understand that from an early age I had feared that if I showed any loss of control—for example, if my hands shook or my voice trembled—people might think I was like my sister, that there was something wrong with me too. I needed to be perfect and came to be terrified of others' judgments on me. As a small child, I had made the decision "not to make waves." I wanted to make life easy for my parents, to make up for their pain . . .
>
> I needed to be perfect, but on another level I felt guilty about all the things I could do and achieve but my sister could not.
>
> I felt a range of negative feelings toward my sister but also incredible sorrow for the life she led. I resented all the attention she received and wished I could have more. When I did get attention, I felt guilty and unworthy. None of my concerns ever seemed as important as hers. I experienced guilt about most of my feelings and couldn't express any of them; they seemed to be pushed to an innermost corner, out of reach to me and to others. If these feelings escaped, I thought, people might see me for who I really was: someone who wanted my own sister to disappear. I was full of shame.[15]

As with anything in life, it helps to feel like you are not alone and others have had similar experiences and struggles—in this case, with guilt and anxiety. While Kate's feelings towards her sister were not the same as mine towards my brother, it is clear that she suffered from similar effects of Caliban Syndrome with her lifelong anxiety and plenty of guilt. As I look back on my reflections on the Caliban Syndrome points, I realize how silly it seems that I may have inadvertently created my own "disability"—one manufactured by my thought life and not a true disability like my brother's. Perhaps by creating my own form of a disability, I was subconsciously inflicting punishment on myself for having a "normal" life and not suffering as much as my brother. I am not a psychologist, but from my own "armchair," this seems plausible. In both cases of experiencing guilt and panic attacks, I now see the common denominator—they stem from voices in my head that are simply lies. I may, in fact, be a textbook example of Dr. Safer's theory of the Caliban Syndrome: I had an odd fear of being disabled myself, I was constantly striving to perform by being a high achiever, and I held onto tons of guilt as well as matured in some ways at a young age.

Of all the four characteristics spoken of in the Caliban Syndrome (premature maturity, compulsion to achieve, guilt, and fear of catching the disability), I have learned that, obviously, the most damaging are the latter two—guilt and unfounded fears. As a secondhand suffering sibling of a disabled/special needs person, guilt may be normal, but it is not beneficial to anyone. (This can also be true if you live and someone else dies.) The voices that spoke to me appeared truthful. After all, it was true that I could do things my brother could not. It was true that it could have happened to me at birth instead of him. It was true that he was still in diapers in his fifties, and I was out by age three (yet, I admittedly wet the bed until I was seven). It was true that Kevin would never marry and have kids, and I married and had three kids. It was true that he couldn't do anything on his own, yet I could do or be whatever I chose, mostly. But were these constant "truth daggers" I was stabbing at myself helping me in any way? No. They were only stabbing small holes in my heart, causing more pain. But if they were true, shouldn't I endure the pain for the sake of my brother? This was my struggle.

"And you will know the truth, and the truth will set you free."

JOHN 8:32

It took me a while, but later in my life, I finally found a reason to stop throwing heart daggers at myself. A psychologist friend of mine once explained it like this: If life is exemplified as a pie, and Kevin and I were both given a full pie, then for me to not eat of my pie (by making myself burdened with guilt instead of enjoying the pie) doesn't make Kevin have any more of his pie. We each get our own "life pie," and there is no sharing. What I did with my pie did not affect his pie in any way. Prior to this "a-ha moment," I was under the impression that if I did not eat the delicious pieces of pie that were given to me, somehow, I was indirectly giving it to my brother. But, in reality, *the pieces of the pie are not transferable.* In fact, when I really thought about it, I knew that Kevin would *not* want me to *not* eat my pie as it does him no good, and he loves me. He would probably say, "Please enjoy your pie, especially since I can't eat mine . . . I want you to enjoy yours for me! Why should the two of us *both* miss out on our pie?" This simple analogy was a turning point in my process of trying to let go of the guilt I carried for enjoying life's goodness using my working mind and body when he couldn't use much of his.

If you struggle with guilt about enjoying the pleasures of life when your loved one cannot do the same, consider this pie analogy. If you don't take what is yours, it goes to waste. You can't transfer it to anyone else, so take the blessings and be fully present and grateful for what you've been given without feeling guilty. I know it is hard, but it is an insight I continue to learn and grow from, and I hope you can as well.

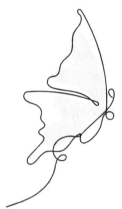

SPIRITUAL REFLECTIONS

Confusion by Multiple Voices

*"I must exchange whispers with God
before shouts with the world."*

—Lysa TerKeurst

At this stage in my quest for truth with God, I was living mundanely with a traditional church upbringing and a distant but good God. My reflections in this section often are what I discovered *later* due to the struggles I had dealt with at the time on my journey. In this case, my struggle was that God was not the primary voice I was hearing in my head as I faced ongoing guilt, unwarranted fears, a need to perform and get attention, and a consistent desire to fit in.

For most of my life, I've struggled with heavy guilt living a full life while my brother stayed in the same institution bound to a wheelchair or a bed without a way to communicate his wants or thoughts or use his hands or feet.

I was so focused on all the truthful facts about my brother's life that were devastating when compared to the opportunities I was given, and I was bound by a deep sadness that kept me in an invisible secondhand-suffering state. However, while these facts were truthful, they taught me some important spiritual lessons later about the source of these "voices of truth" and the ramifications of these voices, which often left me agitated.

Looking back, I grew to understand that the voices I was hearing that whispered these "true statements" were coming from one of several sources: me, God, the world (culture), or from a dark force (lies or the devil). After a lot of growing up and wrestling through these dark, "truthful" thoughts, I have come to see they were *not* from God because they were not edifying or redemptive, and to haunt someone with guilt didn't sound like His character. Instead, they were most likely from my own voice with my slightly pessimistic worldview, coupled with the devil himself, who thrives on haunting people with guilt and lies to bring misery. According to the Bible, Satan is a liar, and he loves to speak some truth mixed with lies or twist the truth for the purpose of discouragement, pain, and destruction. True—I was blessed with the ability to use my mind and body to enjoy life, unlike Kevin. But what was *not* true was that I needed to wallow in guilt and sadness to somehow make Kevin feel better or punish myself for not being disabled like he was. I now see this was the enemy wanting to rob me of what was good for no purpose whatsoever. It didn't help Kevin at all for me to be miserable. And it doesn't help your loved one for you to feel guilty about good things that happen to you or you not suffering as much as they do. So, when guilt, fear, and anxiety get a hold of your mind, take the time to ask yourself whose voice you are hearing before you believe it.

I also used to believe God would proactively inflict trials or tests on us to build our character. Where did I learn that? I was confused about fearing God and the "fear of God" written about in the Bible (the kind of fear that means awe and reverence). I had irrational fears, such as fear that God would give me a disabled child because I was experienced with disabilities, or He would cause me or my family to suffer from a bad disease to teach us humility. When I realized this was not God's whispers to my mind but more likely my own self-sabotaging voice or the voice of Satan, it was a step forward in my understanding the nature of God. Learning how to tell if my thoughts were from God or not was a multi-year learning process. It involved getting to know God's character through studying the Bible, reading inspiring and helpful authors, and spending time with others who invested in me as mentors in the faith. These were a few steps I took that eventually led to my breakthrough in my battle with guilt and fear.

In essence, it was as simple as getting to know what God sounds like and what He cares about. Imagine if you know someone really well, and they are accused of saying or doing something that seems completely out of character. Since you know them so well, you would have the authority to be a character witness to testify that their actions or words they are accused of does not sound like them—and you would be credible. When we know someone intimately, we learn their voice, their behavior, and the heart behind their character. We can speak with authority that recognizes when they are speaking to us or not.

I like what Dallas Willard says about one facet of "The Spirit of God's Voice":

The voice of God speaking in our souls also bears within itself a characteristic spirit. It is a spirit of exalted peacefulness and confidence, of joy, of sweet reasonableness and of goodwill. His voice is not the voice of a bully. It will not run over you and your will. It is, in short, the spirit of Jesus...

The sweet, calm spirit of God's voice carries over to the lives of those who speak with his voice: "But the wisdom from above is first pure, then peaceable, gentle, willing to yield, full of mercy and good fruits, without a trace of partiality or hypocrisy (James 3:17)."[16]

The more we invest in personally knowing the character of God, the more we recognize His voice. So when I began to learn that God's character, as expressed through Jesus's life, does not inflict harm, cause suffering, or twist the truth to project unproductive guilt on me, I could correctly diagnose the issue of the haunting "truthful" yet bullying voices. Truth alone is not the measuring stick. *Tone matters.* My mind needed a spiritual transformation so I could say "no" to the lies, whether they came from my own mind, the world, or Satan. Eventually, I no longer attributed to God what was actually another voice. And this was a major key to loosening the grip of guilt over me. It was like finally pulling the root out of an ugly weed that kept showing up in my mind, bringing unhealthy condemnation.

This is not something I learned overnight. In fact, it has taken a lifetime, and I am still learning how to tell the difference between my own brain telling me lies, the propaganda of the world and cultural icons, or even worse, the "evil one" disguised as an angel of light (2 Corinthians 11:14). I guess I've discovered a short cut—and that is to simply know God better. Just like bank tellers are trained to know the look and feel of an authentic dollar bill so they don't have to know all the various types of counterfeits to tell the difference between true and fake, we don't need to specialize in all the voices that are NOT God's in order to know His "voice." We do this by spending time getting to know God, reading the book He gave us about Him and His ways, and developing a mutual relationship where His voice becomes more and more familiar. For my fellow secondhand sufferers, it is a relationship worth growing as it has the likely additional effect of quieting all the other noise that can pollute our thinking and rob us of a sound mind.

"My sheep hear My voice,
and I know them, and they follow Me."

—John 10:27 (ESV)

One of my favorite descriptions about recognizing the voice of God is one I stumbled on with friends at a book club.

Although His voice is seldom audible, God creates in us hearing hearts. As we walk with Him— listening, noticing, expectant—we begin to discern the inner movement and quickening effect of God's voice, the luminous indelibility of His gentle whisper to our hearts. His subtle impartation shimmers with life and resonates with truth in a way that enables us to distinguish God's voice from all the others. And as we obey, we witness the fruit of "hearing ears."[17]

TOOLS FOR THE HEART

Often, secondhand suffering comes in the form of a parent to a child or a sibling to another sibling. Caliban Syndrome refers to four characteristics people share who have difficult, high maintenance, disabled, or dysfunctional siblings: premature maturity, compulsion to achieve, survivor guilt, and fear of contagion. Guilt and fear are some of the more damaging reactions. Recognize that guilt and fear, if allowed to grow, will paralyze your ability to live the life you were intended to live and does nothing to help your loved one live theirs. Also, it is important to be intentional in discerning the difference between the voices we hear.

Questions to Ponder:

1. Which of the four items from the Caliban Syndrome do you identify with the most?
2. Do you struggle with guilt on a regular basis when it comes to secondhand suffering, where you feel undeserving of experiencing happiness at times? If so, how did the pie analogy resonate with you?
3. If you struggle with unwanted thoughts and ongoing fears, how do you know what voice is speaking? What strategy can you employ to pay more attention to the source of the "voice" so you can better discern which voices are healthy and which are toxic?

Practical Steps:

With any healthy breakup, identifying the root issue gives us the motivation to do the hard thing and cut off anything that is not good for us. However, patterns and habits tend to take a while to break. When it comes to breaking up with ongoing guilt and fear patterns, consider pulling them out by the root. Try these out for growth:

- Memorize this quote from Brené Brown, a research professor on courage, vulnerability, shame, and empathy:

   "The most powerful stories may be the ones we tell ourselves. But beware—they're usually fiction."[18]

- Practice more focus on being present and enjoying the blessings you have instead of letting the voice of guilt or fear rob you of what is rightfully yours to enjoy.

- Study the character of God (to know His voice) by reading the words of Jesus because He said, "If you have seen me, you have seen the Father." Do this by finding a good "red letter Bible" (red letters are the recordings of Jesus's words). For starters, try the Book of John.

- Understand the difference between condemnation and conviction.[19]

- Study this chart and refer to it when you need help telling the difference:

Condemnation	Conviction
Voice produces guilt and shame.	Voice produces a warning signal to offer protection from danger.
Brings feelings of numbness, vagueness, shame, sadness, hopelessness, confusion, chaos—functions as an anesthetic to keep you off the path to healing.	Brings feelings of more clarity, specificity, hope and a path to action; functions as a tool to produce humility with a heart to move forward in right action on a specific thing.
Source: a lie/the devil	Source: truth/God
Keeps you in bondage and stuck.	Sets you free to make things right.
Discourages you to want to give up.	Motivates you to improve something specific.
Rooted in negativity or hate.	Rooted in hopefulness, grace, and love.

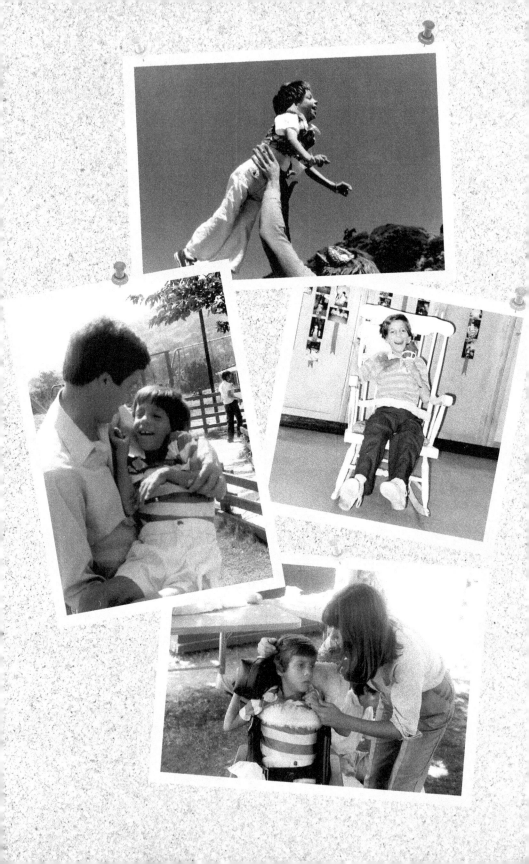

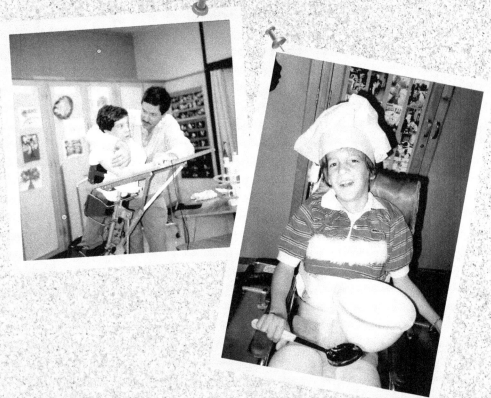

CHAPTER FOUR

Cultivating Empathy—It's a Discipline, Not Just a Feeling

"I do not ask the wounded person how he feels,
I myself become the wounded person."

—WALT WHITMAN, *Song Of Myself*

*I*attended Pepperdine University in the late 1980s and spent most of my years there trying to figure out my major. I think I may have won the record for switching majors the most times. The list included Advertising, Public Relations, Psychology, Sociology, Political Science, Organizational Management, and perhaps a few more I can't remember. In my senior year, my advisor finally told me that he needed to figure out a major for me that included most of these courses if I wanted to graduate in four years. It turned out that there was a little-known major that was as broad as they come . . . Social Science. Bingo! I'll take it.

My favorite class within this major was Sociology. Our teacher told us to think of an experiment we could do that would test people's reactions. It could be anything, and examples included living as a homeless person, standing backward in an elevator, or standing on a street corner in a clown costume singing opera. He recommended it be something we cared about and were curious to see how people reacted. It didn't take me too long to think of my project. I decided to *be* my brother Kevin for the day. Since he is *always* on my mind, I thought perhaps having some kind of experience would help me to understand what he goes through on an intimate level. How would I pretend to be a quadriplegic with severe cerebral palsy for an entire day? Could I actually fool people?

I called the director of the day program at the school my brother attended each day. Before he turned eighteen, he was being bussed to a center for handicapped kids for his "school." I talked to the director about the project I wanted to do and asked her if she would agree to keep this a secret and allow me to come for a day as a new student named "Camille." She would not tell any of the workers/caregivers who I really was, and in exchange, I would agree to act the role the entire day as a fully handicapped Cerebral Palsy teen . . . until the end of the day when we could confess the truth. While I had always secretly wanted to be an actress and had only been in one high school play (where I won "Best Actress in a Minor Role" in the musical *Oliver*, most likely due to me stunning the audience with my dramatic dying scene on stage as Old Sally), I was not prepared for how hard role-playing my brother would be.

The day began with my being greeted in the parking lot by the director, who secured my wheelchair. She rolled me in and introduced me to everyone as "the new girl who was in an accident and was enrolling in the school." Essentially, she gave a background story that sounded "legit" and rolled me around to the place where my day would begin. Because this was my brother's school and he would have recognized me, we waited until a day when he wasn't there (reportedly out sick). No one there had ever seen me before, and it was a life-impacting experience—one I will never forget.

I found myself focusing intently on Kevin and how he acted and must have thought. I guess actors call this "getting into their character." It was a lot of work at first since I am a verbal processor, and those who know me will appreciate how hard it was for me to be mute for a day. But as the day went on, it became easier as I "became my brother." Like Kevin, I forced myself to stare at different people and objects for longer lengths of time than I normally would. I clenched my fists and arms and body so that it looked as though I had spasticity. My arms would stretch out in tightened extensions, and my head would droop to one side, as my brother's does. My mouth would release drool on occasion because Kevin lacks muscle control, even over his mouth. I found myself making noises like Kevin . . . grunts and long vowel sounds in an attempt to make my voice heard, even though no one could understand me. When they got me out of my wheelchair for physical therapy and laid me on the floor, I stiffened up and made myself very heavy to imitate Kevin's inability to bear any weight. Once I was lying down on the mat, I found myself left there for a very long time . . . wondering what the point was other than giving me a break from my wheelchair. I remember the workers saying how heavy I was. I was about twenty-one at the time and 120 pounds. Oh, how I miss that scale number! What I noticed most was how the direct care staff talked about me as if I wasn't there and with a condescending tone. They would raise their voices, as well as their pitch when they talked to me. It was like I was a deaf two-year-old who only understood a foreign language!

"I believe empathy is the most essential quality of civilization."

—ROGER EBERT

My most vivid experience of the day was at lunchtime. They pulled me up to the lunch table and began to feed me. I was horrified as they were serving STEWED TOMATOES! Really? Of all the foods out there, they had to pick tomatoes? Similar to Indiana Jones in the "Raiders of the Lost Ark" when he said, "Snakes...why'd it have to be snakes?" I was thinking the same thing about tomatoes, the *one* food that I had refused to eat my whole life. I couldn't stand tomatoes. Moreover, there was nothing worse on my list of most hated foods than *stewed* tomatoes. It was as if God had decided to test me that day . . . to really show me how poor Kevin must feel when he was fed something he didn't like. I knew I couldn't eat it . . . but how could I do this and not break my character? I wanted a "time out" to tell them this was all a big school experiment, and at that moment, I paused and thought, "Alright . . . what *would* Kevin do if he didn't like something?" And then it all made sense. Kevin often refused to eat certain foods. He would buckle up his lips as if they were a locked safe. When the food came on the spoon towards his mouth, he would pucker up even tighter and not let any bit of the spoon in his mouth. He was stubborn. I could do this.

At least it was worth a try. So, I clenched my teeth, closed my lips, turned my head away, and made a weird noise as the spoon of slimy, mushy, cooked tomatoes headed my way. *This was war.* Unfortunately, before I knew it, the caregiver did the unthinkable. Feeling borderline abused and definitely outsmarted, she took her fingers and forced my mouth open and proceeded to shove the spoon in with brute force. Is this against the rules? Is it even allowed? Astonished and aghast, I had been defeated as the warm, watery, and squishy fruit touched my tongue. I thought I was going to vomit. So, pulling out my next chess move, I did what I had seen Kevin do countless times . . . I spit out the tomatoes all over myself. I know this sounds gross; it was. But I had hit my limit. The lady made some very rude and condescending remark and had the nerve to take the spoon, scoop up my regurgitated red droppings, and shove it back in my mouth! Could she not see I did not want these tomatoes in my mouth? Did I not get a vote? I was ready to forget the whole experiment and run out of there. But, because I was a good A student (high achiever, remember?), I stuck it out till the end of the day.

Later that day, after I had recovered from the tomato trauma, the director came over and gave me the cue that we could wrap it up. We had not rehearsed this, but the plan was for me to reveal my true self. I proceeded to stand up at her wink. At that point, I realized my acting skills should have been Emmy-nominated by the look on everyone's faces. The director then explained what we had been doing and that I was Kevin's sister. No one could believe it, and so I walked away feeling a bit like Sandra Bullock.

*"You never really understand a person
until you consider things from his point of view . . .
Until you climb inside of his skin and walk around in it."*

—To Kill a Mockingbird (emphasis mine)

All in all, it was a humbling experience. I vowed to never again talk loud or babyish to Kevin or anyone with a disability. I would never treat him as younger than he was. I would never force him to eat anything he doesn't want. And I will never forget what it felt like to be in his shoes—helpless, at the mercy of those around me, and frankly, bored. I learned a lot that day, and it brought me another step closer to my very special brother and only increased my motivation to try to bear his burdens.

There are many amazing people with extremely tough disabilities and overwhelming obstacles who have modeled perseverance. I am gripped by the intensity of my brother's challenges and the degree to which he has had to persevere without any aid of communication, physical control, or intellectual stimulation. He fights on without any super-beneficial incentives other than life itself. I think I would have given up long ago. My day is tough when I have a headache because I missed my morning latte or when our air conditioner goes out on a hot summer day. It's hard to imagine a situation like Kevin's to endure...and yet he perseveres with an obvious will to live. It is trendy to talk about being fully present and mindful. Well, Kevin is an expert. And I'm sure you know and love someone who has also taught you the meaning of perseverance and inspired you to increase your empathy capacity.

INSIGHTS FOR THE HEART

Growth through Empathy

*"If there is any one secret of success,
it lies in the ability to get the other person's point of view
and see things from his angle as well as your own."*

—HENRY FORD

My experience conceptually living inside my brother's body for a day at his "school" taught me more than just lessons about being handicapped. In retrospect, I learned much more about human value and worth and how to treat others, no matter what their position or status in life. Trapped inside a body like his, I remember that I still felt every human emotion, and my mind was occupied with being constantly observant of others. When I was forced to use only two of my senses—sight and sound—I saw and heard things I was not expecting. Well-intentioned, extraverted professionals around the staff became unknowingly condescending and aloof to me as a "client." It was clearly an unintentional attitude as these were kind and good people serving a unique group of individuals, but they seemed oblivious to the subtle differences in the way they treated me and the other "kids" versus the way they interacted with the staff. Without me playing this role, I doubt I would have ever noticed. It awakened me to a sensation I had never experienced so deeply—empathy.

"I have found the paradox, that if you love until it hurts, there can be no more hurt, only more love."

—MOTHER TERESA

It also brought to light that if I was not intentional with my actions, I may be unknowingly patronizing children, the disabled, the elderly, or those who look or act differently, simply by the tone of my voice. As I sensed this ignorant, unequal tone of voice by the staff towards me—no matter how loving, kind, and sincere they were—it made me feel less of a person and certainly not as respected as the people who worked there. I also realized how easy it is to treat the helpless this way. Until we are literally living in another's shoes, it is so hard to know how others feel inside. Perhaps if we all had an opportunity to be that other person for a day, the world would be a more grace-filled place, loaded with compassion and understanding.

I had a glimpse of insight that day, feeling like someone helpless, overlooked, a victim without a voice. I felt such a deep empathy for how my brother may feel. The inner actor in me became so intertwined with Kevin's character that after that day, I seemed to begin feeling Kevin's feelings and thinking his thoughts. Training ourselves to mentally and emotionally imagine ourselves in another's world and then intentionally cultivate empathy towards others is a powerful exercise to do before we jump to judgment or form conclusions.

I also think I developed a greater ability to respect others, no matter their appearance, ability, or social status. Being my brother for a day seemed to be a catalyst in my learning to resist shying away from feeling another's pain by "stepping into their shoes" emotionally. To not do so can result in a hardened heart. And if we allow our heart to become hardened to others—usually in an attempt to protect ourselves—we miss out on one of the key components of healthy human relationships.

When my two daughters went to college at Baylor University years ago, they each, at different times, took a course called "Poverty Simulation." It was a weekend spent in the town of Waco, Texas, living as someone without a home. With only a small amount of cash (the students had varying amounts of cash as part of the experience), they were dropped off in town without any phone or food and were forced to figure out how to survive for a weekend without the comforts of a home or any belongings. Both daughters recounted how hard it was to live outside in the cold, being forced to ask for work to get food and without any phone. From their experiences, each of them substantially grew in empathy for the homeless. In fact, afterward, both decided to do something tangible in their volunteer work for the impoverished communities in this college town, rife with poverty challenges.

While allowing ourselves to vicariously experience another's life or emotions, we end up *cultivating* empathy, which, according to Merriam-Webster Dictionary, is "the action of understanding, being aware of, being sensitive to, and vicariously experiencing the feelings, thoughts, and experience of another."[20] Isn't that interesting that it says it is the *action* of understanding . . . and vicariously experiencing? I had always thought that either we are wired to be empathetic (emotional) people, or we aren't. While each of us differs to the degree we are naturally empathetic, I've learned that being empathetic is also a choice—a discipline, not just a feeling—and one that comes with unspoken blessings to those who engage with it.

Further pursuing what empathy means, "Empathy is related to sympathy but is narrower in focus and is generally considered more deeply personal. Compassion, sympathy, and empathy all have to do with having passion (feeling) for another person because of his or her suffering. True empathy is the feeling of actually participating in the suffering of another."[21]

According to a 2015 article from BBC News called "Can you teach people to have empathy?" neuroscience research says that 98 percent of people "have the ability to empathize wired into their brains."[22]

> *True empathy is the feeling of actually participating in the suffering of another.*

The problem is we often don't choose to reach our fullest empathetic potential. I love the way Bruna Martinuzzi explains in her article, "What's empathy got to do with it?" that "at its core, empathy is the oil that keeps relationships running smoothly."[23] In fact, Dr. Antonio Damasio explained in his book *Descartes Error: Emotion, Reason, and the Human Brain* that medical patients who had damage in the part of the brain where the ability to empathize with others resides showed significant deficits in their relationship skills, while their cognitive reasoning was unaffected.[24]

Why is cultivating empathy important? It enhances our ability to connect with others, create bonds of trust, understand human behavior, reduce conflict, identify with others and their perspectives, help us make better decisions, sharpen our "people acumen," and make others feel valued. As someone who works with executives in a recruiting capacity and coaches them in a career transition for many years, I have seen the field of Emotional Intelligence (EQ) flourish in business. More and more, employers are looking for professionals and executives to not just have the right skills, culture fit, and experience, but there is an added quality being sought after in EQ. Daniel Goleman in his book *Emotional Intelligence: Why*

It Can Matter More Than IQ describes EQ as both the ability to recognize, understand, and manage our own emotions and recognize, understand, and influence the emotions of others. No surprise, empathy is one of the key components to EQ.[25]

In his book *Working with Emotional Intelligence*, Goleman cites the Harvard Business School research that determined that EQ counts for twice as much as IQ and technical skills *combined* in determining who will be successful. And the benefits in business? They include: resolving conflicts, motivating and coaching others, creating a culture of collaboration and building psychological safety within teams.[26] So, personally and professionally, cultivating empathy is an important tool and the "secret sauce" in healthy relationships.

While some people are naturally more empathetic than others, anyone can *choose* to be empathetic. At its core is thinking intentionally about others—their thoughts, feelings, and perspectives as if you were actually them. In doing this, we are exercising our heart muscle, showing our humanity, and becoming catalysts for change. Think about it . . . if the person we love is suffering, and we harden ourselves to their plight, what good will we be to them? Will we advocate for them? Will we spend time with them? Will we find ways to help them? Probably not. Empathy is the fuel to spur us on to do what is right and good and treat others as we want to be treated. The alternative is to allow our heart to harden and atrophy until, ultimately, we stop feeling at all.

The downside of empathy for me is the more I experience another's pain, the more I make myself vulnerable to that same pain, resulting in secondhand suffering. Even still, I would rather live with an open and tender heart and be able to relate to others empathetically and risk painful emotions than go through life with my heart locked into a protective box, blocking out the full extent of human emotion. If you struggle with opening your heart to feel the weight of your loved one's emotions as a secondhand sufferer because you are afraid of the potential pain, consider the consequence of locking up your heart to detach from having empathetic feelings. To risk nothing is to gain nothing, and when we risk empathy, we gain a bigger heart and a richer life.

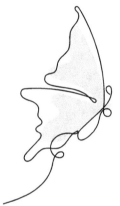

SPIRITUAL REFLECTIONS

Awakening to Something New

*"But pain insists upon being attended to.
God whispers to us in our pleasures,
speaks in our conscience, but shouts in our pains:
it is His megaphone to rouse a deaf world."*

—C. S. Lewis

Growing up in a public school in my same hometown with the same people in my life for over fifteen years, I was in a comfortable place of mediocrity where I didn't challenge myself to reach my potential as a whole person. For instance, I qualified for the honors English class (not math, for sure) and made the mistake of deciding not to take it— even though it was taught by the best teacher in the school—because I didn't want to work that hard. My parents encouraged me, but in the end, they didn't force me. I also picked up bad language habits since all my cool friends spoke that way. And I just never seemed to fit in, so my self-confidence was *very* low. While I knew many people and didn't lack for shallow friendships, I never consistently had "a group" to eat lunch with. I was a floater. It was great to welcome and eat with the new kids who moved to town and introduce them to others until they found their group; I never really found my "tribe" in high school.

All that changed in my later years in college when I was finally in a place of deep discovery and found out what was inside of me, something that was once dormant. I found my tribe with some go-getters, student leaders, deeper thinkers, potential world-changers, and smart people with spiritual values. These people pushed me to pursue what was in me that had never been watered. And it opened up seeds in my heart to press in more to the idea of being the person I was purposed to be. I was feeling more at home in my new environment and enjoyed my new peers. I was becoming a wiser and happier person because of the people in my life.

"He who walks with the wise becomes wise."

—Proverbs 13:20 (BSB)

My senior year I got a new roommate, Stephanie. Something was different about her. She was fun to be around. But she also spent a lot of her time praying for people. Specifically, she prayed for some kids who were suicidal, and she told me about their miraculous stories of being freed from this through her meetings and prayers with them.

She also went on a mission trip to Africa, where she shared spiritual encounters, both miraculous and demonic, which I had never heard anything about until then. She also had a joy beyond my understanding. Even when she was having bad days, she beamed with joy when she talked about Jesus. And instead of just talking about how much she loved Jesus, she spoke about how much He loved her. It was personal. I had sung the "Jesus Loves Me" song in Sunday School and knew, in theory, that God loves people, but something about this friend seemed to take it a step further. She really believed it, and it affected her life. Her spiritual and personal life were intertwined.

I was drawn to this "something more" she had—her joy, confidence in God, the miraculous, and her connection to Jesus in a personal, non-academic way. I still didn't have it figured out, really, but I at least had a vision of where I hoped to be someday. Stephanie's heart was big, and I saw how she cared so much for others and seemed to "feel their pain" and moved to action to make a difference.

Being challenged by my inspiring Sociology professor to step into the role of "being my brother" in his state of helplessness grew my heart to feel compassion in new ways. The fruit of learning how to love another person well is an enlarged heart, and a bigger heart yields empathy for others as an "overflow." By opening up my heart by intentionally throwing myself into the experience of my brother's suffering with the intent to feel his emotions and physical limitations, my heart was becoming tender and fertile ground for an acceleration of faith. In fact, empathy is a quality of God, and because we are "made in His image," we are wired naturally to press in and cultivate this quality.

"To love another person is to see the face of God."

—LES MISÉRABLES

At this stage in my spiritual journey, my heart was growing, and I started attending a few gatherings and opening the Bible. I began to have an interest in checking out this Jesus guy for myself instead of just showing up to church out of moral obligation. I liked that Jesus seemed to be always sensitive to the predicaments of others. He was starting to look different than the old man in the history book I had grown to respect but was not connected to very well. Jesus modeled empathy and a lot of compassion, which I liked. My perspective began to shift from my faith being based on a good historical Jesus with lots of "Christian principles," which shaped my overall character of being a quasi "good person," to seeing Jesus as a powerful force in people's personal lives that transcended simply following religious teachings. I had never really seen a living, active, life-transforming relationship with this God-man from the Bible before, like I did with my roommate and new friend. Seeds were being planted in me, and I wouldn't see the fruit until much later in my life. Something was shifting inside of me that began growing a rich curiosity in the supernatural. But first, I had more questions.

TOOLS FOR THE HEART

Allowing our hearts to fully open and embrace another's feelings, perspective, and suffering grows our ability to love others authentically. The antidote to emotional numbness is empathy. As one of many ingredients to Emotional Intelligence (EQ), empathy is important to cultivate and grow and doesn't always come naturally to everyone. By intentionally working to understand how others feel, we not only bless them but we are blessed. It is a good first step to take before we form judgments about others. As I would learn later, increasing our empathy and love towards others can also help us discover a deeper connection to the heart of God—a huge tool as we face any kind of suffering.

Questions to Ponder:

1. Do you think you are naturally empathetic, or does it take intentional effort? Explain.
2. Have you ever met someone who has something about them that is so intriguing that you wonder what it is and inspires you to want to grow to be more like them? Who is it, and what quality do they possess that you would like to have?
3. Do you tend to pull away from intense emotions of empathy for fear it will cause you to feel feelings you don't want? In what ways?
4. Seeing the benefits of an open and tender heart, can you think of something you can do to cultivate empathy? What is it, and when will you do it?

Practical Steps:

- For fun, find a free Emotional Intelligence assessment and see how you score. One is the EQ Emotional Test by Truity (Truity.com). There are many you can find on the internet, but I think this is a good one for starters.
- A key to developing empathy is to find a way to connect with others to understand them better. Often, when we can learn to be vulnerable with others and more authentic, what follows is a deeper connection. Search for TedTalks and/or go to YouTube and enjoy watching Brené Brown's famous TED Talk from 2010 called "The Power of Vulnerability."

- To get to know the empathetic character of Jesus, read the stories surrounding these Scripture nuggets:

    ◊ "When he saw the crowds, . . . Jesus had compassion on them, because they were harassed and helpless, like sheep without a shepherd." (Matthew 9:36)

    ◊ He observed a widow about to bury her only son, and sensing her pain, Jesus's "heart overflowed with compassion." (Luke 7:11–16)

    ◊ Having lived a human life, Jesus empathizes with all of our weaknesses. (Hebrews 4:15)

CHAPTER FIVE

Finding Your Village—or Better, a Faithful Community

Two are better than one, because they have a good reward for their toil. For if they fall, one will lift up his fellow. But woe to him who is alone when he falls and has not another to lift him up! Again, if two lie together, they keep warm, but how can one keep warm alone? And though a man might prevail against one who is alone, two will withstand him—a threefold cord is not quickly broken.

—ECCLESIASTES 4:9–12 (ESV)

The phone rang. My dad was on the line. Kevin was being rushed to the hospital . . . again. This time, it appeared more serious than ever.

"Should I come down there now?"

"No," my dad replied. "Let me go down and assess the situation, I'll let you know."

I hung up and sat for a moment in silence. We had been through this before. Pneumonia. It seemed to haunt Kevin more than most. My parents had always told me that if Kevin were to die young, it would most likely be because of pneumonia. So, whenever I heard that he had pneumonia, I got really scared. And I would begin praying out of desperation.

Shortly after my brother was born, he almost died of pneumonia, and my parents asked a group of people from their church to pray for him, and they did. In fact, they got together and held a special prayer session for him at our house. I remember it . . . vaguely. The prayer session was one of the most impactful experiences I remember of its kind growing up—so this must have been serious. They prayed for my brother's life, that he would live and not die. This type of gathering was fairly regular, for the people really cared for one another, and it was like a big extended family. Part of what tied a lot of us together was an affiliation with the college where my dad worked, Pepperdine University. We were a close community and did life together.

Another time, I recall a raging fire in the neighboring community. Growing up in Southern California, it was a regular occurrence around October during the "Santa Ana" winds. This fire was moving from Malibu into an area called Lake Lindero in what is now Agoura Hills. Our friends were evacuated, and so everyone came to our house to be together and pray. I remember a circle of chairs in our family room area filled with people who were scared of losing their house but also enjoying being together. It was a fun night for me as I got to stay up later, and it felt like a big adult sleepover.

Now, my parents were not the super "religious type," really. I guess it's all about how you define "religious." If by religious, one means going to church each week, being "good people," being raised in church-going homes with strong morals and traditions, and faithfully saying a prayer at home before dinner, then perhaps they were. But, to me, it seemed church for us was more of a social community that offered support (the churchy word for this is "fellowship") rather than someplace we went because we were spiritually hungry for theological feasts to nourish our souls and make front and center of our every breath and decision. It was a wonderful community of people and a rich part of my growing-up experience. And this church was a life force for our family as they rallied behind us when Kevin was born and they knew things were not right.

I remember one weak moment in my mom's life when she admitted to me that she had wondered if God's plan was to take Kevin early so he would avoid the pain of this life. By asking for people to pray for his life to be spared, I think she secretly wondered if it was the right thing to do since she didn't realize at the time that Kevin's life being saved would mean a lifetime of hardship later. It is so hard for a mother's heart to see/feel her children suffer. I now know this firsthand as a mother watching kids battle different illnesses and experience suffering.

Our church family was truly a community of people who shared struggles, burdens, and celebrations and simply did life together. The community was authentic and full of compassion for our family. Often, our gatherings involved food—church potlucks and dining together at restaurants like Bob's Big Boy or Fish & Chips after church with friends—and families bringing meals during trying times, like Kevin's hospitalizations, or joyful times, like a birth. Seeing this supportive and engaged community bonded through a common faith was foundational for my security as a child. And I know it shaped a big part of who I am today. I just assumed everyone had a community group like this.

INSIGHTS FOR THE HEART

Finding Value in Community

"When we honestly ask ourselves which person in our lives means the most to us, we often find that it is those who, instead of giving advice, solutions, or cures, have chosen rather to share our pain and touch our wounds with a warm and tender hand. The friend who can be silent with us in a moment of despair or confusion, who can stay with us in an hour of grief and bereavement, who can tolerate not knowing, not curing, not healing and face with us the reality of our powerlessness, that is a friend who cares."

—HENRI J. M. NOUWEN
Out of Solitude: Three Meditations on the Christian Life

Sometimes, famous people say things unintentionally that end up becoming idioms that stick. Hillary Clinton popularized an expression she once said, "It takes a village," in reference, I believe, to the government being a network for people. I believe the phrase stuck, not because government is the answer to all things, but because there was an element of truth to it as a principle. We need each other. From my own experience, I believe a community of people with faith beyond themselves is a more intimate form of support than a government institution with financial assistance alone. There is something uniquely powerful about human beings showing love and care for one another.

We hear daily news stories of lives lost. We have friends, loved ones, and acquaintances suddenly dying. Car accidents, viral epidemics, school shootings, suicide, terrorism, cancer—the list goes on. We know intellectually that life is fragile, but often, until it hits close to home, it doesn't faze us much in the day-to-day living we do. Yet, having so many close calls with my brother gave me a perspective early on about the fragility of life. And while not perfect, I saw how my family dealt with these trying times. They did so with a community of faith who prayed for them and rallied with them, and we all—mostly Kevin—persevered through each trial.

While I would later question the effectiveness of prayer and the viability of the God to whom we were praying, as a child I learned the importance of bringing our deepest cries to the Creator of all life, who holds the keys to life and death. I didn't understand how it all worked (do any of us really?), but I couldn't deny that every time it looked like Kevin would die, people came together, prayed, and he would beat the odds. It made me believe that God had a purpose to continue to give Kevin life, and He was not a distant Being uninvolved with our concerns. There was something special about an intimate community of people connected to a higher power as they humbly pleaded for help for those they loved.

As an adult, I have come to believe that having a community surrounding me in tough times is not optional if I want to survive with any degree of sanity. My friends, our faith community, and caring people are what have helped our family through tough times. I lost my own precious mother to a debilitating stroke when my first daughter went to college. The grief was overwhelming, unrelenting, and crippling. I have been held up by my husband, children, and friends—most of them from my own "village of faith" who have shown great compassion, empathy, and love. The meals, cards, emails, phone calls, gifts, flowers, and selfless acts of service carried me during this agonizing time.

The journey of living for those enduring ongoing trauma, such as the disabled or the emotionally afflicted "secondhand sufferer," is traveled most successfully with perseverance. In some ways, a death can feel easier because you grieve through many phases and eventually move on with life. Yet, ongoing trauma has a way of never allowing you to move on. While we are given moments of reprieve, the relentless suffering of our loved ones keeps us living in an elevated sense of worry and anxiety. And even when we have times of peace, we are holding our breath, ready for the next shoe to drop. I don't think we are as wired to endure this state of vicarious trauma at an ongoing high intensity as we may be for shorter-term emergencies that have resolution and life resumes to "normal." It is very difficult to sustain this level of chronic, never-ending grief, as it can paralyze us. So, we develop strategies to deal with it, mostly subconsciously.

Using a popular personality assessment I sometimes use in my career coaching practice, and my own experiences of observation, some of these coping skills and strategies people subconsciously use may look like the following nine Enneagram types. If you haven't heard of it, it is a personality assessment tool somewhat like the Myers-Briggs® test, except this one is uniquely designed to identify an individual's core motivation, which is the power driving their behavior. Whether you are familiar with this tool for a personality assessment or not, you may enjoy checking out the list below to see if you identify with one or more of these coping mechanisms when you deal with grief or trauma as a secondhand sufferer. These behaviors are neither good nor bad, but if we can use this chart to become more self-aware, we can help free ourselves from unconscious knee-jerk reactions that keep us stuck, only responding to pain the same way each time. Each one of these is a behavior driven by a motivation like wanting to do the right thing or staying safe or taking charge. The healthier we become, the more we can employ many of these behaviors—not just the one that comes most easily. But ultimately, none of them is a long-term solution. They are short-term strategies to help us survive. There is more to explore if you are interested. Looking at the chart below, do any of these sound like how you deal with secondhand suffering?

Enneagram Personality Type & Core Motivation	Typical Coping Mechanism for Trauma or Grief *Examples*
1. **Strict Perfectionist:** wants to be good; a reformer or teacher type	Becoming a change agent or advocate to try to fix as much as possible, including reforming systems or righting wrongs, while likely repressing anger trying to hold it all together.
2. **Considerate Helper:** wants to be liked; others-focused	Trying to do as much to help others to feel we are doing something to help, like offering practical help, possibly to feel needed and/or loved deep down.
3. **Competitive Achiever:** wants to be admired; image-focused; goal-driven	Distracting ourselves by focusing on our own success, career goals, or putting efforts into tackling a project or achieving a goal to feel some measure of accomplishment.
4. **Intense Creative:** wants to be unique; individualist; authentic	Feeling deeply sad and seeking relief by pressing into the painful reality and dealing with it head-on emotionally without any fluff while possibly failing to see some of the silver linings.
5. **Quiet Specialist:** wants to understand; thinker; private	Diving into research to find ways to make the situation better; holding emotional feelings inside and boundaries of protection strong, while keeping focus on the intellectual need to understand.

Enneagram Personality Type & Core Motivation	Typical Coping Mechanism for Trauma or Grief *Examples*
6. **Loyal Skeptic:** wants to be safe and belong; values faith and family	Seeking out faith and family for a connection to a higher purpose to rise above the hard reality. Feeling paralyzed at times by fear and doubt, while being uncertain as to which voices to listen to among so many opinions and perspectives.
7. **Enthusiastic Visionary:** seeks variety of experiences; avoids pain	Avoiding the pain by keeping busy with a variety of fun experiences and reframing painful situations quickly in order to avoid dwelling on them. Always focusing on the bright side instead of sitting in the midst of the struggle and hardship.
8. **Active Controller:** protective; strong presence of personality	Getting angry about the situation and trying to control it in whatever way possible out of deep compassion and protectiveness over our loved one. This can result in burning bridges with people if we aren't watching how we come across to others.
9. **Adaptive Peacemaker:** avoids conflict; difficult time making decisions	Becoming numb to the pain and checking out as it is too difficult to bear, or turning off the feelings once it becomes too painful as a way to protect oneself. Avoiding conflict at all costs, which makes it hard to be an advocate and make difficult decisions without some intentional effort.

When reviewing all these coping strategies, I think I have used every single one multiple times, all subconsciously. Having a variety of behavior options in our arsenal is likely better than just being stuck in one pattern. Each of these help us survive when we are in a traumatic situation. While all these reactions to pain work as a coping mechanism for a while, ultimately, we need to find ways to manage secondhand suffering that gets us through not only each day but also to a place of meaning that goes beneath the surface of day-to-day survival.

One of the greatest tools to help the plight of a secondhand sufferer begins with community. Humans caring for humans and showing empathy for one another go a long way to bring healing to breaking hearts. I believe it is a universal reality across cultures, nations, and people that we need each other. And I don't just mean on a video call or phone. Most people came to realize this truth after the global lockdowns in 2020; there is something powerful about being together physically; a face-to-face connection transcends all our coping defenses. A cup of coffee with a friend, a book club meeting, or talking with neighbors on the street can do wonders to give us a lift to our spirit and satisfy our innate craving for connection and community. The more we invest in developing authentic relationships with others, the stronger our community of support and, I believe, the happier we are. Without community, we are left carrying emotional heaviness we were not designed to carry alone. Just as the one who suffers real pain needs people to walk alongside them in life, so do we as secondhand sufferers—no matter what kind of suffering. No one should ever suffer alone.

And as Tracy Brower, Ph.D., a contributing writer for Forbes, states, "Our health and happiness are inextricably linked with our connections."[27] Whether an introvert or extravert or any label on an assessment test, I couldn't agree more.

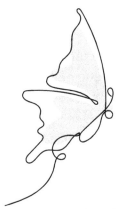

SPIRITUAL REFLECTIONS

Rethinking Prayer

*"Some unanswered prayers are only because
God doesn't want to do something for us.
He wants to do something through us."*

—BILL JOHNSON

While a community of faithful people who cling to hope beyond themselves can be inspiring, there was a time when I questioned whether the "prayer thing" was just a gimmick—a showy way people pretended to be spiritual but just didn't know what else to say. When I used to hear people say, "I'll pray for you," it seemed like an empty cliché to make people feel better. I doubted whether they actually prayed, and I doubted if praying ever really did any good. Did God really change His mind or intervene if we asked? If so, why didn't He just heal Kevin and stop the madness?

Some say, "Well, prayer just makes us feel better . . . but it doesn't really do anything." Others have ruminated, "We pray because we are commanded to, but since God is sovereign, He will do what He wants . . . we just pray out of obedience, but it doesn't ever change anything because God is in control." I've heard others say, "God is the Creator who set the world in motion and let it spin like a top; He doesn't bother with the minor details in our lives." Or did the movie *Bruce Almighty* get it right when Jim Carey played God and answered the world's prayers one after the other in an avalanche of email replies?

The whole thing confused me. If prayer was a waste of time, why did all these smart and kind people keep doing it? Why did the Bible teach us to pray if God had no intention of doing anything with them? That doesn't seem like a very nice God.

I needed an answer to the question, "Does prayer really help anything?" as I saw the obvious emotional benefit of a community that prayed for us. I needed to anchor this social encouragement with the intellectual truth of understanding the reality behind prayer: was it actually a change agent or just a vacuous exercise that comforted us, similar to a placebo pill? In other words, did it just make us feel better, but it really had no power?

While thousands of books have been written on prayer, and I am no theologian, I remember being surprised by a fiction book that opened my eyes from believing prayer was just a theoretical idea to it being an actual act of communicating with God. It played a role in unlocking my only brain-based reasoning to heart-based thinking that allowed room for a spiritual reality to exist beyond the tangible. Frank Peretti is the author of *This Present Darkness,* and he illustrated quite successfully a different dimension that exists beyond the visible world. There may be a fine line between fiction and reality when one realizes that scientists admit there are multiple dimensions beyond what we see naturally. While the book is fiction, I was greatly impacted by the way it revealed what very well may be the reality of the supernatural realm. I began to discover that prayer is the operating system God set up to partner with us to have a relationship with Him. And when we pray, it can be like a power source that fuels and activates God's power since He chose to partner with those who love Him to bring about His purposes on earth. I learned that prayer is about connection to God and is a two-way partnership (including listening on our end). God made us with skills and gifts to do our part in going after stuff, but He also wants us to do it with Him. It may sound so esoteric to someone new to the topic of prayer and having a partnership with God, but consider this short analogy:

> *"The story is told of a little guy valiantly but futilely trying to move a heavy log to clear a pathway to his favorite hideout. His dad stood nearby and finally asked him why he wasn't using all his strength. The little guy assured his dad he was straining with all his might. His dad quietly told him he was not using all his strength, because he hadn't asked him (his dad) to help."*
>
> —Zig Ziglar

Interestingly, the Bible often refers to the prayers of God's people as being like incense—a sweet delight for Him and the key to unlocking a relationship between the Creator of the Universe and individuals made by Him. He loves to hear our prayers, as they are expressions of our faith, something He values highly, according to the Bible. I misunderstood prayer for so long, as do so many of us. But I continue to wrestle through it because I believe there are always answers. And mysteries. But the pursuit of knowing the purposes and heart of God is still a satisfying journey, even with the mysterious.

One thing I have learned is that prayer is often not rightfully understood, as so many of us seem to think that God is a great genie in the sky who just gives us our wishes when we ask. He did address this in the Bible when Jesus taught the well-known Lord's Prayer. It is also a great answer to the question so many Christians often ask, "What is God's will?" Jesus taught that we should pray—and we can know God's will—for what is true in heaven He desires to also be true on earth. He said to pray, "Your Kingdom come, Your will be done, on earth, as it is in Heaven." So, whatever happens in Heaven would naturally be God's will on earth.

> "Our Father in heaven,
> hallowed be your name,
> ***your kingdom come,***
> ***your will be done,***
> ***on earth as it is in heaven.***
> Give us today our daily bread.
> And forgive us our debts,
> as we also have forgiven our debtors.
> And lead us not into temptation,
> but deliver us from the evil one."
>
> —MATTHEW 6:9–13 (NIV) (emphasis mine)

His answers, or lack thereof, are clearly not always what we want, but this may be for so many reasons we can't grasp. One is that we have a limited understanding of what is best for us, and we don't see the whole picture only God can see. But also, there are other circumstances at play. We live in a world by God's design that operates with humans having free choices, and often, those choices hurt us and others. But this doesn't mean this is God's will. Even though God is all-powerful,

He has chosen to operate concurrently with our free will. So, horrible things sometimes happen that free-willed people cause—not God—such as corrupt political leaders choosing an unjust war and someone we love being harmed or killed fighting this war, even though we prayed for them. It doesn't mean God's will was for that person to be killed, but it could mean it was the natural consequence of a poor decision to go to war. Or a child is harmed due to a person choosing to drive drunk. Or a sweet young woman dying of cancer, not because of cancer exactly, but due to the treatments that are toxic when given too much or for too long, harming vital organs. Or an unintentional overdose because of swallowing fentanyl due to criminal activity. I don't see any of these situations where God is the One causing these tragedies, but He does allow the system of free will to operate. Ultimately, it's the only way our world can allow LOVE and FREEDOM to exist. In my brother's case, either a mistake was made inadvertently during his delivery, or a random freak accident occurred without explanation, which caused his cerebral palsy. Either way, I do not believe God caused it.

These tragedies are not always evil or sinister but simply consequences of an error or bad decision. Sometimes, God wants *us* to partner with Him in carrying out His desire for the things of heaven to happen on earth, even in its flawed state. Often, we are His instruments to carry out His desires. So, we can pray but also act to use our minds and talents to partner with Him to make a difference—the abilities He gave us and His power to propel us. In my brother's situation, I can pray and then get involved by being proactive in using my talents to speak up, show up, and do something that God's heart would want. Sometimes, all we can do is pray. I would come to learn later that this could be the most powerful action, actually. God knows these situations, and I believe He sees us and steps in when He wants to exercise His providential right. Of course, God can do an outright miracle if He wants to and still does. In my experience, these miracles are mostly accompanied by people's faith. Yet, understanding when He does this and when He doesn't will remain a mystery on this side of heaven.

There are plenty of accounts in the Bible of prayers having the appearance of God changing course based on a heartfelt plea from His people advocating for something. This is a big encouragement to those of us who pursue God for answers to intervene or even change His mind (or perhaps He had the course in mind all along but was waiting for the prayer to come to unleash His plan). An example is a guy named Hezekiah, who was granted fifteen more years of life after he pleaded with God for more time as he was dying. Also, God honored Moses's request not to bring wrath on the people who worshipped a golden calf after he brought them out of Egypt. In both examples, prayer seemed to alter God's course.

The older I get, the more I realize that God is more concerned with our character over comfort and eternal life over earthly life. So, praying to win the lottery to buy a Lamborghini does not equate with praying to get a job to provide groceries for one's children. Further still, praying to become a more forgiving wife and patient mother is a closer match to the heart of God. And, as I eventually learned, praying just to experience the presence of God as my Comforter and Bridegroom would be one of God's favorite prayers to answer, and surprisingly so, are the most fulfilling for us.

As I have grown in pursuit of God and His ways, I have seen my faith grow as I've both received and given healing prayers on everything from migraines, twisted ankles, frozen shoulders, and hurt knees to an acquaintance being completely healed from a debilitating illness that left him in bed for three years. In the latter case, we were told there was no medical cure, and several friends committed to deep, intercessory prayer for months before there was the miracle. But there *was* a miracle.

In another case, I've seen uncanny answers to prayers about hearts changed, lost items found, addictions broken, and recently, a friend's guitar with a large crack down the neck completely restored without it being repaired—something I wouldn't have believed had I not been a personal friend. And there are countless books with miracles and answers to prayers I've read that have left me in awe. In all these examples, the answered prayer was not a regular occurrence but something that seemed important for that person at that time and became a testimony for them and others. Why can't God do this all the time for any of our prayers? I don't know. But I do see it happen more often when I am asking and spending time with Him. It may also have to do with the atmosphere of faith or the level of darkness around. It is a complicated and deep study, and while one may never understand the fullness of the truth on earth, there are nuggets of wisdom we can find based on reading the Bible and our heart connection of knowing God more. There are plenty of wonderful books on the topic, and it is worth a deep dive, at least I think so.

Do I still struggle with why my brother couldn't be one of those healed physically *fully* with prayer? Yes! But, while God didn't answer my prayer to heal my brother completely, He did answer the prayers to allow him to live and be healed countless times over and over whenever he entered the hospital with a dire diagnosis. Just as a cat is known to have nine lives, I think my brother may have double that. Sometimes, the outcome of a successful prayer is peace and not always understanding.

While I believe we need community to navigate through life's storms and joys, I believe prayer is a different form of community—communion with the most powerful Friend above all else. A community filled with love and faith is a mighty force to help us muddle through life's challenges and ups and downs. Moreover, it is a practical, supportive set of caring people, when combined with a like-minded faith, who can access the ultimate supernatural source from God to have a double benefit. Community with people and communion with God.

I think we all agree that life is unpredictable. God never promised we wouldn't die from this life or suffer. He did promise, however, never to leave us or abandon us. And part of the nature of God is to use people to express support and love through human skin. And He can use anyone—people of faith or anyone He wants.

Some years ago, a musician friend named Kevin from college produced an album with his wife, and I was drawn to a song called "Life is Fragile." Back then, I would listen to it over and over as it connected to my spirit in a way other songs did not. The song is beautiful, captivating, and filled with raw lyrics about real life and the value of prayer. It is worth a listen, but the words are below:

"Life Is Fragile"

Words and music by Kevin Ray Lawson
Copyright ©1995, used with permission

Little Julie's on the back porch
Rocking her little man in her arms
It's just them two and it's always been
And neither of them knows just why or when
It happened that way
But they go on

She's holding his little hand
And singing softly as the evening falls
He's growing fast and the time is flying
She looks at him and starts to cry
A tear of joy
And she goes on and on

She knows life is fragile and a heart is easily broken
in a world of shattered dreams
When no one seems to care
But there's a light of hope she carries
To get them through the dark of life unfair
Life is so fragile
You've got to handle it with prayer

Tommy's in the hallway
Pacing up and down the marble floors

He and Lynne have been waiting so long
To hear their first born cry at dawn
And bring them joy
And he goes on

The doctor comes to Tommy
But there is something somber in his eyes
He says something went wrong
And we tried to save him
We tried hard boy
But he didn't make it
But Lynne's alright
And he starts to cry
And he holds her tight
And they go on and on...
They know life is fragile
and a heart is easily broken
In a world of shattered dreams
When no one seems to care
But there's a light of hope they carry
To get them through the dark of life unfair
Life is so fragile
You've got to handle it with prayer

They may never find the reason
But they always find their peace
When they're reaching out to heaven
To the One who never leaves

They know life is fragile
and a heart is easily broken
In a world of shattered dreams

When no one seems to care
But there's a light of hope they carry
To get them through the dark of life unfair
Life is so fragile
You've got to handle it with prayer
Life is so fragile
Handle it with prayer.[28]

To listen, scan the QR codes below:

TOOLS FOR THE HEART

When we walk through trials, even the trial of being the advocate for someone we love, we need community. I have found the best kind of community is made up of those who support you emotionally and spiritually to the place where your heart feels connected. We can choose to seek out an authentic community that provides ongoing support for us and us for them. And if that support can be from a faith-filled community, even better.

Questions to Ponder:

1. Do you have a "village" you feel is there for you as a support system? If not, what steps can you take to find one and cultivate it?
2. What is your view on prayer? What have you experienced in your prayer life? Have you witnessed any miracles?
3. How do you cope with ongoing grief and suffering for someone else? Do you relate to one of the nine Enneagram strategies mentioned? What is your "go-to" coping strategy?

Practical Steps:

- Make a list of your closest people. Do you have good friends you can count on for support as you deal with emotional challenges as a secondhand sufferer? If not, strategize what you can do to pursue healthier friendships—friends who help carry your load, provide support, and bring out the best in you. This may mean making the first move to pursue others and then be a friend to them.
- Begin a prayer journal. During the week, experiment with writing down your prayers as a regular habit. Don't make it legalistic; just try to do it once or twice a week if possible. Note the date and then begin to watch for answers to prayer, then record them as you begin to notice changes. Try to ask for solutions to things that you know God would agree with your request.
- If you are curious to learn more about prayer and miracles, check out these books:

Prayer: Does It Make Any Difference? by Phillip Yancey
On the Road with the Holy Spirit: A Modern-Day Diary of Signs and Wonders by Ken Fish
This Present Darkness by Frank E. Peretti (Fiction)
The Case for Miracles: A Journalist Investigates Evidence for the Supernatural by Lee Strobel

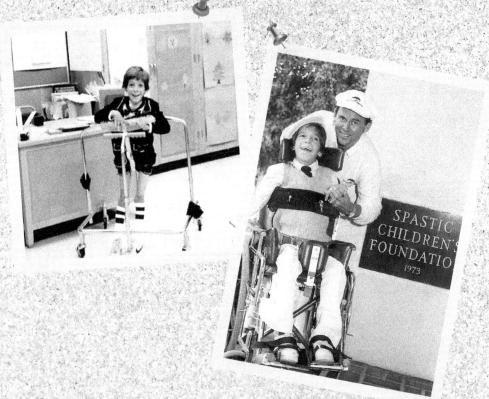

SPASTIC
CHILDREN'S
FOUNDATIO
1973

CHAPTER SIX

Asking Tough Questions

"Judge a man by his questions rather than his answers."

—Voltaire

I **grew up being told that my brother didn't understand much because he had brain damage.** The doctors told this to my parents early on and defined him as "mentally retarded." But I never believed it. I think my mom wanted to believe it because that meant Kevin would be oblivious to his condition. It's hard enough to be someone who can't walk, talk, use the bathroom, and communicate when you also don't have full knowledge of your situation, but I imagine it would be much more difficult to not have all those abilities but to have a fully functioning brain. That would be a "locked-in" situation, a prison of the worst kind. Our family seemed to secretly comfort ourselves in believing that Kevin didn't understand much. That seemed to be a way to ease our pain some. Yet, most who knew him or spent any amount of time with him believed otherwise.

There came a day, many years later, when we had the opportunity to find out the truth. One of our best family friends is a renowned neurosurgeon with a compassionate heart towards my brother. He explained how medical technology had improved such that he could look at an MRI of the brain and tell which parts of the brain were damaged and which were functioning normally. He could let us know if Kevin was mentally retarded (or cognitively impaired) or not with one MRI. By this time, Kevin was in his thirties. Did I want to know? That was the big question. Yes and no. After many family discussions over the merits of accepting our friend's generous offer, I accompanied Kevin to the MRI lab. The poor guy had to endure excruciatingly loud noises circling his head, and since his ears are very sensitive, I could tell he was uncomfortable, grimacing with every loud, grating noise. I held his hand as he lay there locked into the table, looking confused and frightened at his surroundings. He seemed to have peace that I was with him, which made me glad I made the trip.

It's funny because after one of my kids would endure such a procedure (and yes, they have), I would always offer them a "treat"—ice cream, frozen yogurt, a trip to a trampoline place. Yet, I felt helpless over options for Kevin since he wasn't allowed to eat at the time. His reward could only be a verdict on his mental capacity—something purely informational for us and, sadly, not necessarily life-changing for him. Holding his hand and leg during the MRI was something I insisted on. The piercing, loud noises were startling, and he was scared. He had to be strapped in so his head wouldn't move, and the procedure was not fun. But I had to know what was happening inside his brain. Answering my curiosity was a lifelong pursuit.

A few days later, my family met in my neurosurgeon friend's dining room to discuss the MRI results. My mom was beyond anxious. My dad and I were nervous. The verdict? Good news and bad news. The good news was that Kevin's brain showed no damage to his cognitive abilities. In many people with severe cerebral palsy, he told us, there are large portions of missing brain mass. In Kevin's brain, it was all there. His brain damage was not cognitive, it was "just" his motor skills that were affected (the motor cortex part of the brain). The only thing that showed negatively about Kevin's cognitive brain was atrophy around the edges—sadly, for lack of brain use. This meant that all those years of his life, thinking he was incapable of using his brain (according to the experts), Kevin could have been learning to communicate somehow, learning to walk perhaps, or learning to read with the help of a device. If only we had been given hope earlier on, my parents would have surely made different choices that could have affected his quality of life.

What was the bad news? The bad news was the good news. Kevin did not have brain damage to his cognitive abilities. This meant that Kevin *did* understand what was going on. He was "locked in" while his mental abilities were atrophying over time. His brain was like all of ours, except it was not being used to its potential, thus the atrophy. The medical community told us a story about him being cognitively impaired—perhaps it was a story of ignorance, a mistake, a guess, or a lie. In hindsight, thirty-plus years of being labeled as someone without a working brain took its toll. The original diagnosis affected many decisions made for Kevin's life—where he lived, what he did, what training he didn't get, and how the doctors made decisions. This MRI news was a blow.

I am a person who believes when there is a problem, there is always a solution. One of my nicknames assigned to me years ago by a friend is the "fix-it girl." I not only want to fix things, but I usually have some success. Perhaps it's in my DNA, or my persistent mother personified the phrase "where there is a will, there is a way" for me. Whatever the case, I see problems not as dead ends but as mere obstacles to be removed to get to the goal. This quality came in handy in the world of sales for me professionally because when someone told me, "No, thank you," I thought it meant, "I dare you to convince me." To me, no's were invitations to transform them into yes's, thanks to professional sales training early in my career (and my own stubbornness).

When it came to my brother, however, I was paralyzed. I couldn't fix anything. In fact, I was overwhelmed with absolute incompetency! For most of my life, I have been frustrated at the number of roadblocks in Kevin's way for any kind of life change. Feeling overwhelmed by the magnitude of my brother's battles is an understatement. As a young child, accepting that my brother was "special" worked. Strange how, as children, we are so accepting of the simplest explanations. Yet, as I grew older and came to grips with the loss of Kevin's full potential in this life, I was pained deeper and deeper to the point of brokenness.

Ultimately, I came face to face with God—and after the crying, pleading, begging, and bargaining with God for my brother's healing failed, anger set in. *Why the heck can't you just fix him, God? What kind of God allows one of His innocent children to live this way?* I had questions. And every question led down a rabbit trail of even more questions.

Kevin did nothing to deserve this life—he is utterly dependent on someone else for everything except breathing (and even now, he is on oxygen), with no way to communicate his thoughts or needs yet with a real, working, and active brain. This one seemingly unanswerable question in my life—why?—has had such a gripping effect on me and has kept my heart in chains. If the "fix-it girl" can't fix Kevin, one would think the Creator of the Universe could at least. Was I asking too much?

I experienced deep pain, realizing that not only was this problem unsolvable for me, but it was apparently unsolvable for God too. At some point between my early childhood of not questioning my brother's "special" condition, my inherited idea that God doesn't get involved in fixing a lot of things, and Kevin's MRI results, I had developed some sort of belief that maybe God *could* do something but wouldn't. So, if He was allowing my brother to stay in this condition when clearly he had some ability to use his brain, what does that say about God? Had I believed a lie that He was even there? This seed of doubt grew and led me to challenge my so-called belief in God. My faith was being blown away, showing me that my roots of personal faith were not tested, and, frankly, they were shallow and not really my own. I had inherited a cultural faith, truly not one of my own personal convictions.

I believe all of us hit this wall at some time in our lives. Wired into us is a sense of justice, of right and wrong, of a deep longing for happiness, and, if we are honest, perfection. When that reality never comes, and we hit that wall, we all seem to react differently. Some of us may search for some ultimate reason and meaning for our circumstances or pretend that the pain and injustice don't exist by masking reality through addictions or distractions, or we may become hardened to life and end up depressed or worse—living without a sense of purpose. Do any of these resonate with you as a secondhand sufferer? Where are the walls that leave you blocked intellectually or emotionally? Consider this quote by Timothy Keller, a well-respected theologian and Christian apologist, and see if it resonates with you.

> *"A faith without some doubts is like a human body without antibodies in it. People who blithely go through life too busy or indifferent to ask hard questions about why they believe as they do will find themselves defenseless against either the experience of tragedy or the probing questions of a smart skeptic."*
>
> —TIMOTHY KELLER

For many years of my life, I felt guilty for having so many doubts and questions. When I discovered that almost everyone has had them, even in religious communities, I wondered why we all try to pretend we don't. It is quotes like Tim Keller's that, in retrospect, validate the importance of doubt for someone of faith. Faith and doubt are not contradictory; in fact, they can be complementary as long as we don't stop at their intersection but press through to the other side. That's what I'm hoping for you, that you will ask the hard questions and press through your doubts to see what you find.

INSIGHTS FOR THE HEART

Finding Comfort in Conundrums

*"Do not go where the path may lead;
go instead where there is no path and leave a trail."*

—RALPH WALDO EMERSON

I've never been satisfied with shallow answers. I was *that* kid who always asked, "But why?" to my parents and my teachers. Curiosity drove me to an insatiable hunger for answers. Even now, I am often shocked at how satisfied so many are to be content with what someone else taught them, what the news reports tell them, or those who remain complacent in general. Many people seem to settle for a sound bite, a trite phrase of comfort, or resign themselves to "keeping it light." I have been accused of being "too intense" at times as my mind questions itself down so many rabbit holes. Why can't I just keep it simple and let things go, accepting "that's just the way it is"?

I tend to believe that deep down in the soul of every human is a longing for "more." When we stretch our minds and thoughts to search out weightier matters, our spirit feels an impulse that compels us into new understandings that grow us. I guess many people don't feel safe to let themselves go to those deeper levels of critical thought for fear of opening the door to answers they may not be ready for yet. Keeping things simple and on the surface is playing it safe. Perhaps certain people take the easier road to avoid the pain they will face if they hit things head-on. Sometimes, I wish I could be like that. It seems like life would be so much more enjoyable to live in ignorance . . . or would it?

> *"Men occasionally stumble over the truth,*
> *but most of them pick themselves up and hurry off*
> *as if nothing had happened."*
>
> —Winston Churchill

One of my favorite poems is by Robert Frost, "The Road Not Taken." In it, Frost depicts the two paths available to us in every life situation: one is more traveled, and one is much less.

The Road Not Taken
by Robert Frost

Two roads diverged in a yellow wood,
And sorry I could not travel both
And be one traveller, long I stood
And looked down one as far as I could
To where it bent in the undergrowth;
Then took the other, as just as fair;
And having perhaps the better claim,
Because it was grassy and wanted wear;
Though as for that the passing there
Had worn them really about the same,
And both that morning equally lay
In leaves no step had trodden black.
Oh, I kept the first for another day!
Yet knowing how way leads on to way
I doubted if I should ever come back.
I shall be telling this with a sigh
Somewhere ages and ages hence:
Two roads diverged in a wood,
And I—
I took the one less travelled by,
And that has made all the difference.[29]

The Bible also refers to two paths called the "narrow road" and the "wide road" (Matthew 7:13–14). In both literary works, the road less traveled (also the narrow road) is the one that seems to be the better choice. It's the narrow road that leads to life (the Bible's words), and the one less traveled makes a big difference to our life (according to Frost). For my analogy, the road *more* traveled in this context is the road of simplistic answers, shallow thought, and avoidance of pain. This road often leads to a dead end, and while popular, it doesn't typically satisfy our souls. The narrower road, the one less traveled, is bumpier, full of potholes, twists and turns, speed bumps, and even roadblocks. Even still, I believe it is a much more gratifying ride that takes you to places you could never have reached on the wider road. In fact, some of the best destinations may be *off* the road.

My sister-in-law's family lives in a cabin on a lake north of Anchorage, Alaska, which is only reachable by a float plane or a three-mile hike through a forest (yes, filled with bears). According to them (and my son, who has been there), the journey to get there is complicated and treacherous, but the reward of being in this hidden-away destination in nature is worth the journey. It restores the soul.

By choosing *not* to embrace the more narrow road and the tough stuff head-on, we can suffer from spiritual anemia. It's like snacking all day on junk food that tastes great for the moment yet will never satisfy and ultimately leads to poor health. We miss out on the scenery and experiences along the way, which benefit us in ways we cannot comprehend until we are on the other side of them. Diving deep is certainly more painful and dangerous and leaves us vulnerable, but I believe it is also the most rewarding. A scuba diver can witness much more beauty than a snorkeler because they go deeper. They will see things that the snorkeler will never see. And their satisfaction with the experience will be richer as a result.

Ultimately, deep dives into the depths of the "why" mysteries of life do not always lead to exact answers to the original question. One of my best friends and I have a long-standing exchange of news stories that are so horrific that we do not understand why God didn't stop them from happening. We are resigned that when we meet God one day in heaven, we will schedule a meeting with Him, show Him our list, and ask Him why He didn't do more to stop these horrors. For now, we just share the story in a text and say, "Adding this to our list." Somehow, it gives us some relief to share our empathetic pain with each other as it seems to lift the emotional load we bear. Sadly, we have a long list.

Struggling through life's tragedies and heartbreaks is hard enough. But when we meet people who say that God controls all these things (is behind them), it is so much worse. Eventually, much later, I came to understand that God had been misrepresented when I began to unpack the words of the "Lord's prayer." Here, we are told "God's will" (His heart) is that what happens in heaven (everything good) is what He wants to happen on earth—"Thy will be done on earth as it is in heaven" (Matthew 6:9). The clincher, however, is that since God made us to exercise our free will, He doesn't control us, and we can't necessarily blame God for bad things happening. At least we can know God doesn't "will" them.

There is great tension between the mystery of God and the pursuit of answers. I relate to this quote by G. K. Chesterton about Job, the guy who basically goes down in history as one of the greatest sufferers of all time in the Bible.

> *"Job tries to comfort himself with philosophical pessimism like the intellectuals of the nineteenth century. But God comforts Job with indecipherable mystery, and for the first time Job is comforted . . . Job flings at God one riddle, God flings back at Job a hundred riddles, and Job is at peace. He is comforted with conundrums."*
>
> —G. K. CHESTERTON

Being comfortable with conundrums. What a thought. I think it comes easier to some than others. Beth Moore, an author and Bible teacher, asserts in her *Breaking Free* study: "Sometimes when we finally give up trying to discover all the answers to the 'whys' in our lives and decide to trust a sovereign God, unexpected peace washes over us like a summer rain."[30] For me, this peace and comfort from surrendering my need for answers does not come easily. Yet, there is a time to ask, seek, and pursue answers and surrender and be at peace with the mystery when the answers don't appear. The challenge is knowing the time for each.

As a fellow secondhand sufferer, I have discovered that pressing in to ask the tough questions is a pathway to opening new doors. Those doors may be new discoveries for our loved one's healing, new resources for our ability to stay strong as an advocate, or a new sense of inner peace and transformation as we reconnect with God. Think of the possibilities of allowing yourself to "go there" and face one of your own conundrums head-on without denying its existence or staying stuck in paralysis. Just maybe taking the road less traveled will make a difference with your own secondhand suffering. It's worth a shot, right?

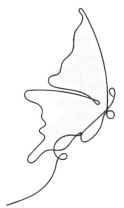

SPIRITUAL REFLECTIONS

Shifting from Doubt to Delight

"Doubts are the ants in the pants of faith.
They keep it awake and moving."

—FREDERICK BUECHNER

It's very common for people in their mid-twenties and beyond into mid-life to contemplate spiritual things and search for answers to their big life questions. Unable to find ways to relieve Kevin from his prison kept me up at night and in an ever-spinning world of mental anguish on and off throughout my life. However, this state of restlessness in my mind played a role in my persistence to find answers about things way bigger than even my brother.

As a newly married professional in my twenties, I interviewed my way into a job in San Francisco that paid well enough to support my husband through law school. It was a job I was not qualified for on paper. Through a connection with a family friend, I was put in touch with someone hiring two wholesale telemarketers for a brokerage firm on the thirty-third floor of a fancy building in the financial district selling to brokers with only high net worth clients. The product was a risky limited partnership, and they were looking for two Ivy League finance majors with at least three years of out-of-college work experience in a similar area. I was a social science major from a small Christian university with only one year of experience in human resources who never took a course in math, let alone knew anything about investments. With my tenacity and sales abilities, I talked the hiring consultant into hiring me over the other candidate from Harvard. I ended up working alongside a very bright young man from Yale for nine hours a day and chatted about philosophical things in between our cold calls. Through these years, he challenged me on my faith—and for good reason. With his prodding and common-sense questioning, I realized my faith was just a shell. It had a nice wrapper but came up empty when pressed for my personal convictions.

This was a turning point in my life, a crossroads of sorts. I didn't like not having reasons for what I thought was my faith, so I decided to tackle what it was that I believed in by wiping the slate clean and starting from scratch. I began reading books on different religions, compared and contrasted them, and then started making lists of all my unanswered questions. I was actually a bit angry that this kid who had never been to church seemed to unravel my twenty-four years of weekly church attendance in just a few months. Why couldn't I answer his questions? What if he was right to ask why I thought I was right and he was wrong? What was wrong with atheism or Buddhism or Judaism? (Yes, he seemed to be all three.)

I don't like *not* having answers for things, but I'm also not afraid to search them out. I realized then that I could never continue to believe something I didn't understand or have a personal conviction on. I was done with borrowing someone else's faith. So, I went on a faith pursuit, a search that took me about two years.

> *"Call to me and I will answer you and tell you great and unsearchable things you do not know."*
>
> —Jeremiah 33:3 (NIV)

My unanswered questions weren't that original. I kept a list of pressing questions of all the basics: If God is good, why is evil and suffering in the world? What about evolution? How do you prove God exists? How do we know Jesus really rose from the dead? Why is there only one right religion, or is there? And my favorite: How do we know that the Bible is really from God and not just a fallible book by fallible people? Can it be trusted?

Around that time, we began attending a church with a new pastor in town. I asked some of the people there about my "brilliant" questions. These were some great people, but I was disappointed that so many of my questions were met with someone quoting me a Bible verse or two. This bugged me as I pointed out that if I didn't believe the Bible was from God, then why were they answering my questions with the Bible? Can't they give me something better than that? That wasn't logical. (This church wasn't sure what to do with me!) As sweet as they were, we didn't get far.

But something was different about this new pastor, and over several weeks, I realized he preached on a lot of the topics I had on my list. I really enjoyed learning from him. I had hoped that someone could help me figure this out; maybe it was him. Eventually, I asked him if he would meet me to discuss my list of questions. Meeting with him seemed like somewhat of a marker in time. He was logical and practical, and when I asked him all my questions, he never responded with a Bible verse. He seemed to get me, and instead, he spoke to me in a way that made sense and gave reasons, historical proofs, and logical, philosophical insights. He honored me with deep, intellectual reasons that resonated as true in my head and my heart. I was a bit arrogant then, for sure, but he met me where I was and helped me tremendously with my doubts.

Slowly, coupled with my own reading about the different religions of the world, I was seeing that many of the religions had interesting philosophies and good theories. But none of them had any figure quite like Jesus, who claimed to be both God and man, lived on earth, performed miracles, and changed the world (even the dating system became divided between BC and AD based on his birth!). He preached life-changing messages, healed the sick, forgave sins, and then went on to be crucified and raised from the dead, where over 500 witnesses saw him post-resurrection. When I learned about the prophecies given in the Old Testament (Tanakh) hundreds of years prior to his life about who was clearly Jesus, the Messiah, my mind was blown. I had heard people say that "all religions basically say the same thing." However, as good as that sounds at first, I didn't see that; in fact, on the fundamental issues, they seemed to say contradictory things.

As I sought out the truth, with each discovered "a-ha" moment, my heart and head were touched, and my soul was satisfied in a way I had never experienced. I felt a true shift in my countenance and spirit. The best way I can describe it was a softening of my heart, followed by a new humility and a hunger and thirst to pursue God even more. But this time, the pursuit was more out of a desire to know Him personally instead of trying to make Him prove Himself to me. It was in the surrender of my strong, combative, and critical will to God that my life truly changed.

Gaining peace about the existence of God, confidence in the evidence that the Bible was actually God's revealed Word, and experiencing a tangible change in my persona proved pivotal for me as I acquired an insatiable hunger to grow closer to this no longer-distant God. The knowledge I had discovered was critical, yet the real change was with my attitude shifting from one of doubt to one of delight. My edges were softened, and my heart more open. I think I finally understood the phrase "born again." Not a physical birth but a spiritual birth based on a breakthrough in my mind that planted the seed of faith in my spirit. And it was only the beginning.

There is no doubt this new birth replaced my "inherited faith" and was a huge tool in my struggle with secondhand suffering. Knowing that there is a God who is real, loves me, and promises to be with me and my brother, no matter the circumstances, took some of the sting out of the empathetic pain I carried. Maybe you are not gripped by the types of questions I was. But my guess is somewhere in your mind, there may be suppressed doubts, hard questions, or deep wounds. I encourage you to deal with them head-on, so you can pull up any bitter roots that may be lodged inadvertently deep inside of you, causing damaging effects perhaps without your realization. Digging up any buried roots of doubt and investing in the process of pulling them out prevents unnecessary bitterness, anger, and resentment and will allow you the freedom to reach your full spiritual potential. Then you will find greater inner peace—and peace with God—as you experience the softening of the sharp edges of secondhand suffering.

TOOLS FOR THE HEART

Often, the road paved with mysteries leads us to deeper and greater places if we pursue where they take us. And even if they lead to more questions, wisdom is earned in the pursuit. Surprisingly, there can be peace as we learn to get comfortable with conundrums. And often, when we allow ourselves to take the risk of asking the hard questions with an open heart without giving up, we discover greater truths than we thought possible. Don't be intimidated to ask tough questions. If you persist, you'll be glad you didn't quit.

Questions to Ponder:

1. When in your life have you hesitated to ask the hard questions for fear the answer may lead you down a "road less traveled"? Have you noticed you give up too soon when the questions lead to messy places?
2. How have you dealt with life's conundrums? Which mystery of life most keeps you up at night?
3. In what ways have you challenged your spiritual questions, and have you felt a sense of peace as a result?

Practical Steps:

- Make a list of all your "stumper" questions about your "whys" in life. Then, spend some time thinking about how best to find answers—do your own research on comparative faiths and how each handles your questions, read books, listen to a podcast of a respected pastor or meet with one, talk with good friends who seem to live a life with wisdom, open and read a Bible in a modern-day translation, beginning with the book of John. Consider praying to God by asking Him to make Himself real to you or ask Him your questions. See what happens over time.

- If you struggle with mind-based questions on faith, consider reading a few books from authors who helped me:

The Case for a Creator; The Case for Christ; Is God Real?
    by Lee Strobel

Mere Christianity and Miracles by C. S. Lewis

The Reason for God and Making Sense of God by Timothy Keller

On Guard by William Lane Craig

Reasons Skeptics Should Consider Christianity by Josh McDowell

The Bible, in updated translations using Biblegateway. com. Here are a few versions to check out: NIV, NASB, ESV, NKJV, The Passion Translation

CHAPTER SEVEN

Embracing the Pain, but Using It for Good

"Turn your wounds into wisdom."

—OPRAH WINFREY

When tragedy strikes, or we feel attacked, we have choices: either fight or flee, engage or withdraw, press in or retreat, turn towards God, or run away from Him with an attitude of anger or apathy. None of the directions are morally right or wrong, but certain reactions may be healthier than others. Both my parents loved Kevin equally and were equally devastated by his cerebral palsy, yet they dealt with it in drastically different ways. I was three and a half years old when he was born, and I still remember a lot of tears and prayer vigils at my house in those early years.

As Kevin grew older and after Brian was born, I remember my mom being very stressed out with three kids, five and under, and with Kevin being "special." Kevin was moved to his new day home and later to a permanent home. Our visits to see him started off with frequency but grew farther and farther apart with each passing year. It seemed that my dad was the one who consistently got our family there to visit, and oftentimes, he would go on his own. My mom always wanted to leave quickly once we got there and had our visit. I'm sure it was very hard on her. I remember she would shift her body position, look around, and obsessively check her watch whenever she was around Kevin.

When she allowed herself to really sit down with him, hold his hands, and look into his eyes, she would be close to tears and then pull away, seemingly looking for an escape hatch. She truly couldn't face his reality.

I remember her telling me that when he was a baby, she would sit with him on her lap on the floor in front of my long-standing red mirror and sing or read to him as they looked at themselves in the mirror. She recalled that in those times, she felt so close to him. But something must have changed once she placed Kevin in his permanent home. Her attitude shifted from an "all-in mom" to an "I-can't-face-this-anymore-because-it-hurts-too-much" mom. Maybe she felt too guilty for sending him away that she couldn't bear to feel anymore. Or perhaps it was when she realized he was never going to be "normal." All I know is that when Kevin left, a part of my mom died. She became numb to survive. For her, it was tortuous to dwell on or get close to Kevin anymore. He was forever trapped in a non-working body, and there was absolutely nothing my mom could do to fix it. So, she checked out emotionally. She would avoid long visits as they required intimacy and coming face-to-face with Kevin's helpless situation. By delaying visits, avoiding visits, and shortening visits, my mom attempted to keep the pain at bay.

Lucky us, she redirected her vast amount of attention and energy and her need to "fix" things on the rest of us—my dad, brother, and me. Obviously, there were a couple of problems with her reaction. One was that she was mistaken in thinking she could "fix" or "control" anyone, and two, she refused to work on "fixing" the only thing she could control—herself. I don't mean this harshly—my heart breaks for the intense anxiety she must have carried. Inevitably, the pain doesn't go away no matter how many defense mechanisms one employs; it simply manifests itself in other areas. In my mom's case, it manifested itself in the form of high blood pressure, anxiety, and a high need to control situations and people, including me. One of the ways she exerted control over me was in picking out my school clothes each year, enforcing the wearing of pantyhose to church, and advocating hard for the color of my college comforter, lipstick, wedding flowers, and bridesmaid dresses (peach). For a control freak, it could have been worse.

Over the years, my mom opened up to me more about her underlying feelings, which haunted her daily. At one point in the pregnancy with Kevin, she took some skin medicine that was powerful. The instructions said that if she were to ever stop the medicine, she should not do it abruptly but gradually. Apparently, she didn't follow those directions and thought that maybe it was her fault Kevin was born with cerebral palsy. However, not one medical doctor saw any connection with her unsubstantiated fear. I remember she would often say, "If I had only been more on top of my pregnancy and told the doctors not to let me deliver two weeks late, Kevin probably would not be handicapped." In those days, they did not have ultrasounds or understand the risks of late delivery. She bore the burden of his birth accident herself and believed she should have "controlled" the situation more by demanding the delivery date closer to his due date instead of waiting for a natural delivery. She blamed herself for Kevin's condition and regretted not doing more to prevent it. Can you imagine living with that kind of guilt?

Consequently, I recall my entire life being "over-protected and controlled" by my mom as she made vain attempts to protect all of us from any kind of pain or difficulty before it happened—thus stunting our ability to learn from our mistakes. It wasn't obvious to me then, but in hindsight, I believe her highly controlling behavior was an effort to prevent anything ever going wrong with me or Brian like she believed she had "allowed" with Kevin. Her God did not stop the birth accident, so it must be up to her to "stop" future accidents . . . or so her theory went.

This theme was an undercurrent behind our day-to-day lives, and it wasn't until I was older that I realized how sad this was for my mom. She actually felt the weight of the world on her shoulders; it was up to her to hold all things together and prevent all harm from coming to anyone she encountered. In essence, she became her own "god" because her God clearly let His guard down, or it wasn't in His job description, and He needed to be replaced. She saw herself, I think, as God's personal Administrative Assistant . . . or more like His Chief of Staff. He was more of a deistic God who "set the world in motion and let it spin." This phrase was a continual voice in my head and put fear into me as I was taught that we are on our own in this world, practically speaking, even if we were created by God. To hold on to her deep-seated belief in a loving God, my mom assumed God must *not* intervene in the affairs of men—otherwise, how could she justify a loving God allowing Kevin's condition? Her motive was good, but I came to believe later her theology was created to protect her from pain and from losing her belief in God.

In contrast was my dad. While he still struggled with his reactions and may have even shared a similar theology, he never seemed to pull away from the reality of Kevin's condition. From my perspective, he "pressed into the pain"—in other words, he allowed himself to feel the pain and for his heart to hurt as he embraced Kevin fully. He never seemed in a rush during our childhood visits and appeared to accept the reality a bit better, though not without deep sorrow. My dad did not appear to articulate his struggles as much but seemed resigned to accept the fate of my brother's condition. And as much as he hurt so badly inside, he found a way to stay strong for us.

"I ask not for a lighter burden, but for broader shoulders."

—JEWISH PROVERB

My mom's anxiety, distance, and lack of peace contrasted with my dad's resignation, intimacy, and even-handedness. Sadly, my mother went on to have an early stroke at age sixty-two, and ten years later, a massive stroke, which resulted in her untimely death. In between these bookended strokes, we had ten years with my mom enjoying being a "Mimi" to her grandchildren but with her brain suffering from progressive cognitive dementia. I believe her anxiety and high blood pressure, which she never addressed, stemming back to my brother's disability, contributed to her tragic end of life. Later, I learned there were additional reasons. In her determination to stay healthy, she had followed poor but common advice about her diet (nonfat diets were the trend beginning in the 80s), and her fear of getting osteoporosis led her to take massive calcium pills. Turned out that studies later revealed that our brains need lots of good fat, and she was starving her brain of needed nutrients (but she had a very nice figure).

I wish we could have gone back in time and freed my mom to eat more butter instead of dry toast. I wish she could have made her favorite hot fudge sauce with heavy whipping cream instead of nonfat milk! And now, new medical science shows taking a lot of calcium pills—her daily ritual for twenty-plus years to ward off osteoporosis—without getting enough of Vitamin K-2 with Vitamin D-3 means the calcium was not able to be absorbed into the bones and may have contributed to her brain arteries becoming weakened, which triggered her hemorrhagic strokes (brain bleeds). She studied her *Prevention* magazine daily and thought she was doing the right thing. Her death was harder for me to handle than I could have ever imagined as I often think about "what could have been" if I had done something differently for her. While our moms are living, we think they are invincible. I struggle with not doing more to help as she used to look at me with her weakening brain and plead, "Camille, can you help fix me?" She didn't lose her tenacity and drive to control what was happening to her, but she lost her ability. Those ten years between her strokes were full of more secondhand suffering for any of us around my mom.

My attitude toward my parents has changed since my mom's death. I was very judgmental about how my mom handled Kevin my entire life. I saw the flaws in her avoidance techniques and her inability to deal with the very issues that reached the depths of her soul. I would beg her to get help, see a therapist, attend a support group, join a Bible study, read books, or simply admit and talk about her feelings. But she shut down every time I tried, and eventually, I gave up—essentially employing the lesson that I could not control or change her . . . that was her job. My job was to help her if she asked for help or was willing to get it. So ironically, in my "right" approach of giving up on her, I ended up also cutting off much of my own emotional connection to my mom in much the same way that she had done with Kevin. I had cut the emotional cord to some degree when I couldn't change her or affect change in her in the same way she had cut the cord emotionally with Kevin when she couldn't change him or his situation. I missed out on a deeper relationship with my mom because I couldn't truly embrace her with all her flaws. I loved her and honored her and was there for her when she became ill after her first stroke, but I think my lack of understanding of her choices, as well as her choices themselves, caused both of us to lose out on a richer relationship. I grieve this loss now in a very deep way.

After losing my mother, I have greater compassion for her inadequacies. I see how life with a son in Kevin's condition stunted her emotional and spiritual growth. I understand her more now in hindsight. Isn't that the way we work? We have so many obvious "lessons" to learn when our parents are in our faces, but so often, it is not until much later, looking back, that we learn from them.

Sadly, though, my mom seemed paralyzed to find the good in Kevin's situation. While my dad still struggled, I believe this area of "using pain for good" was a healthier way for my dad to embrace Kevin's situation. For all the years of my dad's life, after Kevin was born, he chose to engage himself in serving Kevin and supported causes related to the crippling disease of cerebral palsy and other charities. He has served on the Board of United Cerebral Palsy for forty or so years, raising thousands of dollars for the organization every year, and he created and served as president of a family group at UCP in Chatsworth, CA, for many years where Kevin has lived almost his whole life. This family group was a grassroots effort to provide input and extra funds to just one location where the family members lived. It was very instrumental to many amazing changes at Kevin's home.

As a professor at Pepperdine, running the Business Division at Seaver College for over forty-five years, my dad also started a "service learning" program for Business majors, which emphasizes the value of service to the community instead of solely making money. He would take his students to various charitable organizations, including my brother's nonprofit institution (formally United Cerebral Palsy Children's Foundation), to serve as business consultants to help them improve their operations and help with special projects. One such student in his first pilot program class fortuitously showed up in our family's life decades later as the professor of my son's senior year business elective in college. When this professor (Shaun Limbers, the head of Baylor University's entrepreneurial program) realized my son was the grandson of my dad, he immediately asked, to my son's surprise, "How's Kevin?" We learned that Kevin had made an indelible imprint on his life after weekly visits with him for a semester. Following a very successful business career, Shaun is intentional about giving back to causes that impact lives for good and encourages his students to do the same. And coming full circle, this former student-turned-professor honored my eighty-two-year-old dad, his former professor, by inviting him to come speak to his students at the university. What an amazing experience this was for both my dad and my son (and me)!

My dad could have wallowed in sadness, lived his life in denial of his son's condition, and avoided getting involved because it hurt too much, but he chose another way. He chose to take his pain and use it for good. Because he vulnerably shared his own secondhand suffering with his college students, his impact had a ripple effect on many of them, inspiring them to live a life of service for causes that matter. I greatly admire my dad for being this kind of role model for me and so many others.

He chose to take his pain and use it for good.

While seemingly more peaceful on the outside, my dad has had tremendous grief about Kevin throughout his life. I remember him writing an article entitled "How Many Children Do You Have?" when Kevin was eighteen. He reflected upon this common question we are often asked, which resulted in his uncommon emotional reactions as he grappled with its answer. Perhaps if you are a person with a family member who is "not normal," you can relate. As you read parts of his article (the full article is available on my website), do you see yourself having similar thoughts or questions? Does it give words to anything you have found difficult to express as a secondhand sufferer?

How Many Children Do You Have?
By Jere E. Yates

As a child reared in the church and even as an adult, I never recall hearing anything about the disabled and their parents, either from the pulpit or in class. Oh, I have heard in prayers the expression "help the sick and afflicted," but I have never really thought about who these afflicted were until . . .

On November 8, 1970, my first son, Kevin Jeremy Yates, was born. Inexplicably, his lungs did not fully aerate, and thus he suffered brain damage. The diagnosis and the prognosis were not complete until he was four months old: spastic quadriplegic (cerebral palsy), with no hope for being normal.

This frequently asked question, "How many children do you have?" deeply disturbs me. I actually have three children including Kevin; but when I say "three," other questions follow, such as "Do they get along?" "Do the two brothers fight?" Do casual acquaintances really want to know about all of my children? I suspect not because when I do reveal the fact that Kevin is disabled and does not live at home, they appear to get quite uncomfortable. Perhaps I make them feel ill- at-ease by my tone or the way I answer. I try to be matter-of-fact, but sometimes I am aware of a more emotional tone taking over in myself. If my tone changes—or even if it does not—I worry that the person will believe I am asking for sympathy.

I honestly do not do this because I am seeking sympathy, but rather my change in tone is a result of the difficulty I have in controlling the rush of my feelings to the surface. Some people will respond with such a display of pity as to make me regret having mentioned it. Sometimes I respond to the questions about my children without mentioning Kevin, and then I feel guilty for leaving him out, even though I know there are some practical reasons for it; then I chastise myself for taking the road of convenience and practicality.

How Is Kevin?

Some who know Kevin do occasionally ask about him, but most do not. Why? Is it because they are uneasy in asking or because they are afraid I will become emotional? I suggest that it is both. It appears that both sides feel more comfortable not mentioning the fact of his permanent disability. Some parents are reluctant to take a disabled child or person out or to invite friends in to see him or her because they do not want to make others feel uncomfortable. The parents may also fear their inability to handle their emotions in the presence of others.

At times, I have a need to share my son and my feelings about him with close friends, but I usually resist for fear of imposing my burden on them. I know we are supposed to "bear one another's burdens," but this one seems too heavy to share and to expect others to bear. Yet how can one be a truly intimate friend and not share the totality of life?

People seem to know better how to comfort the bereaved following a death in the family than how to respond to the ongoing, agonizing struggle parents face with a disabled child. ... The disabled child continually presents new problems to parents, taxing their coping mechanisms. ... I confess that I block Kevin out of my mind much of the time. I do it out of necessity because the constant load of worrying about him would be too distressful to endure.

Have You Ever Wished He Had Died at Birth?

A few individuals have had the courage to ask whether I have ever wished that Kevin had died at birth. The answer is yes, I have. For a number of years, I thought everyone, including Kevin, would have been better off if he had died at birth. But now I have a different perspective. Kevin's charming smile and genuine responsiveness to people have warmed the hearts of many individuals and deeply touched lives for good in ways that most of us could never do...

In addition, he provides a real opportunity for people to learn the meaning of service and to appreciate their own abilities, which they may take for granted. To wish he had died is to be selfish—it is my seeking to avoid personal hardships at the expense of denying him the pleasures of living...I am convinced that in mysterious ways God has worked through Kevin to bless many lives over the past eighteen years.

How Often Do You See Him?

Kevin lives twenty-five miles from home, and frequently I am asked the question, "How often do you see him?" I feel more guilt about my response to this question than to any other because I do not see him as often as I would like or need to. I usually reason, or perhaps rationalize, that I have obligations to my family, my work, my church, my friends, and myself as well as to Kevin. It is not easy to bring him home; it is hard both physically and emotionally.

Because I know he receives good care and personal attention where he is, I find it easy enough at times to neither visit him nor bring him home.

Was It Difficult to Place Him?

We kept Kevin at home for three years before making the difficult decision to place him. To say the decision was arduous is an understatement, yet in a strange way we had no choice. We (felt) we had no choice if we valued each other, our other children, and Kevin himself. Professionals and other parents in similar situations were one hundred percent sure that placement was the right choice. We heard stories of parents who had tried to keep their disabled child at home for years, only to learn later—after divorce, after their children had suffered emotional problems, and after their own physical ailments surfaced—that placement would have been best all along. Considering all these factors made the rational choice easy, but it did nothing for the emotional trauma I suffered upon leaving Kevin for the first time...The first few years were truly years of adjustment for all of us. Kevin would cry his heart out every time I would leave after a visit at his "special home" or at our family home. Those times were excruciatingly painful for me...

Do You Blame God?

Perhaps I have repressed any thought of blaming God for Kevin's misfortune, but I do not think so. I cannot explain why, yet I have never accused God of causing this tragedy. The classic problem of theodicy (if God is good and all-powerful, why does He allow evil?) has stumped most of us, though some ideas have helped me. The ultimate answer for me is the same as the answer given to Job—a childlike faith. Because I have only finite understanding and perspective, I do not know why God would allow this tragedy to occur. Perhaps Kevin and others like him have been placed here to teach us the true meaning of ministry to one another; perhaps to manifest the hidden goodness in people that a disabled child can bring out; perhaps to cause us to appreciate our normal functioning as contrasted with a helplessly disabled person; perhaps to strengthen our dependence upon God; perhaps to give meaning to the idea of anguish; perhaps to remind us that justice is not to be achieved in this life; perhaps ...

If Kevin's situation worsens in the years to come, I may feel angry toward God; but at the moment, I get some consolation in recognizing that Kevin's ultimate fate is in His hands, and I trust Him. My theology leads me sometimes to dream of being with Kevin in the afterlife when he's fully functioning and to dream that I will know of his thoughts and feelings regarding our decision about him in this life. How wonderful it would be to hear him say we had made the right decisions; how dreadful if he saw it otherwise! I would give anything to have real communication with him now, but alas, I shall have to settle for then.

How Many Children Do You Have?

This question with which I began causes me to reflect on what I really need from others. I believe I need other people to deal with the total me. It is acceptable to be awkward in showing an interest in Kevin or in how I am handling the difficulties of being the father of a severely disabled child. To accept my discomfort in dealing with the very tender feeling generated by talking about Kevin is also what I need from friends. Above all, I do not want Kevin's disability to be a major handicap for him, for me, for my family, or for my friends.

Given Kevin's childlike qualities—innocence, genuineness, spontaneity, love, trust—and the fact that my other children will grow up to be fully functioning adults, viewed from the perspective of a lifetime, perhaps the answer to the above question is "I have only one child, albeit a very special one!"

Truly, it is a poignant article to which many secondhand sufferers can surely relate. It feels hard for me to read in retrospect, but it helps to understand what my parents were going through. Now, many years later, I have noticed a new phenomenon with my dad, and he has also just refreshed this article with an update at age eighty-two. He notes the following:

> It has been thirty-five years since I wrote my article about Kevin. Having reread it several times recently, I don't believe I believe any differently now than I did then. Some things have changed but my answers to the questions I raised in that article have not.
>
> One change is rather monumental. Several years after Carolyn, my wife of fifty-one years, died, I realized that I was grieving more about the tragedy of Kevin's situation than I had for years. In reflecting on why this might be, I believe I found the answer. Carolyn always believed deep down that she did something in her pregnancy that caused Kevin's breathing problem at birth. After extensive examination by attorneys who had previously been practicing physicians, I was convinced that she was in no way responsible; it was an accident with no attributable cause. Because of her belief, she was very uncomfortable being around Kevin for long periods of time.
>
> I always felt that I had to be strong emotionally lest I adversely affected her, leading to an emotional breakdown. With her being gone and my daughter stepping in to deal with issues connected with Kevin's care and health, I

realized that I was allowing myself to grieve more than ever, though I still did not let myself dwell on it for long. Knowing something about stress management, I never allowed myself to focus on his situation very long. My major way of coping became one of blocking out thoughts of him after a short period of grief. I have always reasoned that my being emotionally "down" about Kevin's situation did not help him or me.

The other major change is that I no longer hesitate to mention at a social event, when asked about the number of my children, that I have THREE children. I freely identify that one of my children is special because of his disability. I am much more comfortable sharing about his life without worrying about making people uncomfortable when I identify his disability.

Recently, my dad also admitted that it was hard to see Kevin occasionally visit our home because it makes his disability all the more real. "When Kevin is in his home with others with severe cerebral palsy in wheelchairs and full-time care, it seems to be easier on me," he said. "But, when he is in our home for an occasional field trip, and our family is all around him, it makes me realize all he has missed—I grieve what could have been."

The dynamic of shifting the ability to carry the load of emotional pain from one loved one to another is very real. Perhaps it is subconscious, but it must be natural to allow oneself to "coast" a bit emotionally from hurting when you know someone else is carrying the "suitcase of pain" for you. When I was a child, my parents carried this load. Now that I am at the stage of life where I am a mother myself and a fully middle-aged woman, I seem to be carrying the emotional weight for my dad.

INSIGHTS FOR THE HEART

Finding a Purpose Out of Pain

I have heard there are troubles of more than one kind.
Some come from ahead and some come from behind.
But I've bought a big bat. I'm all ready you see.
Now my troubles are going to have troubles with me!

—DR. SEUSS

While some may call it "writer's block," I call it "not being able to write one more word without pulling an ugly weed up by its root." I was stuck in my writing this story without finding a purpose behind my brother's life of living in the prison of his own body. Do you ever feel similarly in trying to find meaning or a reason for your sufferings? Recalling past memories stirred up so many emotions, which revealed a deep root that was producing ugly weeds of bitterness. That root was being angry at God. I couldn't fix Kevin, but I also needed a reason to write this story. What was this all for? If Kevin's suffering is all meaningless and there is nothing good to come out of his suffering, then why bother with the writing process? I had hit a wall and felt discouraged. I wasn't necessarily looking for a happy ending, but I needed a sense of purpose. I knew that deep down, something good must come out of something tragic.

Sitting in the TV room and ready to throw in the towel, I cried out to God, "I can't do this. I don't see the purpose. Unless you give me a reason to continue writing, I'm done. Give me some sort of sign to keep writing."

I decided to do what most people do when they give up, and I flipped on the TV to dull my senses. At that time, I wasn't a big TV watcher, so I really didn't know what channel to "flip" to. That day, with no destination in mind, I "surfed" the Direct TV channels—all 680 of them—until I paused on one. Some guy was talking and said something that caught my ear. It was something like, "I was mad at God and demanded to know why he would do this to my brother!" I couldn't believe what I heard as I had just muttered those very words to myself seconds ago. I listened more intently. He talked about how his brother was in his early forties with a young family and was killed by a horrible brain-degenerating disease. He had also been a pastor, and the guy talking could not believe that *any* good could come from his brother's life being taken. You could see the emotion in his eyes . . . now this was real. I was tracking with him! He had me glued to the TV.

A Bible quote that many Christians say when tragedy strikes is a verse in the book of Romans. It says, "And we know that in all things,

God works for the good of those who love him, who have been called according to his purpose" (Romans 8:28 NIV). I had always struggled with this verse because I didn't buy it, really. *All* things work together for good? It sounded like some kind of fortune cookie—nice idea, but really? *All things*? I'm sorry . . . how does the murder of a child ever work for good? What about child trafficking? I can't find any good in these things. And, of course, how the heck was my brother being trapped in a body that doesn't work at all work together for good? No matter the circumstances, grief is grief. But this man on TV had such a peace about him, yet he was still grieving the loss of his dear brother. He talked about how his brother's one wish was to preach Jesus to as many people as possible—he said it was what he lived for. This man speaking didn't understand why God wouldn't honor that. As a result of these deep questions about his brother and his passion for spreading the message of God from the Bible, the man on TV decided to write a book that dealt with these brutal questions that haunted him after losing his brother. He happened to have a national ministry, and so his book did quite well. After the book was written and sold, it ended up reaching thousands and thousands of people worldwide.

The man went on to say that one day, it hit him that the "good" that had come from his brother's early death was the very book that he wrote—it took his brother's message to a much larger audience than his brother could have ever done as a small-time pastor. This was his brother's very wish and the purpose he had stated for his life. In fact, the words that came out of the TV that day right after I had given God an ultimatum to "give me a reason to write this book or I will quit" were, "I realized that the good God may have intended to bring out of the tragedy of my brother's death was that I would write this book about my brother and bring healing to others out of my suffering." Upon hearing those words, I froze, and a tear dropped out of my eye while my body broke out in chills. I believe, for the first time, I realized that a piece of the "good" I was looking for all these years out of Kevin's tragic birth accident was possibly resting on me and this book. Could God really use me to take the lessons I have learned from my brother and help others in some small way? If this were true, you (the one reading this) are the "good" that may come from Kevin's life. And if so, then if you are affected positively in some way, what *you* do with the good you have received will affect others in your sphere of influence. Knowing that good is coming out of something so painful as secondhand suffering is one of the tools that eases some of those rough, jagged edges of the suffering and adds purpose to the pain.

That day, I believe I had an encounter with God. I don't say that lightly, as I am sensitive when people claim God "talks to them" all the time. But something shifted in me that day, and for the first time, I began to have peace that I had a role to play—and a responsibility—in bringing purpose to Kevin's life as a part of the Romans 8:28 answer for his suffering. My writer's block was cured. I was starting to feel like some "good" may be possible to come from my brother's suffering. And from that point on, once I had a purpose, words began to flow like a river.

As a career coach, I have seen how people's lives can change when they discover a career, hobby, or purpose in their life that connects their profession to their heart. Fulfilling a destiny that stems from our places of pain can be the greatest gift to the world. Good can be birthed out of bad—we can choose to make that exchange. The Bible refers to this in a beautiful exchange to be like a crown of beauty for ashes, oil of gladness instead of mourning, and a garment of praise instead of despair (Isaiah 61:3). Often, our places of pain are the very places the world cries out for a solution. And when we meet those needs, we find that joy spills over from the inside. Not a joy of superficial happiness, but rather, an inner sense of purpose, calling, and satisfaction. Will you rise to the occasion of making your greatest pain a gift to the world? I really hope you do.

> *"The place God calls you to is the place where*
> *your deep gladness and the world's deep hunger meet."*
>
> —Frederick Buechner
> *Wishful Thinking: A Seeker's ABC*

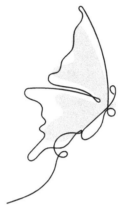

SPIRITUAL REFLECTIONS

Loosening My Grip of Anger

*"Do not be overcome by evil,
but overcome evil with good."*

—ROMANS 12:21

Not long after my spiritual breakthrough of writer's block, I gained a deeper insight into my issues with God after I had the opportunity and compulsion to watch a masterfully produced movie called *The Shack*. This movie unlocked something deep in my heart that needed to get out and something that needed to get in and helped bring healing to a very hardened and wounded part of me. A piece of my heart that had been practically calcified in hardness began to break open, and a piece of God in the form of the Holy Spirit entered that same part of my heart to bring much-needed healing. Certain scenes in this movie tenderized my heart in a way that moved my typical understanding of God from my head to my heart. The Holy Spirit—also known as The Comforter—touched right where my wound was, supernaturally unlocking my heavily guarded heart to release spiritual toxins and roadblocks that had been keeping me stuck spiritually. I know that may seem pretty heavy, but that's the only way I know to explain what happened.

If you've never seen the movie, it is centered around a young dad named Mack, who suffered the horrendous loss of his little girl being murdered. It was a hard-hitting yet tasteful handling of a tragedy none of us can imagine living through. While my brother clearly wasn't murdered, the emotions inside of me resonated with Mack's loss because similar feelings arose at injustice and the realization of "what could have been that will never be." The entire movie was about Mack facing the God he thought he believed in head-on over a weekend he spent in a shack, the very place where his daughter's body was found and the center of his unbearable pain.

During the weekend, the three Persons of God (Father, Jesus, Holy Spirit) were manifested in human form, and this grieving dad asked every question he had of "them." It was powerful and raw. There were so many lines in the movie that resonated with me and brought me to healing tears, and a few are worth mentioning. One was spoken by God the Father or "Papa" in this instance. When Mack challenged God for causing his daughter's evil death, Papa said, "I can work together incredible good in the tragedies, but I don't orchestrate the tragedies."[31] Wait . . . rewind. *God doesn't orchestrate the tragedies.* Thank you,

God. This scene hit my heart with such a shift in my spirit. While it is "just a movie," it somehow validated my instinct that it never made sense to me that God would plan—or cause—the evil that happened on earth. But there was something so powerful to hearing this articulated directly—it hit me at the heart level and not my head, and it felt freeing. In my tears, my anger toward God softened.

I later found out that this statement aligned with so much of what the Bible says. John 10:10 says there is a real enemy (evil) that comes to "steal, kill and destroy," but Jesus came so that "they may have life and have it to the full." Also, the story told in the book of Genesis tells us that this planet is not as it should be, and there has been corruption since the early days of the fall of man, yet this does not mean all bad things that happen are *because* God *makes* them happen. Causation was always my struggle. It's the "why" rising up again. The more I searched the Bible over the years, the more it seemed true that God was not the originator of evil, pain, or sickness. Yes, these things still happen, but God promises to be with us because He loves us, He sees us, and His compassion grieves with us, knowing this world is not paradise anymore like He intended at Creation.

In the same movie, when Mack says he is stuck and can't move on from his overwhelming grief, Papa says, "You're not stuck because you can't; you're stuck because you won't. You don't have to do this alone. I'm here with you."[32] In God's ultimate everlasting love, He chooses to partner with us to accomplish His purpose, and He holds out His hand. Yet, we must do our part and take His hand and embrace that He is right here with us, walking alongside, often carrying us during these tragedies that all of us have faced or will face if we live long enough on this earth. While we struggle to understand so much still, we are told throughout the Bible that God will never leave us and will always be with us to the end of the age. He knows we are carrying heavy burdens, and we were not designed to carry them alone.

"Come to me, all you who are weary and burdened,
and I will give you rest."

—Jesus, Matthew 28:29 (NIV)

In 2023, there was devastation in Maui, Hawaii, with the destruction of entire neighborhoods. Homes and massive human lives were lost through a deadly fire. A dear friend of mine, Nancy, volunteered at the last minute to be a part of the rescue team with a nonprofit organization to help the people in whatever way they could. So much had been lost. Nothing seemed good. Darkness was heavy in that land just a few weeks after the nightmare of evil, and the people who survived were looking for some kind of hope. Working through the rubble, my friend discovered a woman's wedding ring. The news echoed throughout the area, and she sent messages to her friends to celebrate. Something beautiful came out of those ashes. This ring, symbolizing ever-lasting love, was found amidst the devastation. It was a powerful symbol. And, on the same day, a few feet away, she found a fully intact coffee mug with the word "LOVE" on it. The power of love shone through that day for those rescue workers and the people of Maui. While it did not change the fact that so much was taken and destroyed, it was a poignant reminder that if we have open eyes and are willing to search, hope and goodness can still be found.

"When it is dark enough, you can see the stars."

—Ralph Waldo Emerson

As you may recall, I wrote about a favorite childhood hobby of mine in an earlier chapter, watching my elderly neighbor lady paint. My favorite painting of hers (the only one I remember) was of a windmill. Something about that lone, towering windmill captivated me as it stood in the middle of a vast field of wheat. Firm and unwavering, it was planted solidly where it would capture the wind and spin around and around, catapulting power across the community around it. Looking back on that painting, I later wondered why it was the one painting I remember and why it seemed to speak to me. The more I thought about it, I had a bit of an epiphany of sorts. That windmill symbolizes a strong, steady, singular person firmly planted and rooted in the ground, able to withstand all the harsh elements of life. Windmills are often planted in the windiest zones, of course, so they can harness the wind and use it for good to provide power and energy to the community nearby. So, in the same way, how much more can it be true for individuals, and especially those of faith? We can be like strong windmills that are planted (by no control of our own) in a field of harsh winds (the violent elements of life) and stand firm, unwavering, turning our circumstances into a powerful force for good as we churn energy out into our communities.

This imagery provides a picture of how each of us can be used to give power and life to others through our own difficult experiences. *Windmills don't stop the winds of life but face them head-on, taking hold of their power and converting a potentially destructive force into a life-empowering energy.* In my case, while I couldn't control my brother's disability (the harsh wind) or where I have been planted (my life circumstances), I could use the resources within me to turn these hardships into good for others. And so can you.

Let's open our eyes to the fact that God is not the One to blame for the bad, for if we do, perhaps we can be grateful that He walks alongside us on the journey. May each one of us experience some peace and comfort amid the trauma while we search to discover the hidden good.

> *"When the winds of change blow, some people build walls, others build windmills."*
>
> —CHINESE PROVERB

TOOLS FOR THE HEART

While it's true that we can't control many of the circumstances that affect us or our loved ones, we can choose to control how we react to them and how we let them affect our lives. By facing reality and embracing the pain, we may just stumble on ways that good can come from the bad. Each one of us holds the tools to unlock those hidden gems under the rubble of tragedy, and we find our purpose for good as a result.

Questions to Ponder:

1. Do you tend to embrace your pain or run from it? How is either choice working for you?
2. Do you blame God for your loved one's loss, illness, tragedy, or pain? How do you relate to Mack in the movie *The Shack* when he finally believes that God didn't orchestrate suffering?
3. Have you ever been touched by God in some kind of supernatural way that ministered to your heart and not your head? If so, what was it like? Did you feel God's deep love for you? If not, consider asking Him to touch you in a way that brings a form of healing.
4. Have you found any silver linings or purposes that can come out of your secondhand suffering? If so, what are they?

Practical Steps:

- I invite you to watch the movie *The Shack*, a fictionalized story of the heart of God when it comes to suffering and bad things happening. Consider watching it with a few close friends and talking about it afterward, as it is bound to stir some deep feelings.
- Take some time to think about the purpose of your secondhand suffering and how you can use the situation for good to meet the world's deepest hunger. Write your thoughts in a journal as ideas begin to surface. What can you do to cultivate this area of your purpose that stems from your pain? Some ideas may be serving others, speaking to a group, forming an online community, writing a book or an article, or forming a book/discussion group. What are some tangible steps you can take to get started?
- Write a letter about your situation with your loved one—living or gone—which addresses similar questions to the ones my dad addressed in his article. Be honest and get it all down. If you can, share your letter with close friends or family so they can gain an understanding of the things you are going through and begin finding the good in your pain.

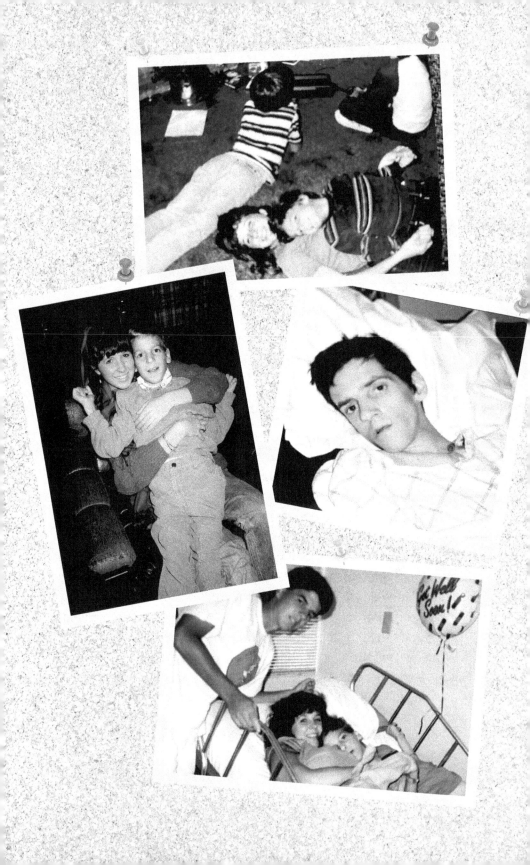

CHAPTER EIGHT

Looking for the Joy

*"Joy is the holy fire that keeps our purpose warm
and our intelligence aglow."*

—HELEN KELLER

Sustainable joy is something I've struggled to understand. My sweet mom modeled this enigma to me throughout my life—she could be happy for short periods of time (she had a great sense of humor!), but she also never reached the point of joy until all her worries got resolved. And her worry list was *never* empty. Yet, when I think about people who have every excuse to be sad or upset, these are quite often the most joyful people I've met. My brother Kevin is one of those people, and he has taught me that joy is possible in the midst of suffering. He lives and models joy to anyone he meets. I can only hope one day, if I ever have to endure this level of physical or emotional suffering, that I can be like Kevin in this regard. Secondhand suffering is hard enough!

As a child, around nine or ten, I remember going through a stage where I refused to smile for pictures when my mom wanted us to take them. She would beg me to smile for the picture, and I would refuse and stand there stoic, puckering my lips to make sure my mom didn't win the battle. I think it was my form of passive-aggressive rebellion. I can't help but think not only was it a battle of control between my mom and me, but it probably reflected that I was not interested in faking a smile when I wasn't happy. This was not the generation where parents sent their kids to therapy, so I may never know why I did this. And come to think of it, I'm sure I needed therapy. But, it reminds me that the expression of inner joy is not something that comes easy for me, though I have always admired it.

When I look at Kevin's life and dwell on it, I feel an overwhelming grief and burden. I stumbled across a quote by author Andrew Boyd that seems to capture a bit of how I feel, and you may also when you think about your situation.

> Compassion hurts. When you feel connected to everything, you also feel responsible for everything. And you cannot turn away. Your destiny is bound with the destinies of others. You must either learn to carry the Universe or be crushed by it. You must grow strong enough to love the world, yet empty enough to sit down at the same table with its worst horrors.[33]

As I have grown to understand the nature of God, my burden, at times, feels some relief as it is lifted in proportion to my connection to God. I can still feel the depth of pain for my brother, and that doesn't go away, but knowing there is an all-powerful and loving God who loves Kevin greater than I ever could helps me not be crushed by it. Some find it easier to become desensitized from pain—thus compassion—and turn to all kinds of coping mechanisms to mask the hurt. But to empty ourselves of compassion can result in a hardened heart. Without God, I see no other way to manage deep sorrows other than being crushed or emptied, as this quote by Boyd so despondently articulates.

Yet, when I switch perspectives from someone like me—a secondhand sufferer—and shift to Kevin himself—a firsthand sufferer—I am struck by his regular attitude of joy despite his severe disability. Perhaps I have had trouble experiencing joy throughout my life because I'm bound to the emotional weight of my brother's lot in life; ironically, Kevin has carried an inner joy in his spirit his entire life. Anyone who knows him sees it. He has taught me much about what true joy is and true love. It certainly cannot be connected to one's circumstances if my quadriplegic brother, without the ability to speak, walk, or control his movements, exudes joy while he sits strapped helplessly in a wheelchair. The simple joy of someone asking him how he is doing that day can light up a smile. Of course, if he is in pain, upset, or sometimes just plain bored, he certainly shows with cries, tears, or depression symptoms. However, his natural disposition is joyful—a true gift to those around him. Clearly, his joy does not have anything to do with what we would call "happiness" because that implies a feeling based on circumstances.

Kevin would not agree that his life is always "happy." Yet, there is something about Kevin's countenance that runs deeper than a feeling. There is something uncanny about the way he smiles and laughs around people who give him attention. He loves all people—he doesn't distinguish them by their education, job title, race, religion, or whether they speak English or not. He has taught me much about unconditional love. When I feel sorry for him, I am reminded of his joy. Recently, I read a quote by actor Ashton Kutcher that struck a chord in me—both an initial shock of disagreement, followed by a later understanding of his larger point:

> My brother was born with cerebral palsy, and it taught me that loving people isn't a choice and that people aren't actually all created equal. The Constitution lies to us. We're not all created equal. We're all created incredibly un-equal to one another, in our capabilities and what we can do and how we think and what we see. But we all have the equal capacity to love one another, and my brother taught me that. When I got older, I spent years and years feeling bad about it, our inequalities. He also taught me that he had gifts that I didn't have. Extraordinary gifts that I didn't have, and that every time I felt sorry for him in life, I made him less. He taught me that and he gave that to me.[34]

While I 100 percent believe that all people *are* created equal, I understand the sentiment Ashton is expressing—all people certainly do not have the same abilities, advantages, or paths in life. Yet, I believe all people are made equally in the image of God and have unique gifts. When we feel sorry for them, we play a role in making them "less."

Like Ashton's brother, Kevin carries an ability to love others, and often he does it with his eyes alone. He is a magnet for people, and people are the hidden source of his joy. When his caregivers talk to him, love on him, and spend time relating to him as a human being and not an object to be dutifully cared for, he lights up. His smile radiates a love that surpasses human understanding. He has the same human needs any of us have—the need to love and be loved. It seems rare that individuals exhibit signs of joy when all alone; it is likely shown as an outward manifestation of an inward feeling when we're around others, possibly for the unconscious purpose of the relationship. I've always said Kevin is a social extravert trapped in a body that keeps him locked in. Yet his smile and eyes escape the prison of paralysis and exude a supernatural engagement with the souls of others—joy despite circumstances.

Most people struggle to understand people like this—people who have nothing and yet can find strength within to still smile, laugh, and love. It must mean we are wired for so much more than our circumstances or our physical abilities. It must mean there is hope for all of us when we see people like Kevin. What does he have that we all need?

> *"The difference between shallow happiness and a deep, sustaining joy is sorrow. Happiness lives where sorrow is not. When sorrow arrives, happiness dies. It can't stand pain. Joy, on the other hand, rises from sorrow and therefore can withstand all grief. Joy, by the grace of God, is the transfiguration of suffering into endurance, and of endurance into character, and of character into hope--and*

*the hope that has become our joy does not (as happiness
must for those who depend upon it) disappoint us."*

—WALTER WANGERIN JR.[35]

Years ago, I saw the movie *The Diving Bell and the Butterfly*,[36] based on the book by Jean-Dominique Bauby. Bauby was a prominent editor of the French magazine *Elle* but suffered an untimely stroke at age forty-three, which left him "locked in" and completely paralyzed, except for one eye. Through a brilliant speech therapist and a patient publisher employee, he learned to communicate with this one eye by blinking at the verbal reading of the alphabet, eventually writing the book telling the story of his life. The movie gives us an inside look at what someone like Kevin may be feeling and thinking. Three weeks after the massive stroke and coma, the movie depicts the scene where Bauby is awake, and the doctors are standing over him. They were talking to him about his condition, and he was asking them questions in his head that they couldn't hear. In his mind, he was talking to them, but in the real world, they couldn't hear him or see any such attempt. In his head, he was yelling at them, begging them to listen. When he realized it was useless, he resigned himself to his new lot in life and sunk into a very dark depression where he wanted to die.

Another scene brought a bit more humor as he lay in his hospital bed watching a soccer match on TV. He was very involved in the game and a doctor kept blocking his view of the TV, and you hear him "yelling" at the doctor in his mind. Then, to make matters worse, when the doctor leaves, he turns off the TV. Poor Bauby wanted the TV to be turned back on . . . but when you looked at him, there was no movement or noise. It was pure silence without any motion. Yet, you hear him talking to himself in his head in a sarcastically humorous way—even through his own dire frustrations, he "entertained" himself with his own thoughts and sometimes off-color jokes about the staff and nurses around him.

While Bauby never recovered physically, and I do not believe he ever would admit to experiencing joy, he did come to experience a quasi-peace that seemed impossible at first. That peace came from seeing his family and kids and using his imagination during his waking and dreaming hours. Eventually, he seemed to gain more peace by being able to communicate so many of his deepest regrets to those he loved via his newfound writing gift with his eye. One of his friends in the movie, who experienced life "locked-in" while being a hostage in Beirut stuck in solitary confinement for four years, gave him valuable advice when he said, "Hold fast to the human inside of you, and you'll survive." The title of the movie comes from the idea that while Bauby's body was submerged underwater and weighted down in a deep sea diving bell suit, sinking slowly into the abyss with no ability to move or escape, his memory and imagination were still free and light like a butterfly's wings: "My cocoon becomes less oppressive, and my mind takes flight like a butterfly. There is so much to do. You can wander off in space or in time, set out for Tierra del Fuego or for King Midas's court."[37] He was still human, which is the ultimate mystery of the source of joy.

Unlike most modern-day movies and TV shows, what I appreciated about this story is that there was no "happy ending," per se. This is true in so much of life. There are no pretty bows wrapped around this movie. It felt sad, with traces of humor and goodness, but also a sinking feeling that the life he had hoped for was over forever. Interestingly, Bauby never indicated any belief or hope in God or an afterlife. Perhaps if he had one, there would have been more joy because there was more to the story of his short life. Yet, even without this hope of God or heaven clearly stated, there must be something in the human soul that transcends life's circumstances, something alive, something untouched by adversity. I believe God created all men and women in His image. As Creator, that makes us creative. As eternally existent, that makes us eternal. And as God is defined as LOVE, that makes us with the capacity to love and be loved. Bauby had all of these traits, and they were given to him by God whether he knew it or not.

"The most beautiful people we have known are those who have known defeat, known suffering, known struggle, known loss, and have found their way out of the depths. These persons have an appreciation, a sensitivity, and an understanding of life that fills them with compassion, gentleness, and a deep loving concern. Beautiful people do not just happen."

—ELISABETH KÜBLER-ROSS[38]

INSIGHTS FOR THE HEART

The Mystery of Internal Joy

*"The deeper that sorrow carves into your being,
the more joy you can contain. Is not the cup that holds your wine
the very cup that was burned in the potter's oven?"*

—KAHLIL GIBRAN

The older I get, the people I've met with the most joy seem to be the ones who have suffered the most or who've been affected by a lot of adversity. I sometimes wonder if that's because they are more surrounded by God's peace than those who seem to have "it all together." I've learned through Kevin and others that adverse and difficult circumstances do not necessitate the absence of joy. I marvel at how people not only endure hardships but show *joy* through them.

Have you ever noticed that something happens to our pride when we face struggles? It crumbles as we give up our will to "be in charge." I saw this with my mom in the last few years of her life. As the dementia set in from her first stroke, she was so upset that she would fight every issue. When we took away her right to drive a car, she fought us for a long time, even when her logic failed her. She had also held the chains of control over her life and often those around her. Yet, there was a dramatic shift when she could no longer articulate her thoughts. When she finally surrendered control, we saw a soft, sweet spirit emerge— one filled with humility, gratefulness, and, yes, even joy. She had lost the will to be in charge and sweetly allowed us to take care of her. Once she surrendered her strong will to control her situation, we saw a joy we hadn't ever seen. It was, of course, bittersweet, but there is a profound hidden gem of truth in her example—a surrendered life can be a contented life.

Even in the smallest of ways, trivial suffering can bring on humility and gratitude. My friend from Texas says that because of the intense humidity and heat there, people often lay down their pride with how they look because no matter what women do, their hair still frizzes, and they still sweat! There is a camaraderie among the "afflicted," resulting in a thread of joy during the suffering Texas heat. While humidity is not exactly what I would call suffering compared to more serious trauma, this light-hearted comment carries a deeper truth. Suffering humbles us, can unite us, and levels the playing field—it is the great "equalizer" among people going through it.

Tough circumstances also seem to polarize people into two camps. They either kick it into gear with their attitude of joy and gratitude for the things they do have or become bitter and give up. I heard from someone recently that suffering either makes us bitter or better. From my experience, suffering rarely brings neutrality. There is a choice involved—we can choose the camp of bitterness and victimhood or the camp of hope and joy. We can't choose our circumstances (usually), but we can choose our reactions. Suffering is real. Contrary to what some religions and philosophies teach, I do not believe it's all in our minds. It is real. Pain is real. Yet, to see my brother Kevin smile at the simplest things—someone walking into a room saying "hi" to him, being pushed in his wheelchair with the wind in his hair, seeing his family approaching him after a long time away, and his beaming smile and giggle at my mention of banana cream pie—these are pictures of joy to me. Even though most of his days are filled with frustration, pain, and anguish as he cannot communicate, move the way he wants, or choose activities to avoid boredom or pain or scratch an itch on his own, Kevin can choose joy, and he can control that.

Finding contentment and joy during intensely difficult circumstances is truly not of this world. Wired deeply in all of us is something that wants to find the good and cling to hope that there is something more. Clearly, good circumstances cannot produce joy alone. Look at the tragedy of comedian Robin Williams. He had all the circumstances money can buy plus more, and he sure knew how to laugh and make others laugh. He had a family, good friends, incredible wealth, success, admiration, fans, a brilliant mind, and was somewhat of a progeny with his sense of humor. He truly "had it all," including what looked like joy on the outside. Yet, at the end of his life, most of us learned too late there was no joy—only a deep, dark depression. People have said, "If Robin Williams wasn't happy, ain't no way anyone can be happy!" Contrast that to those without anything who somehow demonstrate uncanny joy and stick it out with perseverance at full throttle.

"Part of the problem with the word 'disabilities' is that it immediately suggests an inability to see or hear or walk or do other things that many of us take for granted. But what of people who can't feel? Or talk about their feelings? Or manage their feelings in constructive ways? What of people who aren't able to form close and strong relationships? And people who cannot find fulfillment in their lives, or those who have lost hope, who live in disappointment and bitterness and find in life no joy, no love? These, it seems to me, are the real disabilities."

—FRED ROGERS
The World According to Mister Rogers:
Important Things to Remember[39]

Nick Vujicic, a young man who was born with no arms and no legs, is now an inspirational speaker. Recently, he spoke passionately about the topic of joy while in China after a student at a Chinese university asked him what kind of joy he has and why it is so different.

See, there is no joy in the circumstance. There is nothing good about having no arms and no legs is there? No. But there is joy in the purpose of it. What joy is it? Honestly, if I had a BMW, would I have joy? No. If I had a million dollars, would I have joy? No. A billion dollars can't buy me hope, it can't cure me from a disease that's incurable; a billion dollars cannot heal my broken heart, won't heal my mind of memories I wish I could forget...no amount of alcohol, drugs, sex—anything of this world—rock star, fame, money, girls—anything of this world...there is no joy. There is no joy that I have...the only joy that I have is "the joy of the Lord is my strength." That's the only joy I have. There is no joy in your parents separating. If you are in a broken home, I don't know how that feels. But let me ask you, if someone comes in on a wheelchair, and you are not in a wheelchair, who do you think can encourage that person more—me or you? ME—because I know how it feels to be in a wheelchair. If you're in a broken home and you have hope and you find someone else in a broken home who does not have hope or love, but you can give them that hope and love, then it's worth it. That's how I see my life. If my life doesn't change on the outside, then it is more important to be changed on the inside. Love sets me free.[40]

One of the qualities that seems to be a forerunner to joy is an attitude of gratitude. While I can't get into my brother's head and understand what he is thinking, I have to believe that he is thankful for the little things in life—he must be. I don't think he is thankful for his circumstances—I know he desperately wants a new body. But somehow, he finds a way to smile anyway—not all the time, but certainly more than his lot in life should justify. There is a verse in the Bible that says, "Be thankful in all circumstances." It's not a verse I especially am fond of, but I believe it teaches a principle that is good for us. It doesn't say "be thankful *for* all circumstances," and I think I understand the difference. One is a thankful attitude no matter what circumstances life holds, and the other is only being thankful as *a result of* the circumstances. The former sounds possible, the latter, simply insane. People with joy find ways to be thankful for what they do have instead of only focusing on what they don't. They also find something to always be thankful for no matter what. I am humbled in their presence.

"The root of joy is gratefulness...
It is not joy that makes us grateful;
it is gratitude that makes us joyful."

—BROTHER DAVID STEINDL-RAST

Another hero of mine, in addition to my brother and Nick Vujicic, as mentioned above, is Joni Erickson Tada, a woman who became paralyzed from the shoulders down in a diving accident as a teen. Joni has clearly demonstrated a remarkable joy despite her heartbreaking injury. Not only has she made a huge difference in the lives of the disabled through her Joni & Friends Ministry, which provides wheelchairs all over the world to the crippled and disabled, as well as providing countless resources to families, churches, and organizations to help the disabled, but she also has been a role model to so many—including me—for exhibiting joy and choosing to be thankful.

I first read about Joni when I was a teenager and was gripped by her tragic story of diving into a lake head first and becoming paralyzed due to a spinal cord injury. There was a movie made about her story called *Joni* and a book, and then later, she published multiple best-seller books. I appreciated that she was always honest in her struggles and went on to make something amazing with her life despite tremendous pain and difficulties, and even battling several bouts of cancer. In her book, *A Place of Healing: Wrestling with the Mysteries of Suffering, Pain, and God's Sovereignty,* she says:

> As a matter of fact, God isn't asking you to be thankful. He's asking you to give thanks. There's a big difference. One response involves emotions, the other your choices, your decisions about a situation, your intent, your "step of faith."[41]

My brother, Nick, and Joni inspire me as they prove that daily, intense, and prolonged physical and emotional suffering does not prevent internal joy and contentment. This means joy must be something deeper than our external circumstances. It is accessible to all and reflects a character quality that seems unattainable to many. Whatever these beautiful people possess, it is worth more than money can buy.

And how ironic that some people who are the most in chains by the world's standards are often the most free on the inside.

Is it possible that as secondhand sufferers, our attempt to live with joy is even more difficult than those with direct pain, injury, disability, or suffering? It is an interesting question. I don't have the answer, but I think it is possible.

No matter where I look for the antidote to suffering, there is consensus that giving thanks and learning to be content in all things serve as a catalyst for joy to overflow. And by remembering each blessing along the way, they can be a stair step to a new perspective... unlocking a door to joy.

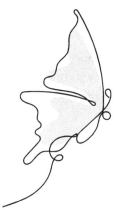

SPIRITUAL REFLECTIONS

Rethinking Pessimism vs. Optimism

*"Anything given to God
can become a pathway to joy."*

—Elizabeth Elliot

Elizabeth Elliot's first husband and four other missionaries were speared to death by the people they were trying to make contact with to serve in a remote region in Ecuador back in 1956. It was all over the American news at the time. Yet, Elizabeth not only forgave and reconciled with the people who killed her husband, but she and her daughter later lived among them and ministered to them for years. She became an inspirational author and global speaker and had a radio program called "Gateway to Joy." From listening to her radio shows on cassette tapes as a very young mom, I remember being moved by her articulate teachings on the connection between suffering and joy. She made this observation,

> The deepest things that I have learned in my own life have come from the deepest suffering. And out of the deepest waters and the hottest fires have come the deepest things I know about God.[42]

Part of my attraction to Elizabeth's teachings and writings was my fascination with how she could find such a deep connection to joy despite her overwhelming life of grief and suffering. It didn't make sense, yet I was drawn to try to understand it.

Being joyful has always been on my prayer list for growth (e.g., "Lord, please help me to have more joy"). Many of my closest friends are very joyful—I am so attracted to it. I see the difference in them, and I have always been envious of their ability to not only be optimistic but also to carry something inside of them that radiates authentic joy no matter what. I have learned throughout my life, however, that the more time I spend with God, the more my joy increases. While I have always struggled with this, I have also always been hungry for it.

On the surface, it's easy to think that having internal joy is similar to being an optimistic person. While I greatly admire the gift of optimism, I have not typically been that person. I tend to be one who says, "Yeah, but...did you consider this?" Even worse, I am often the one who can easily play "devil's advocate" in any scenario. I am not proud of this! But I recently listened to an associate pastor at our church speak, someone with a loving heart and also a man who has suffered much by losing his own daughter to a tragedy when she was thirty. He shared about the role attitude plays in our ability to experience the love of God at the deepest level, raising the age-old question of whether we are a "half-glass empty" or "half-glass full" kind of person. I have always identified as a glass-half-empty person. Trust me, I wish that were not the case. I think it is because my standards and expectations are always perfection or pure excellence, so anything less than full is "less than." I also think that as someone hit with the hardcore reality of having a little brother who couldn't do what I could do, it shaped my identity to carry a deep underlying sadness and anger, which affected my outlook on life. I don't tolerate fake or inauthentic people well, and anyone who told me that Kevin must be disabled for some positive reason, I couldn't be around for long. I sensed "spin" at a young age and would rather someone connect with me about the sadness of his situation than pretend that everything was how God wanted it. Or they tried to make up a reason for why it wasn't so bad. So, when I was asked if the jar was half-empty or half-full, it was a no-brainer for me. Half-empty. But then I also felt guilty about not being able to say "half-full." So, it was not a satisfying answer to the question.

When this pastor spoke about this, I thought he was going to say we should believe it is half-full and give me some Bible verse for why that was. To my surprise and delight, he said something unique. Instead of feeling like we all need to aim to see the glass half-full and be an optimist, we should consider aiming to see the world through the eyes of God. So, he told the story of how one day he asked Jesus (in his mind during his prayer to God), "Jesus, how do you see the world... glass half-empty or half-full?" He felt that Jesus replied, "Neither. It's FULL." And then, this pastor had a revelation: "The half-empty lens is the worldly view. It is true, but it is not the whole truth. The half-full lens is the optimistic worldview. It is also true but lacking the full truth. The truth, when viewed from God's point of view, is that the glass is half-full of water, but the other half is also full—of air. It is a full glass of water plus air—the seen and the unseen in one container. And that means there is great value in God's eyes in the unseen. What we cannot see is still there, and oxygen is powerful. Often, that which is unseen is even more important than that which is seen."

In the case of secondhand suffering, I believe there is value in remembering that we must live within the tension of the unseen mystery when it comes to our loved one's condition and our resulting suffering. The spiritual realm—the realm that is real but unable to be seen—is operating even though we can't see it. Just because we can't see the air in the glass doesn't mean it is not there. The air, in this metaphor, is the substance that, when mixed with water, makes it possible to have the inner joy that we crave. It is different than optimism and different than happiness. It is something that can be reached in our soul (our body, mind, and emotions) and spirit (the place where God's Spirit touches ours) that transcends the visible. So, while we, as secondhand sufferers, see the visible suffering of those we love, we may not be seeing the entire fullness of their glass. If we can muster up the faith to see our situation and our loved ones through the eyes of God, then perhaps we can choose to see the glass is indeed fully full, with both the natural and spiritual realms. And if so, our load is lightened with the new perspective that we don't have all answers because some things are not visible with our eyes but only visible with our spirit. With this new lens, we find hope, and with hope comes an inner joy—most likely not only for us but possibly for our loved ones (even if not readily seen).

"So we fix our eyes not on what is seen,
but on what is unseen, since what is seen is temporary,
but what is unseen is eternal."

—2 CORINTHIANS 4:18

Our secondhand suffering may look like ongoing grief due to losing someone who passed long before what seemed their time and maybe

191

from something very unjust or even evil. Losing someone who has lived a full life of ninety or even a hundred years is hard enough, but to lose someone due to something unrighteous or unexpected at a younger age can be torture. When thinking about the concept of this invisible reality, I think again of the movie *The Shack*. The grieving father (spoiler alert), who lost his young daughter from a horrible crime and came face to face with the Wisdom of God, got to a certain point in his grief, and God allowed him to see into a different reality where his daughter was living and laughing with joy, fully healed. Words cannot describe the emotions that came when he was given eyes to see this unseen realm of reality. If only we could regularly understand that there is more to our story beyond what we see.

I am encouraged the more I focus on the fusion of the visible and invisible reality—life here on earth (temporary) *and* life in the spiritual realm (eternal). When I see more clearly in both realms, inner joy is a fruit. Worldly optimism cannot compete with the joy of the Lord.

> *"The joy of the Lord is your strength."*
>
> —NEHEMIAH 8:10 (NKJV)

As you grapple with pursuing joy, may you be encouraged by the words of Pastor Reggie Mercado as he summarized this fusion of the seen and unseen realities.

> *"We all go through stormy seasons. Hardship is one of those inescapable things that we all wish could be avoided. The same God who can and does deliver us from the storm is also the One who walks us through the storm. Whether He delivers us from or walks us through, our joy must be non-negotiable. We must choose joy in every season. It is the enemy of our soul who seeks to rob us of our joy. Joy is a weapon! We choose joy over hopelessness, despair, doubt, fear, worry, etc. We choose joy and feed it by keeping our*

focus on Him, not our circumstances. It is His joy that is our strength. Joy needs no earthly reason; it's anchored in the unseen yet very real realm of His Kingdom."

—REGGIE MERCADO

TOOLS FOR THE HEART

Joy is not a byproduct of circumstances but of inner strength, fortitude, and a spiritual depth that defies human logic. We can pursue the building up of the inner self through intentional contentment and gratitude and surrender the things we cannot control. It is possible to build joy by looking for the unseen reality beyond the simplistic choices of "the glass half-full vs. half-empty paradigm." Let's choose to intentionally look for how a situation can be viewed differently, such as the glass is fully full and also that the empty parts are filled with a supernatural substance unable to be seen. When we do, we are likely to find increased joy in our spirits and add one more tool to our toolbox leading to hope.

Questions to Ponder:

1. Do you consider yourself an optimist or a pessimist? Do you see life events through a glass half-empty or half-full? Do you have any idea why you lean one way or the other?
2. What unseen reality gives you a greater perspective on a battle you are facing? Is it one that gives you hope beyond your circumstances?
3. What are some of the things in your life you are grateful for? How can you be more conscious of reframing your very real sorrows into also counting your blessings at the same time?
4. Can you think of someone you know—or someone you admire—who has lived in a tough situation yet has also shown to have an authentic sense of joy about them? If so, what do you think is their secret sauce? Consider asking them!

Practical Steps:

- Watch Nick Vujicic's videos and podcasts for inspiration on joy. You can search online for him on YouTube and check out his podcast or website called "Life Without Limbs."

  https://lifewithoutlimbs.org/podcast/
  https://www.youtube.com/watch?v=s5WlD0PMYt0

- To learn about a courageous and joyful woman who lived through great suffering, read the book by Elizabeth Elliot about her husband's life as a martyr called *Through Gates of Splendor* or listen to a recording of her telling the story on ElizabethElliot.com under the podcast tab.

- Without denying the reality of your trials with your life or the life of your loved ones, give thanks for at least ten things and then write them down on an index card. Keep the card by your bathroom mirror or in your car to remind yourself each day of your blessings. This act of giving thanks will contribute to enlarging the "joy muscle" in your brain.

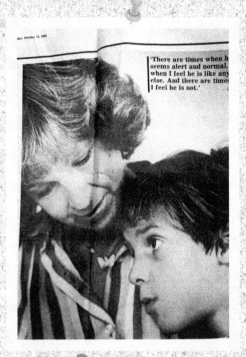

'There are times when h
seems alert and normal,
when I feel he is like any
else. And there are times
I feel he is not.'

'There's also the side of me that
says I hope he doesn't know how
handicapped he is. I would not
want to be smart and know how

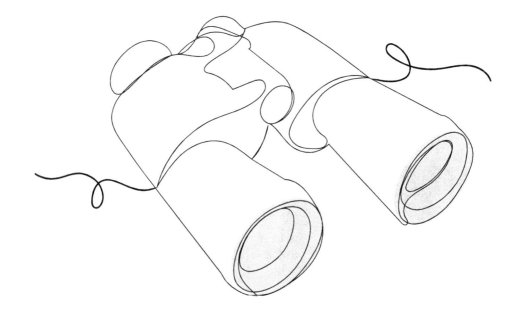

CHAPTER NINE

Playing Hide and Seek With God

"People travel to wonder at the height of the mountains,
at the huge waves of the seas, at the long course of the rivers,
at the vast compass of the ocean, at the circular motion of the stars,
and yet they pass by themselves without wondering."

—AUGUSTINE OF HIPPO

*I*t's natural to ask questions when we don't understand
something or we want to find the underlying causes behind certain
events and behaviors. The answers to our "why" questions help us
understand our world better, quell our innermost fears, challenge our
assumptions, and improve relationships through open and honest
communication.

Questioning "why" became my entryway to meeting God in a
deeper and more personal way. Asking God about my brother was
not my only "why" question, it was my starting point. While other
kids were asking, "Why is the sky blue?" (okay, I asked this also), I
was asking, "Why can't my brother live with us?" or "Why can't my
brother walk or talk?"

It wasn't too far after this that questioning God's very existence
reared its ugly head. After all, if there is no God, there is really no
point wasting time asking why, as there is no intelligent force behind
anything. I could save some painful mental gymnastics and just call it a

day. But the timeless question left me unsettled, restless, and without any true anchor of hope until I pursued whatever train of thought I was on. I think this is a universal human experience as it seems there is something wired inside of us that seeks hope beyond ourselves and drives us to find it...or at least question it.

It does strike me as odd to think that if there is no God, then where do people get the idea to wonder about God or a "higher power" in the first place? The mere fact that most cultures and people groups throughout history have believed in some sort of deity lends credence to the idea that there must be an intelligent Being who created us to crave His existence, so it seems fair to pursue the question, "Is there a God?" And, if there is a God, how do we know? And if there is, then why the heck isn't He doing more to fix all the mess we have in this world? Why won't He heal Kevin? Why does He not stop evil, assuming He is good? And if we can prove there is a God, then which God is He? What is His name? Are there more ways to God than just one? And, if not, who decides which way is true? Are they all true? If not, why not? And why does God allow innocent people to suffer? Was there an intelligent Creator behind our existence, or are we just random accidents evolving through life with no purpose? Why is death so hard on us if it is just "a part of life?" Is there a literal heaven and hell, and if so, who holds the keys to deciding our destination? I was full of questions! And I know these are not unique to me.

My upbringing gave me some basic foundations in the Christian faith, but when I became a young adult, everything was up for grabs again as I pursued these deeper existential questions. This stage of my young adult life was foundational to many of my struggles with secondhand suffering. Yes, I was (and am) a questioner . . . but Kevin was the catalyst to plant seeds of curiosity deep down for truth and hope beyond what day-to-day life offered. I couldn't ignore these questions and simply "Netflix and chill" when looking

> *I was never satisfied with fluffy, religious pat answers from well-meaning people...*

face to face with my brother's plight. I think anyone who has struggled with tragedy, whether themselves or those they love, has an appetite for truth. I was never satisfied with fluffy, religious pat answers from well-meaning people who said, "Well, God must have made Kevin this way for a reason." Or "Since God is Sovereign, He controls all things, so this must be God's plan (or will)" or "Everything happens for a reason." They sound so profound, but they only left me angry. And empty. I couldn't love a God who purposely caused Kevin to live like this. If there was a God and He was good, then those theological answers just didn't resonate with me.

I realize I'm treading on murky and dangerous waters to many in the faith community when I raise these questions, but being raw and authentic in my questioning has led me to a road perhaps more windy, thorny, and dangerous than others. Ultimately, though, I've encountered a mysterious yet richly satisfying multi-dimensional God whose ways and character extend beyond our comprehension. Those "churchy" answers people gave me never satisfied my soul—or my spirit. They didn't seem to represent the heart of God as presented in the Bible either. There must be more to learn than what some people in the Christian community were sweetly saying, probably trying to comfort me somehow. It actually had the opposite effect. With Kevin's disability as my catalytic event, my journey to answer the big "God question" came about because I could no longer swallow the empty calories of "spiritual icing and sprinkles" retorts from a well-meaning world. Some of society's most profound idioms, such as "Life sucks," while often true, didn't satisfy either. Maybe they gave me a momentary split second of being understood, but they left me lacking. Kevin forced me to demand the "steak and potato" meal of answers or else starve. I was ready for an end to the hard-to-swallow explanations that only left me hungry. I needed to make sense of it all. There had to be more to satiate my deep hunger for truth. Maybe not everyone relates to what I was going through, but my guess is that we all hit this path of curiosity at one point in our lives.

"Everyone—pantheist, atheist, skeptic, polytheist—has to answer
these questions: 'Where did I come from? What is life's meaning?
How do I define right from wrong and what happens to me
when I die?' Those are the fulcrum points of our existence."

—RAVI ZACHARIAS

Having been raised in a morally "good people" kind of home, I had been taught the essentials of the Christian faith. As a child, I had loving Sunday School teachers; I memorized the twenty-third psalm and came to understand that there is a God, and I was not Him. I understood the life of Jesus and that He was God who came to earth in the form of a baby, never sinned, taught people some important lessons about God and life, and then eventually was tortured and killed on a cross by people who hated what He said. Three days later, He rose from the dead. As a child, my takeaways were that Jesus was God, we needed to believe in Him in order to be forgiven of our sins and go to heaven, and that we should be good people while on earth. Basic American Christianity, perhaps? We were certainly no Little-House-on-the-Prairie family, nor were we the Waltons (my role model families at the time), but we were decent people with a habit of going to church, trained to write thank you notes and saying our prayers at dinnertime. And somehow, my understanding of my Christian religious affiliation became confused with simply being a good person. I'm not saying this is what I was taught directly, but it is what I concluded.

Yet, as I grew older, like many young adults coming of age, the beliefs of my family of origin needed to be challenged. Through a series of events and meeting new people, I went on a journey as a young adult to search for answers to these questions of the soul. I did not want to believe in a make-believe fairy tale or anything just because I was born into a family religion. Deep down, I knew that if there was no God, then what happened to Kevin was all that more tragic because this is all there is for him. That would seem like a big rip-off. I needed to know for sure. I didn't want to believe a lie.

Eventually, I left my family of origin to marry my college sweetheart and discovered a new facet of myself. Driven by a search for truth, figuring out God became my first quest unexpectedly. At twenty-three, as a newly married young professional, I reached a crisis of faith. I decided I wouldn't be content with either a shallow faith in God or an agnostic/atheistic conclusion without reason. Either way, I needed solid reasons for whatever I claimed to believe. My invisible suffering, which included anger, sadness, guilt, and a restlessness for understanding, needed an outlet or a way to piece together the puzzle. Something wasn't making sense, and I needed to feel more peace. If there was a God, I had some questions for Him, and if He was just something to believe in to make us feel better, I wasn't interested.

Putting God to the test is nothing new for humans. It has happened throughout history from the earliest recorded book in the Bible (Job) to modern spiritual seekers challenging popular cliches such as "to each his own," "what's true for you is not necessarily true for me," and "all paths lead to God," etc. This natural journey seems to be an individual one, not something we can inherit. We enter this world alone and leave this world alone—the in-between time is our opportunity to mine the depths of truth, love, meaning, relationships, and purpose. I contend that it is hard to find satisfaction and peace if we are adopting someone else's convictions. It is not uncommon for adult kids to rebel from their parents' faith as they differentiate into adulthood. Some deny a journey is needed until they face a crisis; some are satisfied with simple answers, and faith comes easily. Some never acknowledge the inner voice whispering in their conscience, tuning out and assuming this is all there is; we might as well "eat, drink and be merry for then we die." But at some point, hopefully, each person will wrestle through their questions to arrive with strong convictions in whatever they believe.

"Because God has made us for Himself,
our hearts are restless until they rest in Him."

—AUGUSTINE OF HIPPO

INSIGHTS FOR THE HEART

The Wonder of the Pursuit

*"It is the glory of God to conceal a matter,
but the glory of kings is to search out a matter."*

—Proverbs 25:2 (NKJV)

Whether it is Indiana Jones in *The Raiders of the Lost Ark*, Benjamin Gates in *National Treasure,* or King Arthur in *Monty Python's The Quest for the Holy Grail*, hunting for hidden treasures is a common theme in movies. There is something powerful about the principles of searching and finding, hunting and discovering, asking and receiving, and sowing and reaping.

While it is possible that the finer things in life fall in front of us like a brick on our heads, it is not as likely. We usually need to put some sweat equity into the hunt. We must go after things if we want to find them—*especially that which is valuable*. The rarer something is, often, the more valuable. Treasures, mysteries, and supernatural solutions are priceless. It is the principle of seeking after what appears to be hidden that I have found to be a discipline worth honing. Finding hidden gems in life is a core insight that correlates to successful people—not necessarily monetarily, but overall. The most common or easy answers are not always the best ones. Often, those are the ones that lead to keeping the status quo and mediocrity and can illustrate the difference between the "wide road vs. the narrow path," as spoken of in the Bible. Truth is worth the discovery process.

A portion of my career was finding talent for companies looking to hire executives. While it sure was nice when those executives were easily found with a referral, almost always, the readily available person with the polished resume wasn't the best one. It almost always took an aggressive hunt and an open mind to search and find the right batch of candidates for our clients. Often, it would be someone more hidden who didn't necessarily have all the requirements on the job description at first glance, or they didn't have a perfectly polished public profile with the right keywords. The best candidates' obscurity made the hunt more fun but also more challenging, as it required thinking out of the box and a good deal of time.

Similarly, when my son got diagnosed with Lyme disease, which turned into a severe auto-immune thyroid disease, I was that relentless mom trying to find the right doctor. Unfortunately, it took six years and eight endocrinologists who all told me there was no cure before we stumbled onto the one doctor who got to the root issue which was addressed. With persistence and a strong conviction that there was a cure, we found answers beyond what we were told was possible and in a package that was not what we had expected.

For my brother, it meant finding many life-changing solutions for symptoms I was told were just "part of his condition." It was always—and still is—an exhausting journey, and finding small and big victories along the way increased my confidence to never give up.

Pursuing solutions that seemed hidden became a way to cope with my inability to fix my brother's physical lot in life. Allowing myself to dream one day of what is possible, I found myself thinking how much Kevin loves speed and motion. My mind wandered to imagining me pushing him on a swing, and before I knew it, I was googling "swings for disabled people in a wheelchair" and stumbled on an invention for wheelchair-bound adults to have a sensation of swinging! It gave me great joy to pursue this idea with a group of families where Kevin lived, and within a couple of years, we were able to raise the money and install a wheelchair swing—something I now use regularly with my brother. He loves it as he gets very relaxed, at peace, and we often see lots of smiles as he feels the soothing motion of going back and forth. When he is really relaxed in this pleasant state, we may hear him make what I call "cooing sounds." It is what peace sounds like to me. So, instead of wallowing in the things my brother couldn't do, I was able to flip it around and find something he could do and then make it happen. A great tool for all of us is when we can't change the hard stuff, find things we can change. I believe it helps empower us to not feel hopeless as we find solutions—no matter how small—to make up for the areas we cannot solve.

Not too long after my mom passed, a friend gave me a book called *My Stroke of Insight,* written by a Harvard-trained brain scientist who, at age thirty-seven, had a massive stroke in her left hemisphere where she could not walk, talk, read, write, or recall anything at all about her life, all within four hours. What was amazing was that her mom, who most likely experienced a great deal of secondhand suffering, ended up moving in with her and taught her everything all over again. It took her daughter eight years, but she eventually made a full recovery. This required incredible belief on her mom's part that her daughter could and would be healed. That tenacious spirit and wisdom to pursue and search out answers is what gave this brilliant woman life again and a role in history to help others with brain trauma find healing.

While it was too late for my mom, reading this woman's story contributed to a deep sadness of unfortunate regret in my life. But the book inspired me that the principle of determined searching, seeking, and hunting for truth—and never giving up—often yields the fruit of finding, discovering, and receiving benefits beyond our imagination. For those wondering if the search for hope and answers for your situation with secondhand suffering is worth it, whether emotional, spiritual, or physical, I believe it is. And it may not be as hard as we think it is if we pursue something attainable at first. It may start with believing hope is possible and getting off the couch that keeps us sunk in depression. I didn't aim to get my brother to suddenly start walking, but I did come up with something that was possible and doable. When we let go of trying to solve the most overwhelming problems, maybe we begin with something a little easier by taking just one step. And before we know it, we may be facing a new direction with fresh possibilities.

Who knows the impact we can make for ourselves, our loved ones, or the world if we dare to imagine what's possible and take that one step?

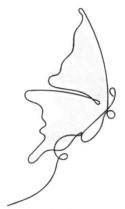

SPIRITUAL REFLECTIONS

The Thrill of Finding Hidden Treasures

"And you will seek Me and find Me,
when you search for Me with all your heart."

—Jeremiah 29:13 (NKJV)

Did you ever participate in an Easter Egg Hunt as a child? If so, do you recall how there were different grassy sections for different-age kids? The area of grass for the little kids had plastic eggs strewn all over the field in plain view. Nothing was really hidden. It was a free-for-all. The only competition for that field depended on how fast you were and how mean you could be as you grabbed other kids' eggs and threw them in your basket. If you were motivated and in the youngest age bracket, there were plenty of eggs to be found without much effort. But the next age group of kids was in the field next door, where there were not as many eggs to be seen visibly, and the majority of them were in holes, behind trees, up in trees, or buried beneath grass-covered mounds of dirt. This hunt took more effort because the kids were older and were expected to think and work more diligently to score the eggs. Finally, the big kids had to go last and were confined to a separate field where the eggs were truly hidden. There were not many "freebies" in this batch of eggs. The kids had to search high and low, look under bushes, in tree bark, and other unsuspecting places. But the thrill of the find seemed to correlate with the difficulty of the discovery.

I would certainly describe this stage in my spiritual journey like a children's Easter Egg Hunt. I recall the endless number of open doors leading to the constant discovery of hidden spiritual treasures that kept me excited to grow my faith. My edge of bitterness was gone, but my journey was still more intellectual as I began studying the Bible, both on my own and in group studies. I had no idea how ignorant I had been of what was in that book! And the thrill of learning so many rich, new lessons with other women kept my mind and heart engaged.

We had the blessing of taking the kids to my parents' country club once a year for an elaborate Easter Egg Hunt. My oldest daughter, Madeline, was the first to experience the tradition at a young age and grew up with the goal of finding the "Golden Egg." Each year, with all vigor, determination, and grit, she set out to find that prize as if her life depended on it. While my other two kids also inherited the "Golden Egg" pursuit, Madeline was convinced it was her destiny to find it. And while we, her parents, couldn't bear one more crying spell of devastation each year when she came up empty, we also couldn't help her find it (and we tried a few times!). It was something only she could do to receive her reward. There was no use in staging our own golden egg hunts as she wanted the "real" one. She would know the difference. Sadly, none of our kids ever found this infamous egg, but it wasn't for lack of determination.

I've come to understand that while God does reveal Himself to individuals, it is not always in the same way. Sometimes, it seems He is truly hiding and nowhere to be found. He desires us to hunt for Him because the hunt is where we are tested and changed, and just like anything in life, we value that for which we have personally invested. When we go on the hunt for truth, or in this case, to find God, our rewards tend to be in proportion to how much we hunger and persevere to find Him. Typically, to keep with the analogy, the more difficult Easter Egg Hunts involve better prizes in those eggs. And the deeper the pursuit of connecting with God, the greater the satisfaction.

For those who give up too quickly, God may design the hunt for Him to be easier, similar to the little kids' Easter Egg Hunt I described above. Depending on our cultural situation, maturity levels, emotions, past trauma, and/or hunger for Him, I believe God provides a way for us to seek and find Him no matter what. He created in us a desire to know Him, but He never forces Himself on us because we are free agents. As "God is love," true love must be free. Out of love, He creates something in us that draws us to Him but then lays out the so-called Easter Eggs for us to find. You might think of learning to follow God as a treasure hunt, where He drops out a trail of breadcrumbs for us to pick up and nibble along the way toward a treasure awaiting us. It is our choice to search for the eggs, follow the breadcrumbs, or opt-out entirely. I have heard it said and agree that God is a gentleman in that He knocks on the door to our hearts but never barges in unwanted.

As I played on the different levels of Easter Egg grass areas, I discovered why the hunt was important. It helped me transfer my inherited faith to one I was figuring out on my own. And I found the slow, methodical, yet persistent search for the depths of the wonder and majesty of God and His love for humanity—and me—was addicting! The Bible was no longer boring. A light bulb had turned on, and it felt good to search out the mysteries of God, having a foundational faith and a belief that God was good. It became a lifetime of pursuit with ever-progressive revelations of who God is and how I grew into a better human being as a result. I learned that often, God is not hiding at all . . . we just need to learn to look in the right places or, sometimes, simply open our eyes to see what is right in front of us.

I may never get answers to every difficult question, but I can find the source of all answers—God Himself—and come to a peace that only He brings. Even having all the answers (impossible, really) won't fully bring ultimate peace because there are always more questions. There is a faith component, no doubt. But, the result of pursuing and knowing God progressively more brings a "peace that transcends understanding" (Philippians 4:7).

Even with many unanswered questions left on the table, I find that life makes more sense with faith in God. When piecing things together, the Bible offers the greatest explanation for how the world works—things like purpose, meaning, eternity, and the human heart. Many people spend their entire lives looking for answers to these grand life issues or trying to avoid thinking about them, but deep down, they know these questions lurk in the pit of their souls. Knowing the "big picture" helps one find peace when they can't locate all the missing puzzle pieces. Yet, some puzzle pieces won't be found on this side of eternity.

The more I get to know God, the more I realize that He is also an interactive Being and not just one featured in a book from 2,000 years ago. God still speaks to those crying out to Him today, first and foremost through His Scriptures, but also through other people, dreams, visions, circumstances, His Spirit, revelations of insight, nature, and endless creative ways. It is a lifelong discovery process that begins small and grows progressively larger as we seek Him continually. In the Bible, "The Kingdom of God" is analogized to a mustard seed, which starts off very small and grows to be the largest of green plants. I see the truth in this progressive growth as we water and feed our souls on the things of God and seek Him through our personal red hotline phone—prayer.

So, do I believe God hides from us? Yes and no. He is always present, waiting to be found . . . but yes, it often feels that He does some hiding. Yet, I think that may be more our feelings, not necessarily the reality, as He promises the opposite: "It is the Lord who goes before you. He will be with you; he will not leave you or forsake you. Do not fear or be dismayed" (Deuteronomy 31:8).

In studying one of my favorite books in the Bible (Song of Songs), a beautiful multi-faceted metaphor of the intimate love between the Bridegroom (Jesus) and His bride (those in relationship with Jesus), I discovered a valuable nugget about the concept of God hiding. Throughout the first half of the eight-chapter love story, there is an ongoing theme of the bride seeking the Bridegroom and going through short periods when He seems absent. She continued her pursuit, however, and in chapter 6, verse 2, the bride had an epiphany that when she thought her bridegroom had "gone," it turns out He had not. The Hebrew meaning for this word "gone" is different from the traditional "gone" in that it is the same word God uses for Himself when He descends or comes down to check in on someone, and it does not mean He actually left or went away. In fact, when exploring this word, it indicates He never left her but was actually indwelling within her heart. While He does leave our conscious feelings at times, this doesn't mean He abandons us. Our feelings are erratic; we don't always feel God's presence, which can make us feel like God is hiding from us. But, we can take comfort that throughout the Bible, it states God never leaves us, and our feelings are not the reliable measuring stick.

God may hold back some of the puzzle pieces for purposes we may never know this side of heaven. While He may indeed appear to "hide" for our own good for a season, He will also transform us in the process of our hunt to find Him. Even Jesus, when teaching parables, admitted these metaphorical stories were taught in such a way that only the ones truly seeking truth will understand them; otherwise, they appear as foolishness to those with hardened hearts and deaf ears. So, God is hidden to some because of the condition of their own hearts *but wide open* to anyone seeking truth (Matthew 13:10–17). Again, God is a gentleman and will not go where He is not invited.

I have learned that it is God's heart's desire that we seek hard after Him to discover who He is, to know Him, and to live out our designed divine purpose. When we realize and feel how much He truly loves us and is the answer to our deepest yearnings, it is a game changer. Our contentment in life is no longer based just on earthly circumstances that often involve suffering, unfairness, and grief, but something greater—a connection with God Himself that is not just for a world after we die but for the here and now as well. Without this revelation of God as a foundation, my journey as a secondhand sufferer would feel more dire.

If you're contemplating this "seek and find" motif, I propose that recognizing the thrill of the hunt for those "hidden treasures" can empower you to keep hope alive. Knowing that persistence can lead to unlocking mysteries, hidden solutions, or greater inner peace, be inspired not to give up your search. Whether seeking spiritual or practical treasures, we are wired to go after the mysteries of life. Don't settle for the "low-hanging" Easter Eggs as your only prize, but go after those harder-to-find golden eggs because of their greater value. And remember, God isn't trying to hide things from you; rather He loves to hide things FOR you.

I believe anyone can find the gold of God when they engage in the thrill of the hunt, and unlike our family hunts for the one and only "Golden Egg," there are enough golden eggs to go around.

> *"I love those who love me, and those who seek me find me."*

> —PROVERBS 8:17

TOOLS FOR THE HEART

Hunting for buried treasure is always worth the effort. Searching is necessary for finding and pursuing the key to unlocking hidden gems. Ultimately, the answer to many of our deepest cries of the heart is satisfied when we search out and find God. It is in the discovery of a (possibly) hidden God that we add another tool to the tool chest of hope for secondhand suffering.

Questions to Ponder:

1. What treasures do you desire that are worth searching for? Have you tried to find them? If not, what is holding you back?
2. What can you do with all the things you cannot fix about your loved one or even things in the world that cause you to suffer? Are there problems to solve you can research? Like discovering a wheelchair swing, is there something you can think of that would help solve a problem that keeps you up at night?
3. Do you sometimes feel God hides from you as you endure your struggles or secondhand suffering? Describe a time in your life when you felt this was true. Looking back, is it possible God was always there, but you simply couldn't feel Him?
4. Do you settle for the "easy-to-find Easter Eggs," or are you willing to head into deeper grassy fields that require more patience yet yield higher returns?

Practical Steps:

- Think of a problem or mystery you have always wondered about or something that is keeping you stuck. Write it down in a journal or notebook, and then spend some time thinking or praying about what steps you need to take to search for the answer or find creative solutions. What keeps you up at night? If you believed there were answers, what would you pursue? Write down what comes to mind and what resources or people can help you. Enjoy the pursuit. It may bring new freedom and growth you didn't realize was possible.

- Have there been certain principles you have believed and thought were in the Bible that have formed your own theologies? Believe it or not, cultural phrases like *"God helps those who help themselves,"* *"Everything happens for a reason,"* *"Money is the root of all evil,"* or *"God won't give me more than I can handle"* are not exactly in the Bible. Look up the following Bible verses for each and challenge your assumptions. Are any of these quasi-spiritual, cultural phrases causing you to settle for a soundbite answer instead of a biblical teaching that may misrepresent the character of God?

Sample Cultural Phrases Often Thought to be in the Bible	Commentary to Look Up	Biblical Scriptures to Look Up (selected samples)	Summary
"God helps those who help themselves"	GotQuestions.org, "God helps those who help themselves"	Psalm 46:1 Psalm 54:4 Isaiah 25:4 Romans 5:6	God's offer of help is unconditional and often He helps the helpless. While He also partners with us to accomplish His purposes, that doesn't mean His help is always conditional on us doing something. His compassionate heart often acts when He hears our cries alone.
"Everything happens for a reason."	Christianity.com, "Should Christians Believe That Everything Happens for a Reason?"	Romans 8:18 Romans 8:28	Usually, this phrase implies that God causes everything to happen. But doesn't this violate God's principle of allowing free will in human behavior? Just because something happens does not mean God caused it OR willed it. The reason something happens could be due to an evil choice or natural consequences of choices or behaviors. But we know that God CAN work bad things together for good to those who love Him because this is clear in the Bible and evidenced in life.

Sample Cultural Phrases Often Thought to be in the Bible	Commentary to Look Up	Biblical Scriptures to Look Up (selected samples)	Summary
"Money is the root of all evil."	GotQuestions. org, "Why is the love of money the root of all kinds of evil?"	1 Timothy 6:10–12 Matthew 15:18–19	It is the LOVE of money that is the root of all evil; not money itself. God looks at the heart.
"God won't give me more than I can handle."	Medium.com, "The Bible does not say God won't give you more than you can handle in life"	1 Corinthians 10:13 James 1:13 Philippians 4:13	This cultural phrase is often confused with the scripture in 1 Cor. 10:13 which says that God won't allow temptation to happen to us without providing a way out. James tells us that we will have all kinds of difficult trials but does not say we can handle these on our own. In fact, often, we can't. We need supernatural help. There is a verse that says, "I can do all things through Christ who strengthens me," but this is different than God won't give us anything we can't handle. We need Christ to do "all things" and the other phrase assumes God is the One handing out all kinds of hardship and we can handle whatever it is on our own. One phrase is in the Bible, the other isn't.

CHAPTER TEN

Being Your "Brother's" Keeper

"It is still true, no matter how old you are,
when you go out into the world, it is best to
HOLD HANDS and STICK TOGETHER."

—Robert Fulghum
author of *Everything I Needed to Know I Learned in Kindergarten*

Have you ever felt like life is an ongoing battleground with only brief moments of reprieve?** Maybe like me, you are often haunted by an underlying fear that, at any time, another batch of flaming arrows will whiz past your head. It might be you who is in the direct line of fire, or worse, a loved one. Regardless of who the attack is targeting, you have a choice—duck and hide or stand your ground and fight back.

As secondhand sufferers, the emotional complexities we experience when our loved ones are suffering can have a physical effect on us, even when we are "just fine." After my mom died, I took on a much bigger role as an advocate with the full support of my dad, who was mentally and physically exhausted from managing Kevin's critical health issues for so long.

I've fought for my brother countless times, but one of the worst battles I've had to fight took all of us—my dad, my brother Brian, my husband, a good friend, and myself. We all had a role to play, and it was the first of many to come that required our full mental energy, grit, and time just to survive. While our medical battles with Kevin clearly are not fought with military gear, the emotions, adrenalin rushes, and pure mental and physical exhaustion that come with them feel like they carry similar feelings to a wartime battle. The enemy we were fighting was invisible, but it presented itself in daily manifestations of depression, defeat, hopelessness, and pure despair. At the time, my seventy-six-year-old dad was feeling the same effects, and we banded together as comrades in the fight to save my brother's life—we were his voice to the doctors, nurses, administrators, CNAs, and therapists, as he had no voice of his own.

It started when Kevin began having recurring screaming fits of severe pain. He would turn red, shriek, and cry at the top of his lungs while his body tensed up in a fit of spastic intensity. This had been occurring for many months and was getting progressively worse. I saw it on one of my random visits, and I was mortified! His staff was loving and did all they could to help by readjusting him in his wheelchair, and sometimes this would help. But, while wonderfully intentioned, when I asked them why he was doing this, most replied that Kevin just wanted attention. What? Let that sink in. How did they know? Did he like attention? YES. But was this how he ever in his life sought to get it? NO. I knew better but didn't know what to do. This was the launching ground to catapult me into a new season of trusting my gut and becoming my brother's voice—my past whisper was becoming a loud roar as I saw him in so much pain.

The tipping point began with an all too familiar call to my dad: *"Kevin is being sent to the ER for low oxygen levels and a high heartbeat, and he's showing signs of respiratory distress. The ambulance is on its way."* Kevin was forty-seven then, and the pneumonias were coming closer and closer together. His hospital visits were becoming all too common. He had been through this same drill only six months earlier and countless times throughout his life. Like the other times, my dad called me, and we got into battle position. My dad said he would head down to the hospital, about a forty-five-minute to an hour drive for him—and he would let me know the status. I was on standby, awaiting my shift after the ER ran the tests. This was not our first rodeo.

Unfortunately, sending my brother to the hospital in an ambulance presents many challenges. The hospital staff don't know him, nor do they understand his communication style, his cries, his sounds, his body, or his needs. Kevin was about 115 pounds of dead weight, which required a Hoyer lift to move him from the wheelchair to a bed. And, of course, he could not communicate with words or move at all of his own volition. When he is in the ER or hospital, doctors and nurses must tend to him. But, with Kevin not having a voice and all the confusing paperwork, it is overwhelmingly disorganized. Nothing is transcribed correctly into the hospital's system, so it is critical that someone who knows him be his spokesperson to answer and ask questions and make decisions on his behalf. This is the role of Kevin's family (and medical conservators). Often, we cannot get there in time, and many unfortunate things can happen in this gap of time between Kevin and our arrival (like the nurses poking him way too many times and in all the wrong places for an IV that won't produce a "good vein" or his right arm pulling out his IV or his oxygen if left unattended for even thirty seconds). Little did we know this first night in the ER would be day one of eight long weeks of non-stop hospitalizations and nursing homes while having a mysterious yet excruciating erratic pain with no relief.

"Speak up for those who have no voice,
for the justice of all who are dispossessed.
Speak up, judge righteously,
and defend the cause of the oppressed and needy."
—Proverbs 31:8–10 (HCSB)

Kevin entered the first of these fifty days with a severe case of pneumonia with the bacteria pseudomonas, a strain that is often resistant to many antibiotics and is hard to get rid of even for physically abled people, let alone a guy who has severe scoliosis, a partially collapsed left lung, a G-Tube in his stomach and lacks the strength to cough in a productive manner. We were in a world of loud beeping noises, IVs, PIC Lines, monitors, random five-minute doctor visits, and round-the-clock shifts of nurses who served as our lifeline for Kevin.

Kevin's fragile body ultimately could not compete with his strong will and inner strength, yet this is predicated on the fact that he needed his advocates. We were his voice and his strength during this crisis—but at times, it sucked the very life out of us.

With this first hospital so far away (about fifty minutes), the toll of not only driving to be by Kevin's side (thus dropping everything else that was going on in our lives) but also being fully present while there in every way was emotionally and physically draining. Thankfully, during this first hospital stay, we had a 4:1 patient-to-nurse ratio, so if we weren't there for a few hours at night, Kevin seemed well tended to. During those first two and a half weeks, Kevin struggled to breathe, get enough oxygen, and cough. His spirits were very low. He struggled with painful episodes, shouting intensely in distress, which tore at my heart because no one knew where his pain was coming from. After being on an IV antibiotic and no real improvement, he was transferred to a skilled nursing facility (SNF) near our home to relieve us from the long drive every day. We were hopeful this would take some of the burden off . . . but we quickly learned the difference between a hospital and a SNF in California and realized our burden and advocacy was only just beginning.

With a 36:1 patient-to-RN nurse ratio, we had our work cut out for us. Patients were constantly pushing those buttons, and loud beeping noises filled the air as background music. No one could really hear the alarms after a while since they never stopped. Sweet older people were wandering the halls in their wheelchairs, just looking for someone to talk to them or find their way back to their room as they struggled with dementia. For fun, many of them circled the main nurse's station and just watched them work. Where were their advocates or family members? It broke my heart that so many of our wisest and beloved parents and grandparents were finishing their days in an institution alone. But at least many of them could walk and talk and push a button. My brother was in a different situation. He needed to be constantly shifted and adjusted, have his diaper changed, receive breathing treatments, respiratory suctioning (four times a day), physical therapy, be lifted in or out of his chair via a Hoyer Lift, and be given regular medicines. He could only be showered twice a week, and only if we hunted down a CNA (Certified Nurse Assistant) and begged them to do it, due to their overwhelming workload.

For every action that Kevin needed assistance, he needed an advocate; it was exhausting physically, mentally, and emotionally. The nurses and CNAs were so overextended, and we learned, very underpaid, and we concluded that Kevin couldn't be left alone for more than a few minutes without us. Plus, he was not well, and new complications were coming up daily, requiring a doctor's help. But in a nursing home, the doctors rarely visit the patients; it's mostly the nurses who will reach the doctor for a phone order by text! We saw the assigned doctor only *once* while there for several weeks—at check-in.

There was no strategy to discover what was causing Kevin's pain; only time to order a drug for a symptom. And only when we advocated hard for it. We were overwhelmed. The only pull I seemed to have had was in my ability to form relationships with a nurse, helper, or respiratory aid. And this needed to be repeated over and over, every shift, every day. I don't blame the people at all; they are part of a system that is broken. Something needs to change in terms of how skilled nursing homes run. They need a major overhaul. Our elderly, disabled, and injured deserve better. And every patient needs an advocate.

There is little doubt that if Kevin had not had my dad and me there (along with my very precious and loving friend, Karen, who we hired for relief), Kevin probably would not have survived. Yet, the toll on my dad and me was almost beyond what we could handle. I experienced something I had never felt in my lifetime—something I only confessed to a few close friends. At one point, I felt like I didn't want to live anymore. A darkness came over me, and while I could never understand why anyone could ever want to take their life, I finally understood the despair of that feeling. Something had overcome my spirit—the secondhand suffering was too much to bear. It was so dark and draining, and there seemed to be no end in sight. I couldn't bear to keep watching my brother suffer so intensely, and yet, I had no choice. It was a "no-way-out" feeling that was crippling my dad and me. That was a very dark time.

If you have ever taken care of a loved one full-time, I know you understand the burden more than most. People would ask me, "How's your brother?" and I found myself somewhat paralyzed to respond as I didn't have the words to answer such a casual question with the weight of an accurate answer. I didn't want to cheapen Kevin's struggles with a pithy short statement that could in no way encapsulate his reality, and I also questioned if they really wanted to know the truth. I worried if they heard my answer, it would make them uncomfortable (and me, for being so vulnerable). And, of course, I was exhausted and didn't have the energy to explain anything to anyone. I was barely breathing.

Towards the end of his stay at the SNF, Kevin experienced severe pain again that manifested in loud, excruciating screams that made his face turn bright red and his countenance radiate sheer fear. It just about killed me to see him like this. If only he could talk and tell me where he hurt. At this darkest point, the pain got so bad in what I began to assume was his abdomen that I insisted he go to a different hospital, one closer to our home than before, and he was taken away by ambulance. This became a turning point and a blessing in disguise. It was here that he would stay an additional three weeks, and here where we became so confident in our advocacy skills that the doctors and nurses practically turned the other way as we approached with our bold questions and requests. After being with Kevin for so many weeks, we knew now what we were doing and what Kevin needed. We became unstoppable advocates. I felt like I was wearing a sign that said, "Don't mess with me—I'm fighting for my brother." When Kevin wasn't screaming in pain, he would often laugh at us as we went to bat for him. He could feel our love by our actions. Maybe he was using his laugh to root me on as I advocated for his needs.

"The one who loves and unselfishly seeks the best for his brother lives in the Light, and in him there is no occasion for stumbling or offense."

—1 John 2:10, AMP

Being with my brother so much gave me the ability to "read his mind" through his eyes, facial expressions, tone of his cry, and gaze. The amount I understood increased beyond what it had ever been. His eyes penetrated deeply into mine (and anyone took the time to truly understand him), and it was through these encounters and being by his bedside through all the trauma that I was able to ascertain the area of his pain. I no longer doubted myself or deferred to "the experts" who didn't know him. We finally got a strong medical team, and we got the right tests done and found some relief—not so much with my brother's symptoms, but with our ability to be heard by the medical team. *We found that there are no dumb questions; doctors don't always have the answers, but the good ones admit what they don't know.* In this environment, I was able to research many of Kevin's symptoms and use my think-outside-of-the-box skills and common sense to put together a list of questions and requests for the doctor. I was surprised that many of my requests were acknowledged, and several doctors seemed open to "outside-of-the-box" ideas. I spoke with nurses about who the best specialists were (the nurses always know!) and requested they see Kevin. We ended up making some switches with the medical team based on the people we met and Kevin's needs. This hospital felt like the Four Seasons Spa compared to the skilled nursing home. We were finally getting somewhere.

Kevin was finally discharged after eight weeks with a new team of doctors that my dad and I pulled together. While not all his symptoms had ceased, I had become empowered to move forward as a partner in his care and advocacy. I was my brother's keeper. And the best part was, he knew it.

Since then, there have been many intense, life-threatening hospital stays for Kevin. Because of some major changes we made from this eight-week nightmare, none were quite as difficult in terms of his pain. Each progressive hospital stay has been hard, but with my increased confidence, boldness, a better understanding of how hospitals, doctors, and nurses work, and my ability to think critically and collaborate with the medical team, we have had many small victories.

Through logic and deduction, I finally figured out that Kevin's pain was coming from the abdomen. This led me to research the ingredients in his G-Tube formula (which ended up being not even real food), and I found there was a direct link to painful gas and constipation. And, while it took a "mere" nine months after this discovery (sarcasm) of incredibly hard work on getting approvals from a dietician, doctor, gastroenterologist, and, of course, his state-funded insurance, we were finally able to make the switch to a healthier formula—not the best one, but one step better. Miraculously, Kevin's screams and pleas for help went away not too long after his new formula kicked in. The staff recognized my instincts were right; I had played a huge role in alleviating my brother's intense suffering, and there was no better feeling or sense of purpose.

The staff recognized my instincts were right; I had played a huge role in alleviating my brother's intense suffering, and there was no better feeling or sense of purpose.

Can you imagine being in excruciating pain without relief but not being able to tell anyone where it hurts? This battleground experience with my brother profoundly shaped me into the caregiver and advocate I am today. Whether you have an aging parent, a special needs child, an adult child who fails to launch, a best friend with clinical depression, a spouse with cancer, or have lost someone you love after a painful battle, I'm sure you have experienced a time when you had to be someone's voice, advocate, or support. It's no small task, and a person's well-being or very life could depend on it. The burden is not light. In fact, it can be overwhelmingly heavy—a huge sacrifice. And, perhaps, like a soldier back from a battle, the trauma may be not something easy to talk about, but for those of us who can relate, I hope you feel understood.

INSIGHTS FOR THE HEART

Keeping the Balance of Giving and Receiving

"So long as you can sweeten another's pain,
life is not in vain."

—HELEN KELLER

Being someone's advocate is not easy and can be very draining. But while it is not only helpful for them, it can also be good for us. I'm sure you have heard the phrase, "Am I my brother's keeper?" It comes from the book of Genesis after Cain had murdered his brother Abel (Adam and Eve's boys). After the dirty deed, God asked Cain where his brother was, which seems like a trick question. With a hardened heart, Cain tried to skirt the question and lied to God by saying he didn't know, followed by the seemingly snarky question, "Am I my brother's keeper?" Clearly, he thought *not* since he had just killed him.

Given that Cain was a murderer and tried to outsmart God (not sure how he thought that was possible when God was speaking to him), I'm certain we can guess how God feels about Cain's answer. When understood in the context of the rest of the Bible, along with our own inner sense of right and wrong embedded in our conscience, it seems logical we are designed to help our brother or sister in need. Yet, is it only our biological "brothers" we are to help, or do we have an unwritten duty to step out of our comfort zones and help anyone in need? Are we to help a friend who lost her job and is feeling discouraged and depressed? I'll bet we could do a lot of good by speaking life back into her with encouraging words, a cup of coffee, and a listening ear. Or what about someone being bullied on the playground, and we get wind of it from our child? Do we sit back and say nothing? Or do we muster up the energy to go to the school authorities, the parents of the child, or train our own child to speak up and face the bully on behalf of the victim? Maybe we have a friend with cancer stuck in a hospital with a family who is uninvolved and needs an advocate to help navigate her situation and stand by her side. There are so many people we can help. I know several people who advocate for foster children they don't even know—they use their time and resources to plant seeds of hope and give a voice of reason in their lives. Many of us have a mother or father (or spouse) with dementia who desperately needs us to do the hard thing and speak for their every need because they can no longer do so. Or perhaps we are a parent or grandparent worried and praying for a wayward adult child making choices that are leading to their own harm.

"Do not withhold good from those to whom it is due,
when it is in your power to act. Do not say to your neighbor,
"Come back tomorrow and I'll give it to you"—
when you already have it with you."

—Proverbs 3:27–28 (NIV)

Being someone's "keeper" can look different depending on who is in your life or what your personal passion or situation may be. And, it turns out that doing good for others benefits us also. A study done by Tristen Inagaki, Ph.D., from the University of Pittsburgh, and Naomi Eisenberger, Ph.D., of the University of California, Los Angeles (UCLA) called *"The Neurobiology of Giving Versus Receiving Support: The Role of Stress-Related and Social Reward-Related Neural Activity,"*[43] and supports this claim. In it, the researchers discovered that giving social support to others may benefit the giver more than the receiver on a neurobiological level. In fact, they outlined three areas of the brain that were positively affected when people were **giving** support to help someone—areas that weren't necessarily affected when they were **receiving** support from someone.

1. Dorsal anterior cingulate cortex, right anterior insula, and right amygdala, which means the **stress-related activity in the brain was diminished.**
2. Left and right ventral striatum, which means **the brain had an increased reward-related activity.**
3. Septal area, which represents an **increase in caregiving-related activity in the brain.**

There were MRIs done on the brains of the participants and these areas showed significantly more activity on the "givers" than the "receivers."[44] I guess the old saying "it is better to give than to receive" is scientifically proven.

So essentially, when giving social support and helping others, our brains are happiest. While this study may provide scientific support for providing practical help to others, my theory is that it may not prove as true when people are facing chronically fatiguing situations with loved ones. As we secondhand sufferers know, long-term circumstances are really tough, and to serve as someone's advocate with a chronic condition, we need to also take care of ourselves and receive our own sustaining fuel for the long haul. While short-term help is one thing and can come with a surge of energy, **we are not able to be superhumans when it comes to a chronic situation.** We must take care of ourselves or risk burnout or failure. For me, during this critical season with Kevin, I learned a lot about taking care of myself so I don't completely collapse, and I've included a few practical tips that might help you:

1. **Get enough sleep**. Without that, we just cannot have the energy or ability to give of ourselves. It's a practical reality we cannot ignore. Sleep recharges and repairs our bodies and our brains. It's our oxygen and fuel. We need more sleep than we think. We just cannot stay healthy without it. If we miss one night, which may be inevitable, we must sleep the following day or evening.

2. **Have boundaries and keep your priorities.** This may mean putting your suffering loved one on hold for periods of time for you to be there for other important family members. For instance, while I was at the hospital, I had to let go of worry and control to get some sleep and trust that the night shift nurse would take care of my brother. Other times my boundary was to stop thinking about my brother's probable boredom as he sat in a room alone when he was being kept in his room during long seasons of isolation and lockdowns. Many times, it may mean you need to prioritize other people or projects ahead of your loved one to keep some balance. Personally, I tend to neglect my husband and even my own kids when Kevin has a chronic crisis. I get so wrapped up in advocating that I become hyper-focused on my brother and forget the need for balance with my other priorities and family members.

Taking an evening to reconnect with my husband, even for dinner or some downtime watching a mindless TV show together, refuels our marriage and me. Don't lose sight of the other people in your life who are important to you. We can't take them for granted. They have needs also.

3. **Get and receive help from other people.** Letting others know what you are going through is important. The mere act of sharing your circumstance with people in your network allows others to carry some of your emotional burden. And, if you are able to hire someone to help you, do it. As you may recall, we hired a dear friend to relieve my dad and me from the long hours every day when my brother was in the hospital and skilled nursing home. It helped our friend, it helped us, and it helped my brother. She was a lifesaver!

4. **Stay healthy physically.** Make sure your body is getting the nutrition and supplements it needs. Find a good nutritional, integrative doctor to make sure you are being proactive about keeping your immune system strong. I'm a big fan of Vitamin D-3/K-2 supplementation, along with sunshine for immune health. Or subscribe to trusted sources online for helpful holistic tips to keep you healthy. You can't afford to be sick because you are needed! Exercise (not my greatest discipline) also relieves stress and keeps us fit. But I'm sure you already knew that.

5. **Pray, Meditate, Spend Time Alone.** Spending time alone in nature or a private area with a journal, Bible, or music can be healing. While it is hard for me to pray when I'm in the middle of a battle, I do believe that God hears our unspoken prayers and worries. Asking others to do the praying for us can be huge, especially when we are empty. I have experienced unexpected blessings, renewed strength, peace during the storm, and practical help suddenly appearing when I humble myself to ask for prayers. Several times, it seemed God sent people as angels to us during our hospital stays, bringing comfort, food, answers, and compassionate hearts.

6. **Turn to your support group and close friends to help hold you up emotionally.** This assumes you have them. As I mentioned earlier about having a community, it is critical to have close friends to support you when you are weak. If you don't have a group of friends, don't wait for a crisis. Invest in a few good friendships. Be a friend to others before you need one for an emergency. Seek out healthy people whom you respect with qualities you would want to have more of in you. Go after those friendships, the ones that make you a better person, and make some investments with your time. And then when you need a friend, they will be there for you if you've already made deposits in their life. We need each other.

7. **Refuel yourself with what gives you joy and doesn't drain you.** While you may not have a lot of spare time in a heavy season, don't neglect your need to refuel. Examples that have helped me include listening to worship, classical, and piano/guitar music; learning something new from a good speaker, teacher, or pastor on a podcast; stretching my body to relaxing music, having coffee with a good friend who can both listen and laugh with me, and putting well-meaning (but draining) people on hold for a season until I have more to give. Some people are fueled by being alone in nature, others by chilling out in front of a lighthearted comedy movie or a few reruns of "Friends" on TV. I know many people who are helped by some form of creativity—painting, dancing, writing, or singing in the car with the sunroof open at the top of their lungs with a favorite song (guilty as charged). Do whatever brings you joy, even if it's just for a few minutes. Personally, my favorite thing is to find what gives me "belly laughs" – you know, the kind that might make you snort. And my friends that make me belly laugh on occasion – thank you; you know who you are!

8. **Take time outs.** We are wired to have time off. Even God rested on the 7th day of creation! Whether it is one solid day of rest or moments throughout your days and week, having some downtime from doing the hard stuff, thinking too deeply and even feeling too intensely is important. While too many time outs may be avoiding

responsibility or difficult, but important, emotions to experience, it's okay to tune out for periods of time. We can't always be on. Learning how to turn the switch from on to off and back again, is a skill that can give us a reprieve without neglecting what is important in the long run.

If you have ever flown on a plane, you can probably relate to the analogy of the oxygen bag. When traveling with someone who is dependent on us, and there is a crisis, and the airbags drop, we are to first put the oxygen mask on ourselves, and only then can we assist the one next to us. We are no good at helping them without oxygen. Being someone's "keeper," especially someone we love and have an emotional attachment to, means we must always "wear our oxygen" before we can be of help.

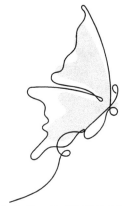

SPIRITUAL REFLECTIONS

Discovering a Modern-day Promised Land

"They open a door and enter a world"
—C. S. LEWIS
The Lion, the Witch and the Wardrobe

You may have heard the trendy term "up-leveling" or "leveling up" as it relates to improving or advancing a skill or a facet of one's life. I hear this term mostly in a business setting. When working with people who wish to achieve their goal of a promotion, often they may need to level up their experience or skills. If you are in any relationship or an athlete or artist, you know the value of up-leveling your competencies to have more success.

For me, when I continued to open new doors as I asked the hard questions and pursued my insatiable curiosity, I was unknowingly being spiritually "up-leveled." I had heard the cliché of life's journey in faith as "walking with God," meant to imply something intimate, personal, and moving forward in a direction.

To illustrate this, I am reminded of the well-known historical story to Jews and Christians in the Bible about walking with God. A time when the Israelites were on a very long walk from Egypt to "the promised land," which took place immediately after God had tasked Moses to free them from hard slavery after 400 years to be His set-apart people, free people. (Think *Ben Hur* or the *Prince of Egypt* movies.) This story demonstrates a significance to my spiritual understanding. To give some background, God sent plague after plague to the Egyptians to assist Moses in getting Pharaoh to let the Hebrews—descendants of Israel who worshiped one God—go free. None of the plagues were very successful until the very last one, which did the trick. God sent a deadly force that affected the firstborn son of a family who did *not* put the blood of a lamb on their doorpost. He gave them a warning, showed them patience, and gave them a way out. The Israelites obeyed and put the blood of a sacrificial lamb on the door, and their sons were spared. Pharaoh's son, however, was not spared, and he finally relented and let them go out of his grief and despair. This historic event is the basis for the Passover celebration today.

Jewish people and Messianic Christians still celebrate with a Passover dinner to commemorate their ancestors' release from physical slavery. Passover holds additional significance for Christians since Jesus, a Jew, was killed on the cross on the day of Passover, a sacrifice of the

"Lamb of God" once and for all to free people from the spiritual slavery of sin and separation from God.

Once Pharaoh let the people go, there was a miraculous escape through the parting of the Red Sea. It's worth reading about in the book of Exodus. You can't make this stuff up! Afterward, the Israelites wandered around in the wilderness for forty years instead of taking the straight path to their destiny. They were guilty of disobedience, poor attitudes, and unbelief. Even after seeing the miracle of the Red Sea parting for them to pass safely to the other side, the Egyptian army drowning as the sea closed once they passed, and even receiving fresh manna to eat each day from the sky so they wouldn't starve, they soon forgot God's presence was with them. They resorted to self-reliance and became convinced they were not strong enough to take possession of the land. Reports came back that there were "giants in the land," and the people were too afraid to cross over into the land God had promised them. They made a choice to basically walk around, stuck for forty years out of fear, unable to progress forward and take hold of the land He was giving them. Taken metaphorically, can you relate their experience to areas in your life where you wandered around in a wilderness due to fear of trusting God for what may be your destiny?

From this story, I could see that for much of my life, I was missing out on what was right in front of me. I had always thought believing in God was all about getting a ticket to heaven one day. But that is the bonus and only part of the story. The Bible's stories are not just historical stories; often, they are symbolic of spiritual principles and analogies of greater truths. If we go back to Moses and the great escape, the first time the Israelites crossed the Red Sea out of Egypt, it represented their salvation as they were literally saved from slavery and bondage and set free from the brutal slave masters, the Egyptians.

Similarly, I learned this is what happens when we accept the gift of eternal life through the offer of Jesus Christ. This incredible offer of salvation is the focus of most churches. Christians call it "salvation" or being "saved," as we are promised to be saved from inevitable death for something eternal. I began to see that "salvation" is analogous to being guaranteed a ticket into God's promised land. I always just thought of that as Heaven. That's the reward, but the analogy continues. And this is where it gets even more exciting—at least for me.

Eventually, the Israelites finally decided to enter the promised land, but they had to cross a *second* water, the Jordan River. When they stepped into the water, it parted to welcome them into the "promised land." With the first crossing through the Red Sea, the massive water parted *first,* and then the people walked (or ran) through. But with the Jordan River, the people took a step of faith into the water *first* before the water parted for them to cross on dry land. It was their faith and a step of obedience that parted the waters this time. Before, God did the rescuing alone. This time, there was a partnership with an *act of faith* as they headed toward their destiny. However, with the Jordan River, crossing the waters into their long-awaited destiny was only the entrance. There were still those "giants" to conquer. The battle was still ahead.

To me, this promised land represents not only the eternal home that we long for—the home that ultimately will solve the problem of suffering—but also the place where God wants us to *fully live* in the here and now. It's clearly not heaven yet with all those giants to conquer still. After our first water crossing (symbolically) with the Red Sea, we may be free from the slavery of our own sin, but it's only the beginning, as we can still wander around in a wilderness without ever reaching our full potential, our destiny, and purpose for our life. We weren't meant to live in the wilderness walking around aimlessly; we were meant to live in the land where we take down giants, walk in the power that God gave us, use the gifts He created in us, enjoy the "milk and honey" God gives us freely and the destiny we were made for on earth and heaven.

> *"In this Promised Land of milk and honey,*
> *they would have a place to enjoy the fruits of their labor*
> *and live in freedom from the chains of bondage.*
> *It represented a fresh start and a new beginning*
> *for the Israelite community."*[45]

My giants have been many. And for so long, as a new Christian, I just assumed those giants are here to stay as we live "in a fallen world" (i.e., Christian-ease for we live on an earth with a lot of issues and injustices and brokenness that was not in God's original design or desire but because people have free will, it is a natural consequence and we are subject to a world not operating in its God-given intention right now). While I always thought the promised land was symbolic of heaven in some far-off future, it never made sense that we would have to fight off giants (bad guys, to keep it simple) as there are no giants (anything bad) in heaven. My eyes were opened to this allegorical "promised land" actually being on earth—a place of spiritual destiny and purpose for each of us to walk out while on earth. A place where God gives us the tools and ability through His supernatural strength to conquer our own giants. I came to understand that to move beyond mere salvation from death and sin into a greater purpose on earth to get that milk and honey, I would need to take out my sword and start slaying some giants. What are my giants? For starters, unbelief, anger, bitterness, an argumentative spirit, self-righteous pride, religious legalism, negativity, envy, fear, and guilt. Phew!

Ultimately, my personal giants seem to be a lot of layers of emotional brokenness and a lack of faith that God is good and that this life counts for something. While I believe I have crossed the Jordan River into the promised land, it is still a slow and progressive journey that involves working on healing from the inside out as I uplevel my skills to slay those giants. The Greek word for this process of holistic healing is called "sozo," an internal healing for the body, mind, soul, and spirit. The actual meaning of the word used is over a hundred times in the New Testament Bible, according to Strong's Concordance, especially when Jesus came to heal someone physically, emotionally, or spiritually: "*to save, deliver, make whole or restore, heal, be whole.*"[46] It is a powerful word that means much more than just saving someone from eternal death for a future heaven. God seems to be interested in a multi-dimensional "saving" that involves holistic health in every part of our being. And I think we all are drawn to this if we are honest and humble.

With a new awareness of the journey of moving from salvation (the rescue from slavery to sin) through the wilderness (where we learn to be dependent on God through trials) to promised land living (where we slay giants and take our authority from God to walk out our designed purpose), I am empathetic to those who have had their Red Sea experience but remain stuck wandering in the wilderness. It seems there may be a lot of "church people" in this land unknowingly. While free from slavery, they miss out on the freedom and power available to them to live in their greater purpose and destiny. *They remain in survival mode looking forward to a future destiny, instead of living in a thriving mode enjoying a present destiny—plus the future thrown in.* I was stuck in that survival location for so many years.

A friend explained it as being akin to getting a free entrance ticket to Disneyland but only hanging out at the entrance and never entering the park with all the wonder and joy the rides, food, and activities offer. The entrance to Disneyland—our ticket in—is fun for a moment, but just like the wilderness, it *is* boring after a while! The wilderness was supposed to be a place to walk *through* as an entrance, not to live in or dwell in forever. No wonder so many church people are bored.

We were designed to live as fully free sons or daughters of God with amazing gifts to use in the territory God has given us to live out our purpose. I believe when we are walking in our purpose using the gifts God created in us, and listening to the right voices and surrounded by a healthy community, we feel a sense of satisfaction and contented joy. It is the feeling of having our deep hunger satisfied or finally getting our nagging itch scratched in just the right spot. We feel a sense that all is right for that moment when we are living out our purpose, no matter how large or small.

Remember the story of *The Lion, the Witch and The Wardrobe* when Lucy leads her siblings through the wardrobe into Narnia? Narnia is a magical land of wonder but also filled with its share of giants and a mean white witch who keeps it in perpetual winter. One of my favorite scenes is where Aslan, the lion who is symbolic of Jesus, gives each of the four children gifts to open. Each gift is suited for each child and is to be used to take down the dark forces that are keeping the magical kingdom in bondage and forever winter. Later in the movie, they courageously do just that in several powerful scenes. In the same way, we are to take the gifts from God to do our part to bring light into a dark world. Whether we believe in God or not, we still come with gifts and talents He created us with. It is with our gifts and talents from God that we are to slay those giants that hold us back from our original design—to "take dominion of the earth" (Genesis 1:26), "subdue it"(Genesis 1:28), then be "salt and light" (Matthew 5:13–16) to a broken world that needs a "sozo" type of salvation.

My pastor Reggie Mercado captures the excitement of living out this way of living in his book *Wildlife* when he writes, "What a privilege we have as co-laborers with God! Every day is a wild adventure because we never know where God will take us and what situations we will face that provide an opportunity for the King to enter someone's world. We get to be dispensers of the Kingdom and see people's lives get radically transformed by a love encounter with God."[47]

When I am walking with God, enjoying the beauty and His gifts while slaying some giants, it offers an antidote to secondhand suffering.

Sometimes, it seems there are seasons in life where I travel back and forth between living in the wilderness on my own strength (tired, rebellious, spiritually dry, bored, and discouraged) and living in my promised land. This is where I tune in to hear from God, live feeling full instead of empty, dream dreams, use my talents to bless others, experience and notice small miracles, and feel alive in my soul. When I am walking with God, enjoying the beauty and His gifts while slaying some giants, it offers an antidote to secondhand suffering. By walking out the destiny God has designed in every one of us, even in the midst of deep, hard struggles, we are empowered to rise above the suffering to a deeper peace that comes when we are doing what we were created to do and be. This type of living gives us a small taste of that milk and honey God designed us to enjoy until a greater day comes.

"Oh, Aslan,' said Lucy. 'Will you tell us how to get into your country from our world?' 'I shall be telling you all the time,' said Aslan. 'But I will not tell you how long or short the way will be; only that it lies across a river. But do not fear that, for I am the great Bridge Builder."

—C. S. Lewis
The Voyage of the Dawn Treader

TOOLS FOR THE HEART

When we act as our "brother's keeper" through our love and actions, we often find purpose, meaning, and peace as we invest in the welfare of others. We also, scientifically, make our brains "happy" by helping others. Yet, we often ignore ourselves when we take on long-term advocacy for a loved one. Learning to put the oxygen mask on ourselves first is critical to be useful to anyone in our lives. God designed us to live on earth not only as "saved" from the death penalty of sin and free from slavery but to live out our destiny and purpose. And, even better, we are made to discover the gifts we have been given to slay our giants and be set free to live without fear.

Questions to Ponder:

1. Do you see yourself as one who is your "brother's keeper," or do you struggle with pulling away because of pain, guilt, apathy, or busyness?
2. What are some ways you can "put on your oxygen mask first" when advocating for your loved one?
3. What are the giants in your life that hold you back from living more victoriously?
4. Do you find yourself living more in the wilderness or in the promised land? If your answer is "the wilderness," what will it take to muster up the courage to step into the river by faith to walk into your destiny, knowing you have to conquer some giants? Are ready to level up your spiritual walk to live fully free?

Practical Steps:

- For a beautiful and inspiring movie on family love and sacrifice for those without a voice, enjoy the three-time Academy Award-winning movie *CODA* (Child of Deaf Adults), about Ruby Rossi, the only hearing person in her family who lives her life both helping her family and living out her gifts and the struggle for that balance.

- If you haven't read the classic book Boundaries by Henry Cloud and John Townsend, make this a priority. If you have read it, consider re-reading it if you feel you need some reminders about keeping yourself protected from overwhelm and unhealthy situations.

- Write down the talents you believe you have that help make a difference in the lives of others and cause you to come alive when you are using them. Now, ask a few close friends the same question. Compare the answers and see how well you see yourself. Look for additional ways you can use your gifts that may scratch your "purpose" itch to help you rise above the pain of secondhand suffering.

- Enjoy watching The Chronicles of Narnia movie series beginning with "The Lion, the Witch and the Wardrobe," based on C.S. Lewis' classic book series.

- For a deeper dive, gather a few friends and enjoy a really great video Bible study on the book of Exodus by Jen Wilken. I was so blessed by this study as it brought the true story of the Israelites' journey out of Egypt into the wilderness and into the Promised Land to life, with deep insights and application to our lives today. I highly recommend both God of Deliverance (Exodus 1–18) and God of Freedom (Exodus 19–40). Visit Jenwilkin.net for more information.

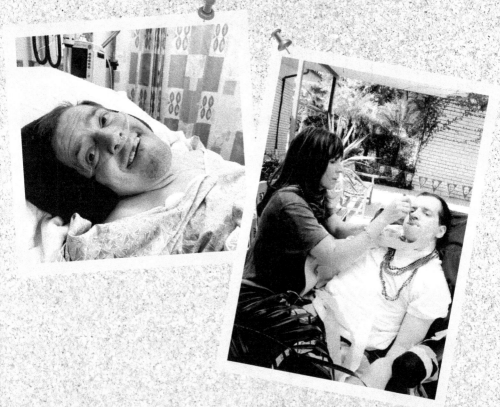

CHAPTER ELEVEN

Living Outside the Box

If you live cautiously, your friends will call you wise.
You just won't move many mountains.

—Bill Johnson

For a period of time, our family had a pet corn snake named Buddy. Buddy was a beautiful coral color, a "nice" snake who came from Santa one Christmas. Our youngest son wanted a pet so badly, and my husband thought a snake in a cage was about all we could handle. He reasoned that it stays in the cage, eats only twice a month, we can leave it when we go on vacation, and the best part—it only poops twice a month! While our son begged us for a brother and a dog—repeatedly—he would have to settle for a snake. Upon picking up the snake from a Craig's List ad, we learned that it had been the pet of a first-grade classroom for a year and was accustomed to being held by the children. The "foster" mom selling the snake said that she also got him out of the cage daily to watch TV with the snake draped around her neck—"He really likes to get out to stretch and enjoy a change of scenery," she said.

Despite my utter repulsion of snakes, my maternal instincts kicked in when I heard this was a nice snake and one that first graders held. I was determined that we would need to make time for him to get out of his cage and "play" and give him some attention. I surprised myself by taking my turn at "cuddling" with Buddy, the name my son came up with for what would become his only childhood pet.

For some reason, leaving Buddy in the cage really bothered me. And, as weird as it sounds, I actually made him his own "playpen" (with a blanket to go with it) that he could go into so he could soak in the sun without fear of slithering away. It was a bit weird, but my motherly instincts extended towards this snake. Inevitably, as it goes in our household, Buddy ended up being an escape artist. Not long after we got him, we had a family New Year's Eve party, and some of the kids were playing with Buddy and forgot to put him back in his cage. He was lost in our house for twenty-seven days! Eeek! It was an awkward time to live in our home, as we were always worried about him slithering into our beds at night from some hidden corner. People refused to visit us (like my mom and dad) until we found the snake. Finally, we found him under our son's bed; the joy of that reunion cannot be overstated.

Over the four years we had Buddy, I couldn't figure out why it upset me that he had to stay in that cage. I'd get frustrated with my son when he didn't let him get out of his cage "to play" in his playpen. While I admit this is a bizarre emotion for a snake, it hit me one day why it bothered me so much. As odd as it sounds, the cage Buddy was in reminded me of the body my brother Kevin was in—his cage. Kevin couldn't get out, no matter how much he wanted to. He was trapped with no way out. What I couldn't do for Kevin, I began trying to do for Buddy the snake. It is one of those epiphanies I'm sure there is a diagnostic code for, but I'll leave that to the therapists to figure out.

What Kevin's living experience has inadvertently taught me is that the freedom of living outside any kind of cage or entrapment is a gift—a blessing—one not to be taken for granted. Metaphorically speaking, "living outside of the box" is a concept of freedom for me. Kevin doesn't have a choice to leave his physical box right now, but I do, and this discrepancy remains an ongoing battle in my mind.

Thinking about Kevin's life and mine in a side-by-side comparison to that darned box (substitute your own examples—wheelchair, addiction, mental illness, emotional paralysis, chronic illness, etc.), I'm flooded with the ramifications of secondhand suffering. More guilt and feelings of imposing limits on my life pair with illogical thoughts of not enjoying my freedom too much because it's "not fair" to my brother. These thoughts continue to creep in, no matter how much progress I've made mentally and spiritually. I lay awake and wonder if Kevin dreams at night of running, driving a car, or traveling on an airplane to a new place. Or giving someone a hug, scratching an annoying itch, dancing to music, making decisions for himself, reading a book, getting married, or having kids. And then I wonder if he is just so tired of being trapped that he wants to call it quits. All these haunting thoughts take me back to the theme of Chapter One, that life is not fair. This emotional mind dance seems to go full circle, but perhaps with a continual upward movement, making it more of a progressively upward spiral so I'm not starting from the bottom each time.

I came across this stanza from a poem by Maya Angelou called "Caged Bird," and I find it captivating. There is something bittersweet about it. I like to think that those who experience first or secondhand suffering are still able to sing as they long for their freedom from whatever is holding them trapped inside.

> *"The caged bird sings with a fearful trill*
> *of things unknown but longed for still*
> *and his tune is heard on the distant hill*
> *for the caged bird sings of freedom."*
>
> —MAYA ANGELOU[48]

I am convinced that if Kevin could talk or sing, he would tell me: "Sister, you are *not* confined to a box, so don't live like you are. Live life to the fullest because you can—physically, mentally, and spiritually. Use your freedom and experience and live as much of this life as possible. Seize the day, and don't let me stop you from living. It doesn't help me for you not to live your life—in fact, go do what I can't do on my behalf. Step out of your invisible box!"

One of my favorite stories about breaking out of boxed-in thinking relates to my traditional religious comfort zone. Many years ago, I heard about a little church hosting a guest speaker on prophetic art, which was an unfamiliar concept to me. Yet, since my oldest daughter was an artist with an interest in the supernatural, I decided to quench my curiosity and go. Plus, I could vet the speaker to make sure it wasn't "too weird" before I bought the book for my high school daughter. I was skeptical but intrigued. I had been studying in the Bible about spiritual gifts from God, and one of them was prophecy. My curiosity was nagging at me since the apostle Paul said, "But above all the gifts, pursue prophecy" (1 Corinthians 14:1), which to me felt a little "out of the box," as I hadn't been exposed to this verse in action. Growing up, I don't recall anyone ever teaching about this in my church. But still, prophetic art? Sounded cool.

Many churches deny any of these prophetic gifts apply to modern times. I wonder how they know that for sure. What else doesn't apply today? What about all those verses on loving one another? Seems like a slippery slope to me, and besides, wouldn't it be super fun to hear from God personally, like a hotline phone? Clearly, one must be cautious before believing anyone who claims to hear from God, but by this time, I was well-grounded in the Bible. I figured I would be on the alert to make sure everything passed the "biblical" test, so I wasn't worried about being deceived (as I've been told could happen).

At that time, I was on the hunt for answers, so if it were true that God could speak by giving people thoughts or pictures via art, why not check it out? How cool that would be! I was finally free enough to explore the topic. I walked in alone to this small church, and I really didn't want to talk to anyone and wanted to remain anonymous. I sat in the back row, slouching down, trying to be invisible. As I watched the worship team sing, I noticed several artists were up on stage painting on blank canvases to the music. It was interesting to watch as their colors and strokes began to form new life. I had not seen anything like this before in a church.

After several songs, the artists made final touches to their paintings, the music faded, and the main speaker came up to the podium. Before starting her presentation, she introduced the artists and asked them to speak about their paintings. Just then, I felt a unique sensation. I can't describe it other than to say it was peaceful, warm, exciting, and unlike anything I had ever felt. Looking back, I can say it was the presence of the Holy Spirit in the room syncing up with my spirit inside of me.

The very first artist to present her work began by looking out to the back of the church (as I scrunched down behind the tall person in front of me) and said, "You there," as she pointed my direction, " . . . the one in the back row with the red shirt." Her eyes caught mine, and I instinctively turned behind me, hoping there was another person in her view. Yet, to my disappointment, I was facing a wall as I was in the back row. "Yes, you," she said. "You who are turning around in the red shirt . . . please come up here." I thought to myself, "Are you kidding me, God? I'm supposed to be invisible! I don't want anyone to know I'm here . . . Can I just run out the back now?" Reluctantly, in front of about one hundred-plus people and having no real choice in the matter, I sheepishly walked to the front at the beckoning of this young artist's bold command. She pointed to the painting and explained that she'd had a vision on her nine-hour drive down to the conference of the painting she was to paint along with an image of the person it was to be given to. When she saw me in the back row, she knew I was the one in her vision and the person to receive her painting and message. While I was nervous and definitely out of my box, a part of me felt very excited. It was like I was being seen—seen by God.

She went on to describe the painting: it was a woman with brown hair, the same as mine, at the top of a cliff, running off it with her hands up and holding on to what looked like wings. The girl was wearing a yellow shirt, and the background showed that it was during a sunset, with orange and peach tones in the sky. The girl had a smile on her face, showing no fear as she leaped out in faith to the unknown. The artist described that she believed the Lord had given her this image to tell me that the girl was me and there would be many things coming up in my future that would be somewhat out of my comfort zone—a bit scary, but new territory. My circumstances would require me to hold on to God and not let go, as His wings would carry me. She said to open my eyes and face the unknown without fear because if I didn't let go of God's wings, He would carry me.

I walked out of that church that night a little shaky, but in a good way. I was impacted similarly to getting the "chills" when something stirs our soul. Though still a bit skeptical, I felt an excitement in my spirit that I couldn't put into words.

The next year held a series of events that seemed to make sense of that piece of art. I began a brand-new season in my life with a whirlwind of progressively challenging events that required me to shift into higher gears with God to survive.

It started the day after I left that church with my painting when my ten-year-old son was diagnosed with Lyme disease, followed by an autoimmune disease, which turned out to be a seven-year-long health battle that was anything but easy. It involved a solution that was very out of the box and took years of battles with doctors who said there was no cure.

How could I have known then that this was only the beginning? Enter another few rounds of secondhand suffering to take me further out of my box.

That summer, our extended family on my husband's side took a vacation cruise to Alaska, where one of our excursion options was to go down the world's largest and longest zip line in North America (Ketchikan, Alaska). Obviously, since I have those awful panic attacks, fear of heights, fear of speed, and fear of being out of control, I had no intention of going, but my teen girls had signed up. At the last minute, the cruise line informed them that to be able to go, they needed a parent because both girls were under twenty-five. Had only my eighteen-year-old gone, it wouldn't have been a problem, but because my fifteen-year-old wanted to go, they needed a parent over twenty-five for a chaperone. Trying to find every loophole possible and coming up unsuccessful, my fears were temporarily overshadowed by motherly love, and I signed up with my petrified body and anguished spirit dragging behind.

It was truly the scariest thing I've ever done and a direct test of being out of the box. I was used to controlling, which kept me comfortable. There were eight zip lines that took you through a magnificently high forest (with bald eagles flying *below* us), and each leg of the zip line was *very* long to the point that we could not see the end of the line at each run because it was so far away. Let me repeat that—we could *not* see the landing platform at the end of the zip line because it was so far away. It is a tremendous understatement to say I was scared out of my mind. When it was our turn, I was instructed to literally *jump* off this tiny platform and fly through the air with my feet up, and if I made any mistake, I would risk dangling in the middle of a rope 135 feet above the ground with my only hope relying on a seventeen-year-old summer employee to climb out and rescue me. I became paralyzed with fear as my girls passionately encouraged me, rattling off every Bible verse they had ever learned in Sunday School (I was surprised how many they knew!) in front of a group of fifteen people, as everyone's trip depended on me going. My girls gave me several mini-sermons to

> *"Trust the harness. Don't let go and let it do the work for you—all you have to do is have faith that it will carry you and enjoy the ride."*

help me with my panic attack. The entire tourist group was cheering me on as well. The instructors reminded us to *"Trust the harness. Don't let go and let it do the work for you—all you have to do is have faith that it will carry you and enjoy the ride."* The only way I could get off the first time was to hold the harness tightly, close my eyes, and let the instructor push me. Yes, push me. The first five zip lines I did in total fear with my eyes closed, missing the beautiful scenery and bald eagles flying with me, but by the last two runs, I had a shift.

While in the air, I finally opened my eyes in an attempt to capture the moment and enjoy the scenery when I was suddenly reminded of the painting and the words of the artist. It came to me in a flash as I looked around at the beauty, "Trust the wings that are carrying you as you jump off the cliff; hang on and let God carry you through the unknown in front of you." Remembering the color of the girl's shirt in the painting, I looked down to see what color shirt I was wearing—it was yellow. Just like the painting. And yes, goosebumps—what I now call Holy Spirit chills—came all over me.

It seemed God was "circling back" to remind me of the power of that "out of the box" prophetic painting. It was the perfect metaphor for my life and my need to learn to trust God, hold on tight, and let go of fear. He knew what was coming and that I was going to need to be carried as I soared over the valley of things I would soon be experiencing that was already beginning.

Shortly after that zipline epiphany, a physical fulfillment of this spiritual lesson hit me hard. We dropped off our oldest daughter to college out of state, and I was an emotional wreck. My marriage also seemed to be falling apart, and as if it couldn't get any worse, my precious mother died suddenly from a massive stroke—all within a three-week period. The deep and unrelenting trauma and grief were almost too much to carry. I was hanging on with all my might to those wings in order not to fall off the cliff. It was *no doubt* the hardest year of my life. And this was on top of the ongoing burden I carried for my brother and seeing his tears at our mom's memorial service.

Having the painting to look at and reflect on is a gift from God that touches my spirit in a way that reminds me that He can speak to us in unique ways, to hold onto Him for hope and not let go. It gives me great comfort to know that God foresaw what was coming, and He gave me this gift so I would know He sees me. Only He knew of the very difficult season I would be going through right after that night, and He was there for me to hold on tightly. Thus began my "out-of-the-box" living, both in the hard times and the good.

As humans, it is so natural to settle for life in our comfortable box of routine, limitations, and self-preservation tactics as long as we can. But life has a way—if we live long enough—to kick us out of those boxes.

Sometimes, this happens fairly suddenly as we no longer fit inside them comfortably and have to face the outside elements of hardship, both for others and those we love. Perhaps we can think of these times as opportunities to fly while being carried by angel wings. And no matter what the box represents, getting out of it seems inevitable—for both the adventure to grow us and for the reality of life to humble and refine us.

INSIGHTS FOR THE HEART

Unsticking and Rewiring a Stuck Brain

"It's snowing still. And freezing.
However, we haven't had an earthquake lately."

—EEYORE, WINNIE THE POOH

Growing up with "God in a box" (where our ideas of God kept Him limited, not all that powerful and under our control) made Him a little boring but perhaps safe. Accessing the keys to unlock the box I had kept God inside of has been an exciting journey as I have learned He is available now and not just as a reward one day in Heaven. One of my favorite quotes from C. S. Lewis in his brilliant book (and movie) *The Lion, the Witch and the Wardrobe* is when Lucy, one of the four children who discovered Narnia through a wardrobe closet, correctly describes Aslan's (the lion representing Jesus) character. She profoundly stated, "Aslan is *not* safe, but He is good." My desire to stay "safe" (in control, skeptical, risk-avoider, fearful of the unknown, etc.) was keeping me from experiencing much more in life, and when I finally grasped that God is good, I found there were treasures I was destined to discover. But first, I had to step out of the boxes I had created for myself and God.

"To the degree that we believe God is good
is the degree that we are willing to be intimate with Him."[49]

Speaking practically, becoming aware of those things that keep us locked in our own boxes is an important step. What keeps you locked in? Is it being overly concerned about what others will think of you if you speak up about something important but maybe controversial? Is it a fear of making waves at work, or worse, losing your job when you voice your ethical opposition to the direction they are taking for a product or policy? Is it not having the confidence or belief in your abilities or your God to think you can be a difference-maker for causes you care about? For me, a lot of my "stuckness" was rooted in my mind.

We have heard so much over the last decade about "mindfulness." At first, it sounded a bit hokey to me, but it turns out that mindfulness is a very powerful concept people and businesses are embracing as important to success. While mindfulness has several nuances to its definition, depending where you look, it is essentially: "A technique in which one focuses one's full attention only on the present, experiencing thoughts, feelings, and sensations but not judging them: The practice of mindfulness can reduce stress and physical pain."[50] I struggle with toxic thoughts that haunt me about my brother being stuck in his box all the time, and it seems like my constant focus on his situation with so much judgment and negativity probably affects my stress level. I'm not a fan of pretending the reality of a situation isn't true, yet there seems to be a practical and spiritual truth to the fact that replaying negative thoughts on the reality of a situation over and over in my head is not healthy nor helpful.

Knowing something is not helpful and overcoming it are two different things. Over the last few years, there has also been a strong fascination with something called "neuroplasticity," simply stated, "the brain's ability to change and adapt due to experience."[51] This is an "out of the box" type of breakthrough, in my opinion. If we are stuck in familiar thinking patterns that are pulling us down into negativity or paralyzing thoughts, changing our brains to support new "out of the box" types of thinking that can give us new freedom as secondhand sufferers—or anyone, really—can be an onramp to a new tool. There are two types of neuroplasticity that enable major changes to our brains:[52]

- **Functional plasticity** is the brain's ability to move functions from a damaged area of the brain to other undamaged areas.
- **Structural plasticity** is the brain's ability to actually change its physical structure as a result of learning.

My focus is more on structural plasticity that through learning and experiences, we can literally rewire our brains! Dr. Caroline Leaf, Communication Pathologist, Audiologist, Clinical and Cognitive Neuroscientist, has much to say on this topic and offers practical steps for those wanting to override and change toxic thoughts and stress to control one's thought life. According to Leaf, "Today, there is an increasing body of evidence that the brain changes according to experience. The anatomy and physiology of the human brain is much more malleable and plastic than we once thought—the brain changes according to how we use it! Yes, life can certainly be challenging, but our minds are actually more than prepared to stand up to these challenges and overcome them—all we have to do is *think!* Our ability to think is truly phenomenal. Our brains can change as we think (neuroplasticity) and grow new brain cells (neurogenesis). Using the incredible power in our minds, we can persist and grow in response to life's challenges. We can take our thoughts captive and change the way we think, speak and act!"[53]

Dr. Leaf goes on to provide some ways you can develop your mental resilience and change your brain:

- "When you find yourself feeling hopeless, stop and tell yourself that your brain can change. Tell yourself that your brain is plastic, and you can use your thinking to change your mind and take control of your life. Write down your thoughts if you find that this will be helpful. Practice doing this for 3 weeks (it takes 21 days to start changing neural pathways).

- "Over the next 21 days, pay attention to what other people say to you. If it is negative, do not meditate on their words. Forgive them and fight the desire to take any negative comments into your mind. Remember, whatever you think about the most grows, affecting your ability to think, speak, and act.

- "Spend a few moments every day for the next three weeks focusing on challenges you have overcome in the past. Remind yourself of your strength and ability to not only survive but also thrive."[54]

Finding ways to keep our brains out of the "boxed-in" thinking patterns that can keep us in bondage is a worthy endeavor. But it takes intentionality. And it is a process. Currently, I'm working on re-wiring my thoughts by choosing more where my focus lies. There is additional excellent research in this area by one of the most well-known psychiatrists in the field of interpersonal neurobiology and an original voice in the field of neuroplasticity, Daniel J. Siegel, MD, a clinical professor of psychiatry at the UCLA School of Medicine, founding co-director of the Mindful Awareness Research Center at UCLA, and author of several best-selling books. One of his many discoveries is that the more we pay attention to something, the more our brains are changed. According to Siegel, "We can learn to use the focus of the mind to actually change the connections in the brain itself."[55] This is just a part of his research on how having a truly connected life of integration is a secret to health and happiness. He calls this reflective ability "Mindsight," similar to the popular field of "Mindfulness." This involves how you can "learn to use the focus of your attention on the mind itself to actually transform the connections in the brain, to move the brain to a more integrated, harmonious way of functioning."[56] For a simple yet more academic definition from Siegel's book *AWARE, The Science and Practice of Presence*, changing the brain is possible because "Where attention goes, neural firing flows and neural connection grows."[57]

For me, I am realizing that the more I focus on something I want to change in my thinking, the more I am successful. When a toxic thought pops into my head, I'm working on not always vocalizing it and automatically giving that thought "air time." It had become a bad habit to give voice to something that is bothering me, even when it is reality. I can be a bit of an "Eeyore," one of the Winnie the Pooh characters, if I'm not careful. While there is a time and place for authentic venting, and I certainly am not recommending stuffing hard feelings, I have seen the benefit of my mood and ability to be more emotionally balanced when I work on training my brain to think before I speak, pause, and reframe my words.

One of the many benefits, according to Siegel, is the notion that "the mind itself . . . can be something that we learn to master and (we) become in many ways, the captain of our own ship, where instead of just riding things and being passive as a participant to just see where the mind takes us, we actually can become empowered to move our minds in a way that is healthy, enriching, and creates a much more flexible way of living."[58]

*"Do not be conformed to this world, but be transformed
by the renewal of your mind, that by testing you may discern what is
the will of God, what is good and acceptable and perfect."*

—ROMANS 12:2 (ESV)

Of course, there is so much to uncover with how we can use neuroplasticity to improve our thinking patterns that add to our secondhand suffering. For example, I am choosing to rewire my thoughts about my brother by affirming that while Kevin may not be able to live out of the box physically and fly with the eagles on a zip line through a rainforest like I did, I believe he can do so mentally perhaps in daily conversations with angels where he can soar freely on the inside of his soul. Finding an additional reality to focus on that brings hope and helps "unstick" me from habitual negative thoughts is a practical tool to keep handy. The more I understand that my words and thoughts have power over my situations and attitudes, the more I aspire to change my brain to think thoughts that are more inspiring rather than discouraging.

No doubt all of us are guilty at times of allowing our negative thoughts to consume us, creating worry, stress, and emotional despair if taken to an extreme. Let's face it: life is hard! And if it's not, just wait. I realize that happy thoughts alone do not change circumstances and I'm certainly not a fan of burying our true feelings and slapping on a happy face sticker to every thought. Yet, if we as secondhand sufferers can find a better balance of living in the tension of life's hard realities and finding ways to keep hope alive—albeit it may be better termed "messy hope"—shouldn't we do so? One of the ways we can do this is by focusing more on what we focus on in order to make our brains just a bit more resilient, positive, and hopeful. It may not change our loved one's pain, but it just may make ours that much more bearable.

"As someone thinks within himself, so he is."

—PROVERBS 23:7 (NASB)

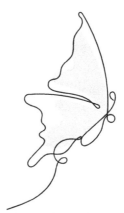

SPIRITUAL REFLECTIONS

Meeting the Holy Spirit: He Had Me at "Hello"

*"The goal of the Bible is not
so that we can memorize the Bible
but it is to get to know the Author."*

—Kris Valloten

My zip line experience was a pivot point in a new season of freedom that continues to grow to this day. My spiritual momentum was speeding up as I acknowledged I had been confining God to a theological box He could not fit in, except by my limited thinking. I began to understand that God is not just words in a book but that those words point to a Person interested in a private and personal relationship that we can access when we "tune in" to His voice. God never promises to fix all of our circumstances in this life. But through it all—the good, bad, and ugly—if we hold on to Him through faith (sometimes clinging for dear life amidst screams and cries), He will carry us by His wings through the unknown valleys ahead. And while we may not see where we are going or the landing spot ahead, we can hold on and try to enjoy the ride because we know He has us. We just have to remember to keep our eyes open to capture those bald eagles along the way.

Reflecting back, being raised in a relatively small "box" by my parents to keep me safe, something in me has always yearned to cross the lines of normal, "challenge the status quo," and "break free from mundane and monotonous day-to-day" kind of living. A part of me craved the thrill of breaking the mold, stepping out of a self-imposed cage, and allowing my mind to question, challenge, and pursue ideas that were a bit different than the norm. Clearly, one of these "out of the box" areas foundational to battling secondhand suffering was my view of God. When I was younger, my spiritual box was filled with many "should's and shouldn'ts" and "bad and good." But, after getting over my intellectual obstacles about faith, my heart began to unlock . . . slowly. I learned God is more than a puzzle to be solved with all my mind-based questions. He is a Person (capital P) to know, converse with, and connect to, as well as someone to be loved by and respond to by loving in return.

Over time, I learned the best "out of the box" gift that God gave me was an introduction to the missing secret sauce of His very being—The Holy Spirit. At first, this third Person of the Trinity (Father, Son, and Holy

Spirit) was a bit like Jiminy Cricket on steroids (remember that little dude who whispered in Pinocchio's ear?). However, for many years, "Jiminy" was hard to hear as he mostly whispered, and unless I was intentionally listening, I only heard static.

"What comes to our mind when we think about God is the most important thing about us."

—A. W. TOZER

Learning to hear from God in a supernatural 3D-multi-dimensional sense instead of just in a book written 2,000 years ago felt like a new dimension that was deeply relational and personal instead of simply intellectual and philosophical. To think that He cared enough about me to use this artist to awaken my senses, soften my heart, and carry me through a very difficult time was profound. And to realize that this same gift of hearing from God is still alive today and something the Bible says is for all of us to pursue (1 Corinthians 14:1) felt like such exciting news. I had to come to terms with the fact that God doesn't always fix things or prevent bad things from happening; rather, He desires to be with us through it all (and for us to want Him) and provide peace that surpasses understanding (Philippians 4:7).

My experience with the painting transcended any theological doctrinal argument for God's existence that I could study. It was the beginning of a shift in my faith from constantly trying to figure everything out, making sense of suffering from an intellectual perspective to pursuing a spiritual encounter with the living God. This shift in gears felt fresh and real but grounded in truth. My journey of eighteen inches from my head to my heart had begun.

My ever-growing pursuit of "the more" of God began to unlock my understanding of the Holy Spirit—the very presence of God who lives inside those who accept the free gift of God Knowing Jesus, God's Son, the Messiah, and Savior who came to earth in human form to be the bridge to reconnect us back to God and His Kingdom is something I had understood in theory, but connecting the dots with the fullness of God took some time. I grew up missing this third part of God . . . the **powerful and exciting** aspect of God in the Holy Spirit, and it finally clicked when I realized these three Persons of God came as a package deal. This part of God is a difference maker in this life, and not just the "ticket to heaven" part of God. But so far, I only knew this Spirit as a name said at the end of The Lord's Prayer ("in the name of the Father, Son and Holy Spirit, Amen"). I had no idea what I was missing. And my guess is I was not alone in this, even for those who walk into a church one day a week.

"but whenever a person turns to the Lord, the veil is removed."

—2 Corinthians 3:16 (HCSB)

Once I took that step of faith, and like the above verse, I made a "turn" to the Lord and laid down my self-rule of being my own god. He flooded me with His Spirit, which opened my eyes and gave me a greater understanding of God I had been oblivious to before. The Bible refers to this as the veil being lifted and having "eyes to see." I don't quite get why God set it up like that . . . it seems to me He should make Himself a bit more understandable first, and then people would choose Him. Maybe a big sign in the sky? But I guess even when Jesus walked the earth and did all kinds of miracles, there were still those who didn't believe who He was. And the religious people seemed to be the worst—they knew a lot of Bible passages, but most of them completely missed the identity of Jesus. He often spoke in parables (like riddles or veiled truths) as a way to attract only those who sought Him out in faith and had the right hearts. Faith seems to be God's currency to assess our hunger for Him. There is a power in our divine hunger and the process of surrendering our will to God's that yields a greater revelation to our hearts of the nature of God and His love for us.

During a trip to Paris, I began asking God to help me understand the gift of prophecy. At the time, I was trying to make sense of those verses about spiritual gifts in 1 Corinthians. I was taking a tour of Notre Dame with a young man who was our tour guide when I became overwhelmed with a feeling that I was supposed to share with him a message; this compulsion to tell him something wouldn't leave me alone throughout the tour. I kept pushing it out of my head, thinking I was just making it all up and how silly I would feel if I said what I was thinking to him. But by the end of the tour, my family and I walked away, but I could not get that nagging feeling out of my head that I was to turn around and tell him this "message."

I remembered the question I had asked God about understanding the gift of prophecy before we left on this family reunion to Paris, and it hit me that perhaps this was God's way of answering me. So, I turned around, leaving my family, and ran back to find him talking to a couple who had been on the tour. I waited patiently, and when they left, I did my best to tell him something like this: ". . . *I know this may sound funny, but I have had a nagging sense the whole tour that I was to tell you something, and it is that 'God is calling you to be a pastor one day as He sees your heart for Him even though you don't fully know Him yet and to keep searching and you will find Him and one day you will speak for Him to so many who need Him*." As I was speaking, I could sense the words were not mine. They flowed out of me with power. And then I looked into his eyes after I finished, and there were tears. He told me that he was overwhelmed with what I shared since he had been questioning if there was a God, and part of the reason he came to Paris for the summer with an ecumenical group of people to give tours of museums was to discover the answer to the "God question." He said I helped him more than I could know. And then I had to run off to find my family wandering in Paris somewhere. The feeling I had inside me was one of the best I had ever felt. It was indescribable . . . partnering with God to bless others with His words was more fun and purposeful than I could have imagined.

*"Earthly wisdom is doing what comes naturally.
Godly wisdom is doing what the Holy Spirit
compels us to do."*

—CHARLES STANLEY

It seems in our culture, there is a public acknowledgment of this greater "Spirit" existing, yet they are calling it something different. I'm hearing more and more a popular phrase in the media and entertainment industry, "the Universe spoke to me." Clearly, more and more people acknowledge there is some Higher Power, and many yearn for some kind of supernatural connection to it. For me, if people give credit for the Universe directing our paths, it's not a hard leap to see that some power must have created the Universe. It makes more sense to invite the God *of* the Universe into our lives as Lord (ultimately the One who is in charge of our life) and Savior (the only One who has the power to save us from ourselves and eternal death). If I were to hedge my bets, I'm going to align with the Creator of the Universe and not just the Universe. The Bible says the Holy Spirit is the deposit God gives us of Himself so we know He is with us and gives us some extra powerful doses of His presence and power while we live here on Earth. I love that God doesn't force Himself on anyone—He must be invited. The Holy Spirit has a robust job description: speaking to us, comforting us, giving us His power, feeling His presence, revealing truth, and convicting us of sin, righteousness, and judgment. I had known about the convicting-us-of-sin part of the Holy Spirit before, but the rest was new territory.

Experiencing God's presence inside of me has had many benefits, including increasing my capacity for love, forgiveness to others, and a new form of wisdom with a newly transformed mind. When the Bible talks about the "Fruit of the Spirit"—love, joy, peace, patience, kindness, goodness, faithfulness, gentleness, and self-control (Galatians 5:22–23)—these have become more organic to my character and less dependent on implementing religious behavior.

In addition to this "prophetic Paris" example, I had an experience with a very sensitive topic for me—healing. A couple of new friends of mine were with me on the beach, and I had an ever-growing headache that was entering migraine territory. Asking them for an Advil became an entry point for them to ask me if they could pray for my headache to go away. I was a bit confused at first because a third friend was looking for the Advil, and I thought that solved the problem. Why pray if there was Advil? But they seemed to think prayer was a better idea, and so, staying true to my pursuit of the "more" of God, I said, "Sure, why not?" They gently laid their hands on me and my head—on a public beach—and prayed for my head to be healed. And when they finished, they asked me if it was better yet. I laughed and said, "Uh, no. Not yet. But thank you." I expected to go on and grab the Advil. But then they said, "Okay . . . let's pray again." I was so confused. I had never seen anything like this—pray again? And their hands were back on my head and shoulders. We went through this three times, and inside my head, I was thinking, "Oh my, they are not going to stop until my head doesn't hurt," so I figured I better get with the program and add my faith to the whole thing. Not long after, I was shocked to have a sensation I had never felt. I can only compare it to my head feeling like a pressure cooker, and I felt the top of my head become like the knob at the top that unscrews, and a ton of intense steam and pressure began to be released out of my head as my pain lifted up and out. Within just a few minutes, my headache had lifted and was gone.

The Bible says we are to "heal the sick" (Matthew 10:8), so why was this so shocking to me? The written word of the Bible was coming alive for me in such new ways. But of course, I immediately think, "So why does God heal my headache but not my brother or not so many others who ask?" Who decides who is healed and who is not? What is the secret formula? I have no clue. But I do know that I was in the process of asking God to show up in my life in a new way, and these experiences probably were more about God working on my heart to know Him differently than just academically. I'm sure the Advil would have also done the trick for my head. But I'm so grateful for my friends taking the risk to expose me to God's willingness to be involved in my life with their healing prayers, as it played a catalytic role in my increased faith and hope.

God is a gentleman, and He doesn't force Himself on us. As I've discovered, this "out of the box" Holy Spirit loves to partner with us if we invite Him in. Using the driving metaphor, either we can steer the wheel of life on our own, we can drive on our own but ask for directions, or we can hand over the wheel to Him and see where He takes us. Whoever is driving determines not only the speed but the route, power, and destination—and also the enjoyment of the ride. I learned to drive on a stick shift Honda Civic, and I see a correlation with our role in accessing the power of God. From my experience, it seems when we find God (or perhaps He finds us), we usually begin that relationship in first gear. For me, it was humming along very slowly for so much of my life, and we didn't go very far. But as I grew spiritually through all the stories I've shared, plus more, I began shifting gears at each progressive stage, gaining more power and speed. And when the Holy Spirit came on the scene, it was like shifting into the fourth and fifth gears, and we were driving on a scenic route on the freeway. With each hard push of the clutch with the left foot and gear stick up and in with the right hand, I've experienced greater speed and greater power and avoided burning out the engine, something I would have easily done if I had stayed in first gear moving through life at an increased speed. Translating that metaphor into my Christian "walk," without the growth in knowing the Holy Spirit, I would have most likely reached burnout trying to do life with my own power and frustration as I hit the wall trying to do religion without a relationship.

> *"But when He, the Spirit of truth, comes,*
> *He will guide you into all the truth; for He will not speak*
> *on His own initiative, but whatever He hears, He will speak;*
> *and He will disclose to you what is to come."*

—JOHN 16:13

I have found that many people who maybe don't have a traditional faith do have a hunger for the supernatural. They pursue psychics, tarot cards, meditation, Ouija boards, spiritual yoga, horoscopes, and things like that. They know something more is out there, and they feel it, but the world has fed them alternative answers. There is no judgment here as sometimes (and perhaps often) these spiritual seekers are more hungry for a powerful supernatural God than regular churchgoers. I share this because one of the critiques I used to hear from people in churches that I went to in the past when I expressed interest in pursuing the Holy Spirit more is to "be careful" because "once you open the door to the supernatural, you can let those demons in." That sounded scary, and I decided I wouldn't open that door to be safe.

However, God is by definition supernatural and beyond the natural realm, and so eventually, it seemed silly to stay away from all the mysteries He has for us as He created us as spiritual beings, in addition to the physical (John 3:6–8).

What helped me is to learn that only God is a Creator; Satan cannot create anything new; he can only copy and pervert something from the original. *So, why settle for a copy when we can have the real thing?*

Understanding there is a supernatural realm that exists of dark and light, angels and demons, and good and evil explains so much of life. The greatest movies from Hollywood have at their core these themes. Think *Lord of the Rings*, *Star Wars*, *The Incredibles*, *Avengers*, and *Harry Potter*. These movies are successful because they resonate with people's reality by touching on emotions and thoughts we have had, wonder about, or long for deep within—good triumphing over evil, truth winning over lies, underdogs beating out the bullies, superpowers being real, good guys beating bad guys, hardships having happy endings, etc. So, it makes sense that we are physical beings living in a spiritual world. Most people have that sense, so being able to choose the right spirit to follow is critical if we want to be aligned with the true Holy Spirit. One easy clue is that we can know His nature by the person of Jesus and what He says in Scripture about Himself. (An easy way to know this is to read a "red letter" version of the Bible with Jesus's words in red.)

For a quick, incomplete, and oversimplified summary of the biblical story of good and evil, and in my own words (not a theologian's) and with my eventual conclusions, God is the Creator and made us in His image, but Satan—the Father of lies—is a created angel who chose to rebel and attempt a coup d'état over God (even he had free will) as his desire to be God overtook him (major pride issue). While Satan has some power like an angel, he will never have the authority or power like God, not even close, unless we give it to him through agreement, open doors, or worship. One of Satan's goals seems to be revenge for being thrown out of heaven and jealousy for not having the power of God. Since humankind was made in God's image, and the angels were not, he has some major resentment because he knows he cannot win against God, so he goes after God's kids—that's us.

One of the ways Satan does this is by trying to deceive us by imitating God to throw us off course. If he can influence God's children on earth to follow him in some way, he is getting back at God indirectly and having his field day, although short term, to rule and reign over the only place he is allowed, in the individuals who let him (perhaps inadvertently). He was kicked out of heaven, so he only has earth to operate. And he seems to be keeping plenty busy here. The allure of the supernatural to humans is just one of his many tactics. Thus, when we hear a lot about the supernatural realm in our culture, we need to discern the spirits, a spiritual gift the Bible teaches about in 1 Corinthians 12. Just because there is power in other spirits without Jesus doesn't mean it is good or from God. We can know the character of the true God by knowing Jesus as He was revealed on earth. The Bible records Jesus saying, "If you really know Me, you will know the Father" (John 14:7–11), and if we know Him, we can discern His Spirit and not be thrown by a counterfeit. If we have the mind of Christ (something we are taught is possible), then we shouldn't be afraid of a counterfeit spirit because we will be able to discern the spirits (1 John 4). Knowing this gave me confidence that I didn't need to close the door to the supernatural realm, as this was God's domain. I just needed to know the difference between the real Spirit of God and the counterfeit.

As secondhand sufferers, will we accept the invitation to kick our spiritual life up a notch to a fifth-gear experience, where we are able to go to beautiful places with ease and power and enjoy His company on the long road of life? Whether we are driving or He is taking the wheel (I think both are okay depending on the road conditions), we can experience the thrill of His guidance, an accurate GPS, a satisfying conversation, and feel the peace and joy of His presence along the drive.

I believe it is ingrained in all of us to desire the things of God and pursue to fill the empty places in our hearts with something beyond this world. The question is, will we spend our lives filling those places with worldly answers that won't ever satisfy us? Or will we fill them with deposits of God's very essence and experience the satisfaction of our spirit finally being connected with God's? When we choose to break free to live out of the box with God, we can be untethered from unwarranted fear, infused with new strength and hope, and gain a brand-new perspective on life with supernatural insights that satisfy many of our deepest longings to be seen, known, and loved by our Creator.

TOOLS FOR THE HEART

Pursue the courage to live outside your comfort zone of a self-imposed box locked from the inside, as it does nothing to help your loved one if you don't. Embrace the gift from God to live the way you were intended—in freedom and living out your purpose. Rewire your brain to find workarounds to toxic thoughts. Consider seeking after the out-of-the-box God for a peace that surpasses understanding, even if circumstances don't change. Enjoy the adventure of driving in fifth gear with the power and presence of the Holy Spirit, who infuses your life with supernatural gifts to take you to new places and experience greater purpose.

Questions to Ponder:

- Where do you find yourself in a box that is holding you back—perhaps out of comfort, routine, or fear of risk? What areas would you like to explore to step outside your sphere of enclosure?
- Do you feel that you have understood the depth of the Holy Spirit? If not, what do you think you could do to begin the discovery process? If so, what are the areas of growth you would like to see over the next year? What can you do to cultivate that?
- Using the stick-shift car analogy, if you were to evaluate your life in terms of how well you are using the engine inside of you to reach your potential, what gear would you say you are driving in right now?

Practical Steps:

- Apply the principle of re-wiring your thoughts to be more free from burdensome negative thinking to your situation related to secondhand suffering. Intentionally catch yourself thinking and verbalizing negative thoughts—that may be true—and then practice finding something more hope-filled to say. You can practice giving voice to these additional and alternative perspectives more often to change your thinking.
- If you consider yourself to be a Christian, try taking the "Spiritual Gifts" test to discover how God has wired you to live and serve as you live your life. A good one I've seen is Lifeway Christian Resources
- In addition to reading the Bible (book of Acts, 1 and 2 Corinthians), check out some other books to get to know the Holy Spirit:

Holy Spirit Power by Charles Spurgeon

Surrendered to the Holy Spirit by Hayley Braun

Hosting the Presence Every Day by Bill Johnson (a daily devotional)

The Wildlife: Our Supernatural Journey with Jesus by Reggie Mercado

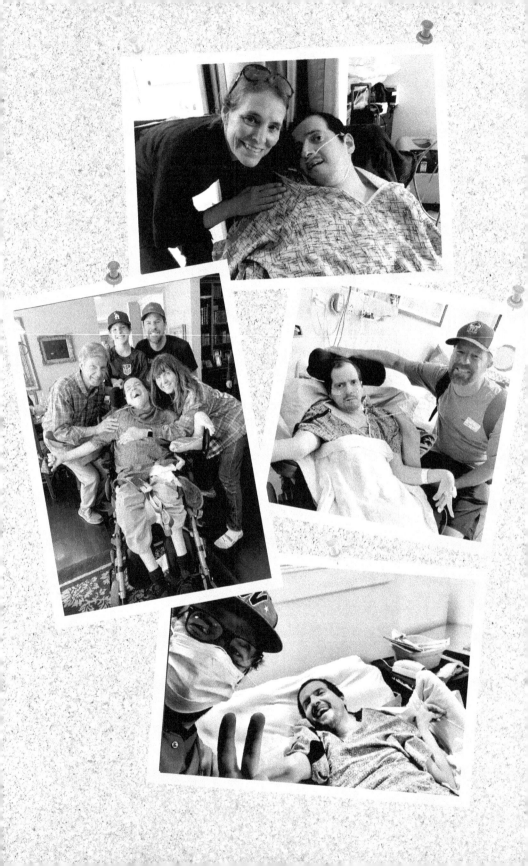

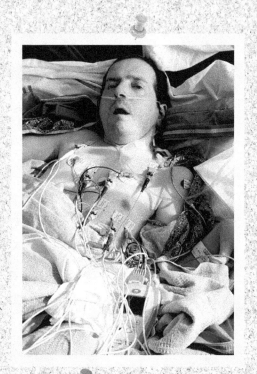
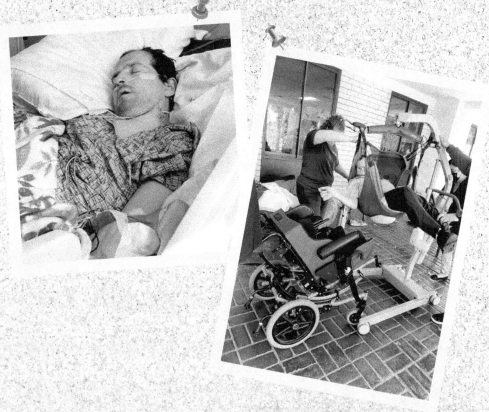

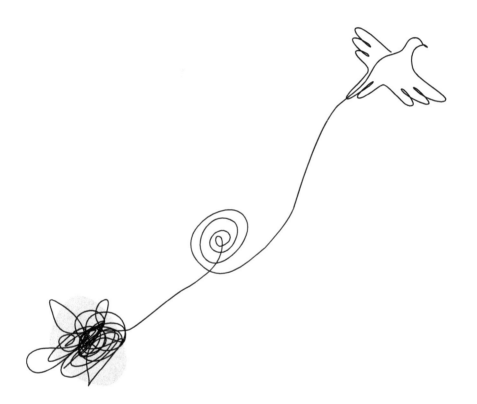

CHAPTER TWELVE

Clinging to Ultimate Hope When You Can't Fix It

*"If I find in myself a desire which no experience in this world
can satisfy, the most probable explanation is that
I was made for another world."*

—C. S. Lewis

In my guest bathroom, I have had for years a little book in a basket for guests to flip through called *Don't Sweat the Small Stuff . . . and It's All Small Stuff*. Someone gave it to me a long time ago; I guess they thought I needed it. As a dutiful friend who didn't want the gift to go to waste, it has been my entertainment for guests for thirty-plus years. I never real

ly identified with the premise fully, although I realize I probably could benefit from its lessons. I related more to Beth Moore's response to this little gem of a book when she said, "I'd like to stuff a sweaty sock in the mouth of the person who first said that. It's not all small stuff. I have a friend whose son was paralyzed in an accident his senior year of high school. I pray almost daily for a list of people, from ages 4 to 74, who are battling cancer. Two recently came off my list and into heaven. My precious friend's husband, an honest hard-working man with a son in college, just lost his job—again. Not long ago, three tornadoes whipped through my hometown—stealing, killing and destroying. No, it's not all small stuff." I echo "Amen" to that. Yet, somehow, the book remains in our guest bathroom. I would like to be that person who sees life this way. Things would sure be simpler.

When I think about Kevin and what he has gone through being locked up in a body that cannot communicate or function, there seems little hope for this "wrong" to be made right on earth in this lifetime. There is not a day that goes by that I do not wish this was *not* the case and some doctor would find a cure for fixing his motor cortex so he can talk, walk, eat, run, read, and experience the gift of life here on earth to the fullest. Or better yet, he would one day simply experience a miracle and get up and start walking and talking! As a child, I prayed for God to heal him, but I'm not sure I ever really believed it would happen. Perhaps this contributed to the problem, as the Bible clearly speaks of faith being a powerful factor when healing does happen on this side of heaven. I know that God is not a genie in the sky who instantly fixes all problems on earth, heals anyone who is sick, or doesn't allow people to die. But *can* He do all of these things? I believe He has the capability, of course. *Does* He do them? At times, yes. But most of the time, it seems not. If we can be honest, there is a great mystery about if, when, how, and why God does and doesn't intervene. We cannot ever know the reason why, when we pray, some are healed and others die. And should we really be blaming God in the first place? When I focus on the here and now and the injustice in this life, I crumble in hopelessness. Let's face it: bad things happen. Suffering happens. Hearts break. People die. Babies and young adults seem to get cancer now. Life can seem ridiculously unfair and leave us in despair if we let it. Yet, one thing gives me hope no matter what. It is that there is more to our story—a life beyond this life. I believe there can be a happy ending that all of us long for—and it's not a Disney movie; it's real.

While finding God has been the greatest gift to me in terms of how I live my life and the peace this connection brings, I'm sure the continual pursuit for answers will never be fully satisfied on this side of heaven. And ultimately, heaven is the greatest answer to many of our unsatisfied longings, especially those things we cannot fix in our lifetime.

> *"The wizard [of Oz] says look inside yourself and find self.*
> *God says look inside yourself and find [the Holy Spirit].*
> *The first will get you to Kansas.*
> *The latter will get you to heaven.*
> *Take your pick."*
>
> —MAX LUCADO
> *Experiencing the Heart of Jesus: Knowing His Heart, Feeling His Love*

When I see Kevin and am at a loss for what to say to him, I often tell him about heaven, where he will have a new body and be able to run. He never fails to smile when I talk to him about running. I've often thought Kevin would have been a baseball player or a track runner if he'd had a normal birth.

I've come to embrace the concept of heaven in a fresh way since I first learned about it in church. Then, whenever I thought about heaven and how it was described, it made me want to stay on earth. It seemed boring, frankly. Who really wants to go to a place where all you do is sing songs, float on clouds, and play with harps? No offense to singing or harps or clouds, but this kind of life for all of eternity made me want to stay right here with my comfy couch, books, meaningful work, movies, friends, family, chips and guacamole, and foamy breve lattes.

We must admit that the elephant in the room of life is death. Most of us avoid talking or thinking about it until we go to a memorial service of one of our friends. I recently went to one for a twenty-five-year-old who left his fiancé for heaven three days before their wedding, dying from a horrific form of fast-moving cancer. All eight hundred of his closest friends were face to face with this injustice during this emotional service, but the hope of heaven from his faith-filled community—and the faith of the young man—gave us a reason to go on. It's likely most people believe in some sort of afterlife while also carrying some fear of dying. It seems to be a certain outcome for all of us at some point. Even atheists, I'm sure, secretly wish they were wrong. The book of Ecclesiastes in the Bible says, "God has set eternity in the hearts of men." I take this to mean we are wired to want to live forever. When people we love die, we weep, grieve, and ache in our bones because it feels so wrong, so lonely, so final. I believe we are not made to die—but to live forever. That's why it hurts so much. Living forever was the original plan in God's story.

When it comes to the personal pain of suffering or experiencing secondhand suffering for others, the hope of heaven can be a welcome thought. But, of course, I have a lot of questions. Pursuing them is how the hope of heaven becomes more than wishful thinking but something to embrace as a key tool to handle the pain of my brother's suffering and losing my mom and close friends. I am no theologian, but the following is my thirty-thousand-foot overview of the basis for my ultimate hope that a future heaven brings. It took me a while to get here, but taking the time to do a deep dive on eternity from a biblical perspective helped turn a nice fairy tale soundbite about an elusive "heaven" into a tangible hope that makes sense as I battle ongoing grief for those who suffer. Here is how I see it.

When God created man (and woman), He designed us as eternal beings. Death was not His plan—paradise on earth forever was. In the book of Genesis, God is shown to make all the creation progressively until He reaches man and woman. With each day of creation, He called His work "good." God clearly created man and woman with the ability to make free choices, as when He placed man in the garden and said to him, "You are free to eat from any tree of the garden, but you must not eat from the tree of the knowledge of good and evil, for on the day you eat from it, you will certainly die" (Genesis 2:16). An odd command, yes, but one that tested the concept of free will and submission to God and also revealed the heart of humankind. Shortly after, the woman was created, and apparently, she got the message as well (though maybe Adam didn't do the best job of communicating the details to his wife). God gave Adam and Eve the authority to rule the planet—essentially,

He gave them a set of keys to manage this place of paradise ("take dominion"). A good picture of this is God as the owner (or landlord), and He made us the managers (or tenants). God then gave them instructions for how to enjoy the planet and each other, yet also one command for them *not* to do—eat of the one tree of "good and evil."

The scene shifts in chapter three, and a new character enters—the serpent (Satan). He tempts the woman to eat the fruit of this forbidden tree and tells her, "You will not die but instead become like God—knowing good and evil" (Genesis 3:5). Becoming like God was the temptation she couldn't resist, and wanting to be our own god has been one of man's downfalls ever since. The resulting problem from Eve eating that fruit was not only that Adam and Eve disobeyed God but that they *obeyed* the devil. They switched gods and, therefore, switched kingdoms from living under God's full rule in the Kingdom of God to now living in a world where God's enemy finally got some power as the ruler he had wanted to be for eons. The human race was now tainted with sin—similar to getting the DNA gene for a disease that may be passed down from generation to generation. This sin now separated God's children from Him, and even though they were warned, they were blocked from the Tree of Life (enter death).

With the introduction of sin, out of love for us, it makes sense to me finally that God needed to allow death—not to punish us but to prevent us from living eternally in a corrupt or sinful state. "The LORD God said, 'Since man has become one of Us, knowing good and evil, he must not reach out, take from the tree of life, eat, and live forever . . . He drove man out and stationed the cherubim and the flaming, whirling sword east of the garden of Eden to guard the way to the tree of life" (Genesis 3:22, 24 HCS). So, if "we" didn't disobey God's one command, allowing the knowledge of good and evil to enter our world, then the tree of *eternal* life would never have been blocked from us. While I'm sure this didn't surprise God, it is clear why death feels so horribly wrong to us. We weren't designed for it.

Free choice is a big deal to God—without it, true love is not possible. While the devil is certainly a factor in the evil unleashed on earth, we don't have to take it like a victim, as we have also been given authority to resist, fight back, and even choose not to let us lose hope. This sneaky serpent figure is more like a parasite, sucking the authority and power God gave humankind out of us by deceiving us into doubting God and trusting him instead. When we do this, we are left with the consequences of a world filled with evil, suffering, and death because this world is no longer God's original design. While we also have so much goodness, righteousness, joy, and life as we obey God, walk under His rule, and carry His identity as we are made in His image, there is always a part of living on earth that isn't heaven yet.

> *"The most tragic strain in human existence lies in the fact that the pleasure which we find in the things of this life, however good that pleasure may be in itself, is always taken away from us. The things for which men strive hardly ever turn out to be as satisfying as they expected, and in the rare cases in which they do, sooner or later they are snatched away . . . For the Christians, all those partial, broken and fleeting perfections which he glimpses in the world around him, which wither in his grasp and he snatches away from him even while the wither, are found again, perfect, complete and lasting in the absolute beauty of God."*[59]

> —RANDY ALCORN, HEAVEN

Fast forward to the end of the story. Towards the end of the Bible, there is a picture of the throne of God where on both sides of the river is the tree of life . . . and there is no longer any curse. In other words, true living without a curse—eternal life—will be restored to all those whose names are written in the Book of Life. The Book of Life? Where do those names come from? If just anyone could make that list, we would be back to the original problem where the DNA for sin, evil, or corruption would enter eternity. That would make heaven more like hell. Can you imagine heaven being a place where we still have evil, tyranny, slavery, murder, lies, and cancer? No, thank you. So, the Book of Life must be full of uncorrupted, perfect people then. There's the rub . . . those people don't exist. Jesus even tells us in the Bible that no one is good except God alone. There goes that "I'm a good person" defense. So, what's the catch? God is just and good, so evil must be judged. If even we desire and demand justice in our world, how much more would a good and just God demand justice in all of eternity?

Humans can never work hard enough, be good enough, or obey God perfectly enough to be holy—a necessary "entrance fee" to heaven. It seemed God needed a Plan B. Plan A was for humans to freely obey God perfectly so there would not be evil or sin operating on earth forever. Plan B was for God to find the only perfect human being He could and have that person take the punishment for everyone else's sins and put sin to death once and for all—so there is justice. Make no mistake: God is outside of time and knew this would be necessary—nothing surprises Him. (So, perhaps Plan B was His Plan A all along?) Since there was no human on earth who met the perfection standard, God decided to solve this problem Himself. And as if right out of a science fiction movie, the God-man was born: the ultimate transformer action hero. Enter Jesus, stage right.

"For God so loved the world that he gave his one and only Son,
that whoever believes in him shall not perish
but have eternal life."

—JOHN 3:16 (NIV)

You've likely seen the Bible verse John 3:16 on signs at football games. This is one of the most profound verses in the Bible as it explains the motive of God (love) and the reason for Jesus's coming to earth (our salvation from evil and death). Jesus was the "human form" of God . . . yes, God humbled Himself to become one of us for a time to both communicate who He is and then to take on the sins of the world—past, present, and future—and put sin to death once and for all. He did this because "He so loved" each of us and all of us, desiring us to not only know Him and love Him but also to live with Him forever in a perfect place like the original Paradise (garden of Eden) He created—the place we were created to live. Yes, paradise on earth! That was always our intended destiny. A real, tangible and uncorrupted beautiful place.

When Jesus gave His life for ours (all of humanity) on the cross, He, in essence, also took away the curse of death and now holds the keys to death (Revelation 1:18) so that the kingdom of God can rule again over the earth—and individuals' hearts. By overcoming death as a perfect human being (but still being God), He also conquered death for all because the "wages of sin is death but the gift of God is eternal life" (Romans 6:23). He essentially put to death ultimate death! Isn't that good news?

The only thing God has asked us to do in return is to humbly accept His unconditional gift of Jesus's sacrifice through our personal repentance. In exchange, God also gives us a new heart and the Holy Spirit as a deposit of things to come[60] —a promise that this life for us is *not* the end of the story, and our names are now written in the Book of Life. This Book of Life guarantees our hope for heaven, or eternal life, without broken hearts and suffering.

According to the Bible, heaven seems to be much more like earth and not a place of floating clouds and harps; in fact, it appears it will be a "restored earth" (Revelation 21:1, 5). We have good reason to believe this redeemed life will be full and one where we will use our minds, have friends, learn, laugh, have meaningful work, and where animals like the lion and lamb play together—a place where our bodies will be whole with no fear of cancer or dementia or wheelchairs.

*"And God will wipe away every tear from their eyes;
there shall be no more death, nor sorrow, nor crying.
There shall be no more pain, for the former things
have passed away."*

—REVELATION 21:4 (NKJV)

When we are given a difficult hand of cards, and we find ourselves hitting a wall after doing all we can to walk through the many tools at our disposal, sometimes all we can do is sit in the pain and surrender. In that surrender, remember there is ultimately good news beyond the here and now of life. And, with that news, it is possible to feel a peace that surpasses understanding that will comfort us in those times when things are just not fixable.

INSIGHTS FOR THE HEART

Developing an Appetite for Eternity

*"Aim at heaven and you will get earth thrown in.
Aim at earth and you get neither."*

—C. S. LEWIS

When we plan a vacation, we often research where we are going: the hotels, the drive, the activities, the food . . . We anticipate it, talk about it, budget for it, and study it. It seems funny that while no one argues that we are all going to die, no one really wants to discuss, plan, anticipate, or study where we are going or what happens after this obvious point in time. It's the huge elephant in the room that few want to mention. But ignoring death and the question we all have deep down about "what's next" doesn't make the issue disappear. It reminds me of my son when he didn't want me to see him doing something he wasn't supposed to, and he would cover his head under a blanket. I still saw him; pretending he wasn't there was funny but nonsensical. He was right in front of me, no matter how much of the blanket covered him. In the same way, the topic of death is right in front of us, so wouldn't we be better off acknowledging it? Why not anticipate it like we would our next vacation? Study about it; think about it; talk about it; prepare for it . . .

It is vital for life to have hope. A verse in the Bible captures this: "When there is no vision (or hope), the people perish" (Proverbs 29:18). No one wants to die, I don't think. It is a scary thing to imagine because we don't know what happens exactly when we leave this life. I often wonder if a baby fetus was given a choice in the womb to stay inside where it is cozy and warm, with a seemingly endless supply of food, or come out into the bright lights, cold, and feeling the sensation of tears and hunger if it would choose to stay put? Clearly, with their limited knowledge, they may choose to stay inside the womb. Yet, because we are outside of the womb and have experienced life to the fullest on earth, we would say, *"Are you crazy? You don't know what you are missing! Come out and experience life!"* In the same way, I believe dying may be like exiting another "womb" into a life we just haven't experienced yet.

Another thought is that life continually drops tastes of heaven (amazing goodness and experiences), but they don't always last and, ultimately, leave us hungry for more. This very hunger leads me to believe that there is, in fact, more. For example, if you've enjoyed a very fine dinner experience, you can relate to the feeling of savoring a tantalizing appetizer for starters. By nature, an appetizer is a small amount of food that will not satisfy alone. Yet, it awakens the tastebuds to prepare for something greater and larger. Imagine being offered this appetizer and then quickly escorted outside, never to enjoy the meal. We would be left not only still hungry but also left without closure on our initial enjoyable experience. We would know that there was something more coming, but we may feel somewhat "robbed" from what we had been looking forward to—a full, satisfying meal. In the same way, the beautiful and satisfying part of life is a little like an appetizer. It is good to enjoy, but it doesn't last, doesn't satisfy, and only leaves us longing for more. And without eternal hope, there is no coping mechanism to balance the finality of the death of those we love.

Hope is a part of how we humans are wired. And I'm convinced the greatest fulfillment of hope for any of us is heaven. To me, heaven will be like the satisfying meal and dessert that is to come . . . and unlike an expensive and enjoyable meal that still leaves us hungry the next day, it will be an eternal feast that will delight every sense, right every wrong, redeem every tear, and satisfy our souls beyond our wildest dreams.

On the flight to say goodbye to my sweet mother-in-law in Alaska, who had been battling a debilitating disease, I re-read a classic book on the topic of heaven. Originally published in the early 1980s, *Within Heaven's Gates* was written by Rebecca Springer, a woman who had suffered a terrible illness and near death yet had a profound experience during this fragile state of existence between life and death. The small book is the recollection of her experience and has given me great hope about heaven. After describing several amazingly vivid events, she writes:

> I can only lightly touch upon these heavenly joys. There is a depth, a mystery to all that pertains to the divine life, which I dare not try to describe. I could not if I wanted to; I would not if I could. A sacredness enfolds it and curious eyes should not look upon it. Suffice it to say that no joy

we know on earth, however rare, however sacred, can be more than the faintest shadow of the joy we find there. No dreams of rapture, unrealized on earth, approach the bliss of one moment in that divine world. No sorrow, no pain, no sickness, no death, no parting, no disappointments, no tears but those of joy, no broken hopes, no mislaid plans, no night, nor storm, nor shadows even. There is only light and joy and love and peace and rest forever and forever. Amen. And again, my heart says reverently, Amen.[61]

Have you read the story of the little four-year-old boy who claimed to go to heaven and back after a life-threatening car accident? I read the account of this true story long before the movie *Heaven Is for Real* was made, and I found one of the more powerful statements this little four-year-old gave was when he told his dad about meeting "Pop" in heaven—his grandpa who had died before he was even born. What was fascinating is that when his dad showed him pictures of "Pop," the boy said, *"No, that's not Pop."* The dad said it *was* Pop, and they battled it out for a while. Then the dad had an idea to retrieve pictures of his dad when he was in his early twenties from his mom's attic. He left one of these pictures lying around the house because he didn't want to tell his son that it was Pop. Amazingly, when the boy came home one day and saw the young picture, he exclaimed, *"That's Pop!"* It was a picture the little boy had never seen before. The conversation the boy had with Pop when he died was with a man in his early twenties, not an old man. Since the boy had no idea what Pop looked like, I found that testimony to be fascinating.

Perhaps even more convincing is the account of Harvard-trained Neurologist Dr. Eben Alexander, who had a near-death experience as he suffered a coma from a deadly form of meningitis and claimed to be escorted to heaven by an unknown woman. A skeptic and non-religious person prior to this event, he came back a changed man, fully convinced this vivid experience was real and not a hallucination.

One of his many convincing proofs is that the woman he met while he was in his coma ended up being the exact same image of a biological sister he did not know existed since he was adopted and they never met, who died a few years earlier. He went on to write a book about it, which I've listed at the end of the chapter.

"Only an imperishable hope can satisfy the human heart."

—Timothy Keller

While I have struggled and cried out to God my entire life about the injustice of my brother's life, ultimately, the only thing that has always kept me going is the hope of heaven. When my hope lies only in this world—finding a cure for cerebral palsy or cancer, righting wrongs, eliminating conflict with others, stopping violence, world peace, etc., I am left either in a state of constant agitation, anger, and emotional exhaustion, or defeated and empty because I cannot ever truly right every wrong on earth. It doesn't mean I shouldn't fight for these things—of course, I should, and I do, but the ultimate cures for these societal ills may never be perfectly solved in this life. Yet, when my hope lies in the heaven where evil is overcome, and I can enjoy life as originally intended on a restored earth with a twenty-three-year-old body (my vote) with more no tears . . . that is worth looking forward to!

As you know, secondhand suffering can carry a grief that may even be more potent than firsthand suffering. Putting one's hope in heaven can be a powerful antidote because it offers a full resolution to an earthly heartbreak. It is what gives me ultimate hope that my brother will one day be healed. It is what gave me hope when my mother died that one day I would see her again. And when my heart breaks because of the pain of relationships or tragedies and injustice that happens in this world, I have the hope that it will all be redeemed. And I believe the hope is real, not just a wish.

"In the world you will have tribulation,
but be of good cheer,
for I have overcome the world."

—JESUS, JOHN 16:33 (ESV)

About a week after my mom died, I was awoken by a vivid dream or vision—I'm not sure which. Mom appeared to me wearing the bridal shower outfit she had bought me. It was white with bright red, yellow, and purple flowers—a skirt and top that overlapped to form a sharp-looking suit dress. I wondered why she was wearing my dress. And she looked like she was in a magical forest of some kind. She was joyful and radiant and looked like her old self, a younger version without any signs of that distant look that dementia brings. She let me know she was okay. And then she vanished. If I ever doubted if heaven was real, this was my cure. This wasn't my imagination—it felt so real. It wasn't until later that I thought about the significance of her wearing my bridal shower dress. She was married to the bridegroom. It was God's way of saying that she is a bride of His and celebrating in that great banquet feast talked about in the Bible. If you are suffering from the death of a loved one—secondhand suffering on steroids—I pray you will feel the peace that comes from such a dream or vision.

The grief that comes with losing a loved one can be debilitating. Similar grief can come with someone still living but who has chronic pain, loss of mind, or who is fighting a terminal battle. Picking up the pieces of a broken heart is something we all struggle to do successfully. And the broken heart may not be about losing a person either. It could be about difficult times of persecution, abandonment, rejection, betrayal, or even living out the consequences of poor choices and feeling the pain of regret and the bitterness of unforgiveness from others and for others. Being stuck in old patterns, holding on to old wounds, and living in fear or lack of transformational faith can cause your heart to become hard or frozen. Pain is pain. Suffering is suffering, no matter the trigger. Sometimes, feeling that someone understands what you are going through takes the edge off sharp pain. Finding that person, community, or support group is critical, as we discussed earlier. But sometimes, the simple random act of hearing a song on the radio can hit your spirit at just the right time, and you feel instantly "seen" as you connect at a heart level with the music and lyrics. For me, that happened when I heard a poignant song on the radio recently called *Tell Your Heart to Beat Again* by Danny Gokey.[62]

With beautiful instrumental music in the background, the lyrics seem to articulate so much of what any one of us feels while in an emotional place of suffering—feeling shattered with your life in a thousand pieces on the floor. We feel hopeless and without words as the world drives us to our knees. There is a new beginning ahead, and love's healing hands are pulling us through. All we need to do is get back up and take a step, leave the dark places of our lives, and feel the warmth of the sun. Our journey is not over; things can begin again. We can tell our hearts to beat again, letting shadows fall away and taking that step of faith into the light of grace. And part of this journey involves letting go of our yesterdays, saying goodbye because we don't live there anymore—or shouldn't. But we can let every heartbreak and scar remind us of how far we've been carried and how heaven is working together things for our good, even through our shattered hearts. I hope you'll consider listening to the song for yourself, as my paraphrase of the lyrics doesn't convey the full power of the song.

For me, that song touches on so many pieces to the puzzle of my life journey—the interweaving of brokenness, shadows, darkness, heartbreaks, and scars with new beginnings, sunlight, hope, healing, and things working together for good. Through the ups and downs of life, I will continue to climb as I move forward, sometimes falling back and other times sprinting ahead. But I—and we—need to move on at some point. We can't live stuck forever. The ebb and flow in life is reality.

Allowing some doors to close as we welcome new doors to open paints a picture of how we move from yesterday to today to tomorrow. As secondhand sufferers, moving forward doesn't mean we don't have scars or need to forget where we've been. But it may mean making a choice to rise above our feelings and take that step forward—into our destined promised land—to get unstuck and cross over into a greater reality.

Is there someone you need to forgive who you've been holding a grudge against that is only causing bitterness? Or do you need to forgive yourself because you have held onto unnecessary shame, guilt, or resentment? Have you believed lies that have held you back in your yesterdays instead of being freed into your tomorrows? Are you secretly relishing your pain over your loved ones as an excuse to avoid the messy unknowns ahead that could lead you to achieve your God-given potential? Are you so overwhelmed with grief over the loss of a loved one that you think you cannot go on?

All of us have a choice to tell our hearts to beat again and jumpstart us back into hope for the long game of eternity and the present moment. Whatever the reality is you are dealing with, at some point, you must say your goodbyes so you can invite your hellos.

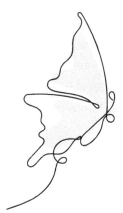

SPIRITUAL REFLECTIONS

Hunger + Surrender = Transformation

*"Therefore, if anyone is in Christ,
the new creation has come.
The old has gone, the new is here!"*

—2 Corinthians 5:17 (NKJV)

For so long, growing up in an environment where I attended church, was basically a good person, and looked forward to going to heaven when I die, I felt like I was doing my best. On those occasions, if I was spurred on to grow "in my faith," it usually involved reading a self-help book, joining a Bible study with homework, and improving my character through behavioral modification techniques such as praying more, memorizing a verse, and not raising my voice at my kids. (The latter was my biggest challenge for a season.) I worked hard at being a "good person" and got fat with knowledge with some wisdom thrown in. But I was busy trying to check all the boxes of expectations, make everyone like me by jumping through their hoops, and gobbling up whatever the latest trend was in parenting or acceptable theological dogma of whatever church I was attending at the time.

Overall, my spiritual journey hit a breakthrough after discovering the Holy Spirit piece of the puzzle, and it may be best simplified by the story I used to read to my kids called *The Very Hungry Caterpillar* by Eric Carle.[63] If you haven't read it, it's the story of the small caterpillar who was born off a leaf and proceeded to be hungry all the time and eat all kinds of foods nonstop (one apple, two pears, three plums . . .) until he was about to pop. He grew to be a big and fat caterpillar. But there came a point in time when the caterpillar was stuffed. He could no longer eat anymore. At that point, the caterpillar curled up into a self-made cocoon and rested.

Similarly, as I pursued the things of God on and off throughout my life, what kept me growing was my hunger. Hunger breeds growth, for sure, and I got to a point where I had all the right intellectual arguments and retorts to anyone who didn't believe in God. I was so bloated in my head knowledge of spiritual truths, and I thought I knew it all. But I was missing something greater but didn't see what it was or how to find it.

Through my continual hunger for the knowledge of God, almost to a fault, there came a point where I didn't want answers anymore; I wanted something without words, reasons, or arguments. My pivot point was when I discovered the power of surrender by going into my own cocoon, held together by God's womb-like enclosure. I was at the end of my life as a fat caterpillar, ready to give up my fight to play God, fix my brother, be a good person, read all the self-help books, fill my mind with every proof text for God . . . I had gone as far as I could on my own, and so to move farther, faster, and shift into what I was created to be, something new had to happen—I needed a complete transformation.

At the right time, just as the caterpillar must feel compelled to poke its way out of its temporary home to emerge as a completely new creation, my ultimate surrender to the cocoon of rest came about. I bet the caterpillar is a bit astonished at first when it looks and feels differently as it breaks out. After getting used to its new body, it finds itself free to fly, enjoying its new beauty, abilities, and utter magnificent but messy transformation. Likewise, I was finally understanding what being God's "new creation" means—a transformed mind, soul, and spirit. It has nothing to do with doing a lot of good stuff or being filled with many spiritual facts (although that was a big part of my process). It is something that takes time and involves a surrender of striving—a new birth of sorts. And, continuing with the metaphor, when the caterpillar transforms into the butterfly within the cocoon, its "caterpillar DNA" is essentially turned off, and the "butterfly DNA," which was suppressed and hidden before, is now turned on. It is always in the caterpillar but dormant. And, even more interesting, the butterfly's brain is bigger than its caterpillar brain. It is a whole new creation with advanced capacity in every way, yet it is still the same being.

> *"When it comes to religion today, we tend to be*
> *long on butterflies and short on cocoons.*
> *Somehow, we're going to have to relearn that*
> *the deep things of God don't come suddenly."*[64]
>
> —SUE MONK KIDD

303

Like the caterpillar, each one of us has the full potential of our "inner butterfly DNA" all the time, even as we are crawling around and eating everything we can find as slimy and fat caterpillars. Our potential to become our fullest created selves is already within us, but until we surrender and submit to the transformation, we will remain wandering around as a fat caterpillar, missing out on our greater ability to soar.

For so long, I thought that our "butterfly stage" of being free to fly and be at our best potential had to wait until heaven. Of course, we will be at our best selves then, but living as a new creation makes for an even greater hope for us to reach our potential while still on earth. So, as a fat caterpillar, who found her way into a cocoon, I was ready to reach the beginning of life as a butterfly, a transformed follower of Jesus able to live more freely, live more fully with increased abilities, and find intimacy with the Creator—a process much harder to do with my head but much easier through my heart.

Think about how dark it must be inside that cocoon, or a womb about to birth new life, or even right before death. The darkness is temporary until the light begins to creep in at the moment of the new birth. I love the old English proverb, "The darkest hours are right before dawn." To birth into something new, we often go through a "dark night of the soul." The hard times, trials, and sufferings are often what bring us to that desperate state of surrender. And only then can the new birth and transformation begin. It is also never instant or a magic pill. Like the dawn, it is gradual, and with each step forward, the light shines brighter in us and through us.

I have found my spiritual transformation to be slow and gradual, full of twists and turns. But the freedom of life soaring as a butterfly does not happen without the caterpillar's trek into the surrender that leads to transformation.

"Hunger is the escort to the deeper things of You."

—MISTY EDWARDS IN "SOUL CRY" SONG (PERMISSION GIVEN)

TOOLS FOR THE HEART

No matter how bad life is, there is always hope. Cling to the hope of heaven where all wrongs will be made right and the inner longings of the soul—for you and your loved one—can be fulfilled completely. This hope is the remedy for the restless soul on earth to satisfy the longing for which we are designed to fulfill. To embrace all that is ahead involves an intentional focus on hope and a willingness to surrender what keeps you from reaching your unrealized growth. There is a time to grow as much as we can, doing life, crawling around, grabbing, and doing all we can on our own like a caterpillar. But then, when we can't do any more on our own, we must surrender, rest, and allow God to set us in His cocoon for our transformation. Only then will we become all we were designed to be and fly as a beautiful new creation.

Questions to Ponder:

1. When you think of heaven, what do you see? Have you ever thought much about this potential future destination, or do you prefer not to think about it? When you think about your current situation with a loved one you cannot fix or bring back after their physical death, how does clinging to something beyond this world comfort you? Or does it?

2. Can you relate to the hungry caterpillar story? Have you exhausted all you can do on your own to the point of surrendering to your customized cocoon that leads to reaching your created potential? What do you need to lay down, give up, or surrender to move into your spiritual transformation?

Practical Steps:

- If you are still skeptical about heaven and need some encouragement, check out these resources for some fascinating real-life, evidence-based stories for further exploration. Some of these have movies and interviews you can watch on YouTube or Amazon. I encourage you to look them up.

  Proof of Heaven: A Neurosurgeon's Journey into the Afterlife by Eben Alexander, M.D. *(NY Times #1 Bestseller)*

  Heaven Is for Real: A Little Boy's Astounding Story of His Trip to Heaven and Back by Todd Burpo and Lynn Vincent

  Within Heaven's Gates by Rebecca Springer

  The Case for Heaven Documentary: Experience the Evidence for Life After Death by Lee Strobel

  Imagine Heaven – Near Death Experiences, God's Promises and the Exhilarating Future That Awaits You by John Burke

- To explore the depths of the ultimate meaning of heaven as expressed in the Bible as being "heaven on earth" instead of heaven in the sky somewhere, check out this classic book: *Surprised by Hope: Rethinking Heaven, The Resurrection, and the Mission of the Church* by N.T. Wright.

- Take some time to slow down and listen to some music that touches your heart in a way that can release some of the emotional heaviness you carry and gain a greater perspective on life—music that offers hope to your soul. Just be still and let the music and lyrics speak to you at a heart level. To start, below are a few songs that have ministered to me:

Tell Your Heart to Beat Again, Danny Gokey

You're Not Alone, Meredith Andrews

Letting Go, Steffany Gretzinger

Rescue, Lauren Daigle

Soul Cry, Misty Edwards

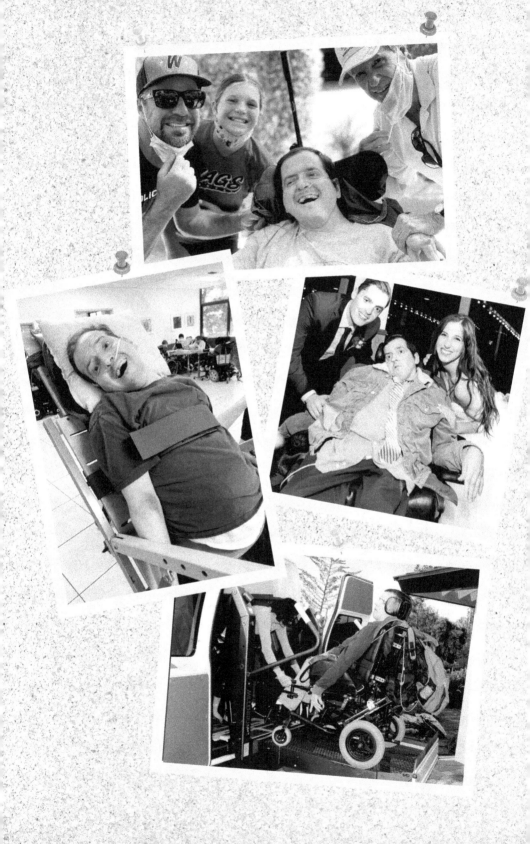

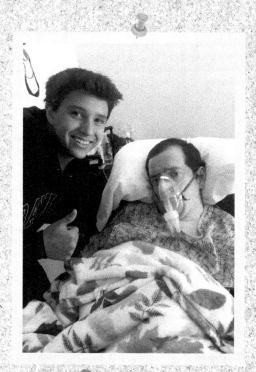

CHAPTER THIRTEEN

Blooming at the Intersection of Hope & Suffering

*"They wander on earth and live in heaven, and although they are weak,
they protect the world; they taste of peace in the midst of turmoil;
they are poor and yet they have all they want. They stand in suffering
and remain in joy, they appear dead to all outward sense
and lead a life of faith within."*

—DEITRICH BONHOEFFER
THE COST OF DISCIPLESHIP

Do you remember as a kid playing the sidewalk game? I recall my friends telling me the point of the game was to not step on any cracks between the slabs of concrete. Of course, I thought the better game was to make sure and STEP on every crack. I was alone in my interpretation but to this day I still like to step on the cracks instead of avoiding them.

With my focus on those concrete dividers, I remember my fascination as a child with those rare times when a beautiful flower emerged from one of those cracks. How was that possible? I wondered. I knew no one planted it under the concrete; it didn't seem to have any soil other than cement, and growing up in Southern California meant if it didn't have a sprinkler on it, it wouldn't get water. It was a paradox to have something so beautiful and full of life break through a hardened, ugly, man-made slab of cement.

Similarly, the quote from Bonhoeffer above speaks to this paradox in us as humans. How is it possible to wander on earth but live in heaven? Or to be weak but still protect the world? Or taste peace amid turmoil? Be poor but be satisfied? Stand in a state of suffering, yet remain in joy? Appear dead in all outward appearances, yet lead a life with internal, sustaining faith?

It's one thing to have a hope for heaven in the future to escape the hardened concrete-like existence in our earthly lives that often brings trials and suffering for us and those we love, but another thing altogether to be able to vibrantly bloom where we are planted, no matter our surroundings that we cannot control.

Originally, I assumed I would conclude my story with the last chapter on the hope of heaven as my greatest "tool" to offer for secondhand suffering. After all, what could be a better ending than having the ultimate happily-ever-after ending for us or our loved one's unfixable heart pains? But as I pressed on with living my life, I became more aware of the challenge to pursue the paradoxical possibility of living in the tension of both hope and suffering, much like a flower growing out of a concrete crack.

Once I gave a name to this experience of secondhand suffering and shared it with others, from their reactions I have seen a palpable connection with their heart and, for the first time, they admit they feel seen, not alone, and drawn to ponder this new sense of validation. I believe by defining a reality that already exists, it provides a needed onramp to a discussion that has too long been ignored.

The hope for the ultimate healing is important, but the day-to-day journey is still there and isn't always satiated with a distant hope of heaven. Often, as much as I was growing, my internal joy was still dependent on my brother's circumstances (or my child's or my dad's).

My story, like yours, is a progressive journey, still in process and one that won't end on this side of eternity. Something still stirred in my restless heart, though, and I knew my story was not quite ready to be told, which is why I couldn't end with chapter twelve. Yet, my journey seemed to be at a tipping point to discover the missing piece. I knew it could only come if I experienced it first. It could not be manufactured. And wouldn't be learned from a book.

So I pressed in. I spent increasing amounts of time with God, not just learning about Him with my mind but spending time with Him with my heart. There was a hunger to grow and an openness to being vulnerable, an "all-in" type of focus. My thoughts were becoming more and more like His thoughts as I intentionally surrounded myself with people and environments supportive of emotional healing. The more I tuned my ears to God's frequency to hear better, the more obvious it became. All the time I had spent spinning my wheels with the wisdom of man and even beautiful theological doctrines could only take me so far.

Kevin continues to have countless battles with a myriad of issues, from respiratory crises, emergency room visits, G-tube complications, and random wounds popping up at times to difficulties with changes in staffing, bureaucratic regulations, and ongoing evaluation and monitoring of his medications and quality of life concerns. And as emotionally exhausting, draining, and deeply frustrating these battles are, I've noticed they are balanced by an increasing number of blessings, miracles, and sweet surprises as I see the fruit from my advocacy blossom. I am experiencing some relief from guilt, living more out of the box, new victories for health battles, and my spiritual eyes being opened to more interplay between ongoing battles and hardships with encouraging anecdotes and answers to prayer. Without hope rising, at least intermittently, I was likely to burn out.

Not too long ago, I was checking in with one of Kevin's caregivers since he had recently been released from the hospital. This trusted caregiver said something unusual this time. Always on edge, expecting another shoe to drop, I asked him to repeat what he said when it sounded too far-fetched. He repeated, "When I came in for my shift this morning at 6 AM, the night shift nurse and I talked briefly. She told me that when she was here last night, she heard a man speaking in Kevin's room. She thought maybe one of the male staff members wanted to greet Kevin since he just got back from the hospital. However, when she went in to see who it was that was visiting Kevin, she saw no one was there. She looked at Kevin's face, and he was beaming with a big smile and looking radiant." I exclaimed with a new sense of faith and excitement, "Oh my goodness! I think Kevin was talking with angels!" Kevin's self-proclaimed agnostic caregiver said, "I know—that's what I thought!" There was no other explanation. We took a moment of holy awe to absorb that possibility.

I have often prayed in desperation for my brother to be visited by angels when he was alone. But, deep down, did I really think it would happen with audible voices? I think if I were to be honest, my answer would be "not really." Even with my growth, I still struggle with optimism at times.

To reinforce my desire to believe my brother interacted with angels, my intellect reminds me that throughout the Bible, angels are regularly mentioned as real beings that show up to serve people, often appear in response to prayer, and can communicate with humans, all to bring the goodness of God to a situation or need. This account about my brother speaking (or listening) to/with angels was a huge lift to my spirit. This time, instead of remaining in a state of doubt, I rested in faith and chose to believe it was true. And joy flowed out of me. Kicking doubt and skepticism out of my head ended up growing my heart.

Another small miracle that lifted my spirits recently was when I got a panicked call from Kevin's nurse that he was on the way to the ER in an ambulance because his heart rate and vitals were extremely low. They thought he was crashing due to sepsis. The call seemed dark and dire and felt different from the others. It seemed like they thought he could be dying, although they wouldn't say that. To make things worse, this call came to me on the same day I was preparing to serve as a greeter at one of my very best friend's memorial service, and I was grieving deeply. It was not a day I could handle anything more. I had already come out of five months of watching my friend suffer and lose a battle, and my grief was already over the top. I knew that if my brother went to the hospital, I would have no choice but to go and enter battle mode, something I had no emotional bandwidth for that day. I was broken, weak, and desperate, and I had nothing in me other than tears and the words "NOT TODAY GOD . . . NOT TODAY!"

I texted a group of praying friends, and my husband stopped what he was doing pray boldly. They knew my tone was *not* "Dear God, if it is Your will, please consider healing Kevin so I can go to my friend's funeral." No—my boldness emerged, and this time, I asked my friends and husband to demand a miracle from God on my behalf. I knew from Scripture that we are given authority by Jesus to heal the sick, but at that moment, I had nothing in me except desperation. My tears and hysteria flooded out of me, broken and undone. Within ten minutes, an incredible gift was delivered to me via text from the caregiver and supervisor, saying, "Kevin's vitals are 100% back to normal and better than ever." I collapsed in tears of a different kind and felt in my spirit this was an all-out miraculous answer to prayer. God's love overwhelmed me in that moment. I still had to meet my brother in the hospital to have him tested and cleared, and as I was driving there, I had a vision of my dear friend in heaven telling Jesus something like, "Okay, Jesus, now you need to hear my friend Camille's prayer right now because I need her to be at my party tonight. It's my day, and I want Kevin healed right now. I need her to be fully free and available for my celebration event." (And, yes, I believe people we love who are with Jesus can be our advocates in the heavenly realm!)

The story ended with a heavenly touch when I walked into that emergency room to see Kevin fully smiling and laughing at me (he thinks it's funny when his shenanigans get him an extra visit with me). The miracle was confirmed when his tests came back perfect and in range, and then he was released within just a couple of hours (a first). Now,

I could be fully present to celebrate my dear friend's life that evening. The doctors were all in shock, and no one knew what happened, but I chose to believe God answered my prayers and reminded me to look for the small miracles amidst the tough stuff. It changes momentum and the atmosphere when we do.

In the same month, Kevin had an opportunity to enjoy a wild ride in a golf cart at a golf tournament for his home organization. This may sound like not that big of a deal at first, but trust me, it was. He doesn't get out much, and thanks to a very "out of the box" and super-fun head nurse, Kevin was allowed to get off campus, be lifted and strapped into a golf cart with a few of us surrounding him, and experience a wild ride through a very hilly 18-hole golf course. Kevin's nonstop laughing and cackling with sheer delight as he experienced his own Disneyland ride made this secondhand sufferer feel the happiest she had felt in a long time. Being fully present in these moments makes the harder moments more tolerable.

So, there *are* good days. I'm opening my eyes to them and being present when they appear. Having an attitude of joy, gratitude, and courageous faith instead of fear, negativity, and doubt plays a role in ushering in the momentum for discovering more of these moments hidden behind the veil of a despondent attitude. For all of us in the community of secondhand sufferers, during our times of overwhelming worry, fear, anger, and desperation, we can choose to look for the light in the darkness, silver linings in the dark, stormy clouds, beauty from ashes, flowers growing out of cracks, and promising hope even as life is intertwined with the reality of suffering.

INSIGHTS FOR THE HEART

Unpacking "Living Hope"

*"God is the only one who can make
the valley of trouble a door of hope."*

—CATHERINE MARSHALL

Have you found that often the most important lessons in life are ones we must learn over and over again, each time dealing with a different layer of the same obstacle, until the change or transformation sticks?

For me, it was my underlying anger toward God. And yes, I thought I had checked that box and moved on, yet I realized I had only gone part way. I had done the work to loosen my grip on anger and deal with the surface-level hostility I felt toward Him, but it was more like I had only scraped off the top layer and left the deeper wounds anesthetized so I could continue tackling other areas of growth. But as those deepest wounds were thawing out, I was a mess . . . My anger toward Him was deep-rooted and needed to be excavated by its roots to free me from being stuck.

I thought I had taken care of the surface bitterness with my intellectual, philosophical, and biblical pursuits, but there was still more I needed to detox. Turns out I still was mad at God for not fixing a lot of things—my brother's disability and the untimely deaths of dear friends and family (might as well throw them all in the mix). I've always admitted my disappointment with God rather freely; however, the root of all disappointment is often anger. Uprooting the seed of anger became key to being authentic with God, myself, and you, the reader.

> *I thought I had taken care of the surface bitterness with my intellectual, philosophical, and biblical pursuits, but there was still more I needed to detox.*

The act of admitting I had not stopped being mad was an anchor holding me back from moving forward. So, I figured, knowing He already knows my thoughts, I might as well just be honest. I told Him out loud—not metaphorically, "Yes, God. I have been mad at You. I had hope as a little girl that You would heal Kevin in this life, but You didn't. The Bible even says, 'Hope deferred makes the heart sick,' and my heart has been sick for a very long time. And angry. And sad. And on top of that, I miss my mom and now several close friends who left too soon. And my kids all moved away and have gone in new directions. Life is hard. I just wish you would fix it all. I need to be free from my anger. Help!" That's when I felt a shift happen.

I'm pretty sure God appreciates our raw honesty because then He can partner with us for our healing; He doesn't just wave a magic wand, though. Our humility and open heart are a part of God's "pre-reqs" for our growth. Many of us are angry at God, and admitting this becomes our starting point. Sadly, for many people, it is also their ending point.

Our hearts can either turn hard or tender towards God, depending on our choices. If we only keep an open heart towards God depending on IF our lives are free from pain or suffering or our prayers are answered our way, we risk missing out on a deeper journey of growth towards a different kind of wholeness—the kind that can exist despite unanswered prayers. We can remain stuck in unforgiveness, bitterness, or avoidance or simply stay spinning in place without moving forward.

I now see that the confession of our heart initiates the healing process. Without it, we can only get so far. God doesn't do shallow very well. He looks at our hearts, and that goes deep. Even though God knows our heart, admitting it affects something. With my own confession of this angry root gnawing inside of me, there was a release. Just like when the chiropractor twists a very stiff neck, and we feel the "pop," and a rush of relief goes through our body and lessens the tension all over, something snaps in the emotional/spiritual sense when we get raw with God. Often, it is then that He releases more of His power and jumpstarts the healing process. And things become clearer.

God never promises a pain-free life. While I had wrestled with God theologically, biblically, intellectually, and spiritually and had come up with satisfactory answers, I had been ignoring something deep down that needed to be "outed." After I declared out loud what was really bothering me, I felt God's peace release in my heart as the Comforter said, "I know.

Thank you for being honest . . . finally." It seemed a large roadblock was moved aside. My theological veneer with all the answers was stripped away, and I was naked before God. "Now I can get somewhere," I felt Him say. And, since that day, the bitter anger has dissipated.

> *"Between stimulus and response there is a space.*
> *In that space is our power to choose our response.*
> *In our response lies our growth and our freedom."*
>
> —VIKTOR E. FRANKL

The confession of honesty broke something in me. It broke my pride that I had already arrived as a solid, strong, faithful Christ-follower. Who was I trying to impress? While my theological conclusions helped me never to fully blame God for all the trauma in life, deep wounds can defy logic and require a change in heart and humility of the will to be released.

One day, I was invited to a "prophetic" prayer meeting. While I had already begun exploring this concept of prophecy (a fancy word for hearing from God's heart) on my own, making myself vulnerable to others was something new. Ten years prior to this, I would have thought going to a meeting like this was bizarre, if not close to heretical. Yet, experiencing something trumps forming judgments about something you haven't experienced.

As background, the Bible says, "Pursue love, and earnestly desire the spiritual gifts, especially that you may prophesy" (1 Corinthians 14:1). In the New Testament, prophecy is understood to be a gift that anyone can receive, and it is mostly used to edify, comfort, and encourage one another (v. 3). While there are many prophets in the Old Testament (or Tanakh) who speak on behalf of God about future events and warnings to repent, the prophetic gift in the New Testament is more spoken of as one who hears the heart of God towards a person and reveals it to them to strengthen, comfort, and encourage. To the recipient, this can naturally bring a greater intimacy with God.

Who doesn't want to be able to hear from God? I am guessing we all yearn to hear God's heart for us or how He sees us, yet many suppress this yearning due to unbelief, lack of awareness of the Scriptures, genuine skepticism that God speaks to us, fear of false teachings, and the list goes on. I've wrestled with all of these, and my studies and experiences have led me to believe that this gift is for anyone to pursue.

As I walked up to a group of three individuals to receive prayer at this meeting, one gal told me that as I was approaching them (without talking to me or ever seeing me before), she saw a picture in her head of a dilapidated old tree house that was falling down, broken, and unfinished. It was not in its working shape yet, and she saw me next to it with a very ornate and over-the-top "Bob the Builder" outfit with a huge tool chest of tools. In her mind, she saw me banging away on it with all my tools, trying desperately to fix the darn treehouse with the best "fix-it outfit" and tool accessories out there. She saw me trying every tool in my tool chest in desperation to try to fix IT, but nothing was working. I had done everything in my power, and I even had the outfit, the gear, the fancy toolbox, and the latest and greatest expensive tools. But the treehouse remained broken and falling apart. My efforts weren't working. She then saw the Lord step in and say, "Stop working so hard to fix something you were not meant to fix. Lay down all your tools and rest, and let Me do the fixing."

The funny thing about this picture given to me is that, at that time, we actually had an unfinished, dilapidated, broken embryonic pre-treehouse in our backyard. When our kids were little, this project began and never finished because we had a big family argument over the whole thing. For years when the kids were still young, I longed to have the thing built and fixed, but it stayed there, completely nonfunctional and an eyesore for years. My own son was heavy on my mind when I went to this prayer meeting as he has been through years and years of health battles, and I was pleading with God for help, exhausted from fighting his sickness and going on our eighth endocrinologist in eight years. After hearing this treehouse analogy, it resonated with me about my son, as I was experiencing secondhand suffering with his illness, which seemed insurmountable.

My takeaway from that experience was that I needed to surrender these battles to God and lay down all my fancy tools. "Cast all your burdens on Him because He cares for you" (1 Peter 5:7) was a good starting point. We simply can't carry the full weight of life's burdens, and I don't think we are meant to. While I have identified many tools for the heart to alleviate the blow of secondhand suffering, I now understand that the "fix" isn't found with the tools alone. The key "tool of the heart" to address our empathetic pain is not a tool at all. In fact, the real key to living in a situation that feels hopeless and traumatic is the very act of *laying down* the tools and giving them up in exchange for a Person, the ultimate Tool Maker.

About the same time as the "fix it" revelation of Bob the Builder, one of my clients said something else that stood out. This client was dealing with a long unemployment situation and had been anxious about it. When I asked how he was holding up, given how many months he had been out of work, he replied that he was doing wonderful as he was really focusing on his true living hope and not his circumstances. I asked him to repeat what he said about "living hope" and explain it more as I felt its "shimmer" on a missing piece on my journey. So, after we hung up the phone, I immersed myself for the next six hours in understanding this "living hope." Up until then, that phrase had always felt flat to me. It was a theological concept—sure, we have living hope because when we die, we get to live again in heaven. That was what I thought it meant. My yearning for an end to suffering for my brother and me in the "secondhand" sense has been mostly about a future hope. Having a living hope—something for today and not for just some time in the future—was a new idea that caught my attention.

My focus on defining "living hope" led me to read about one of the worst forms of suffering for millions of people, mostly Jews, during the Holocaust as they were placed in death camps. Most people in these horrendous camps lost all hope as they saw friends and family being tortured, starved, and killed. However, a now famous doctor and survivor who was in one of those camps, Viktor Frankl, wrote a book about this experience. The book is called *Man's Search for Meaning*, and in it, Frankl speaks of four different ways people responded to this monstrous suffering. The first type of response was that they became brutal and cruel, even the nicest people. The second type of response he saw was those who gave up all hope. The third type of response was those people who decided to hang on to the hope that if they could just stay alive, they could get their hope back, and their life would be restored fully as it was before, including their achievements, things, and way of life. And the fourth type of response was only held by a few people. Frankl discovered these people had an inner strength that carried them through those dark days of despair, even knowing what their fate may be. They stayed kind, and they kept an inner liberty inside, knowing they were likely to be killed. His focus was on this last group of people. Why were they carried by an inner strength no matter what the circumstances? What made them different from the rest?

Suffering in a concentration camp, according to Frankl, tears open the human soul and exposes its depths and foundations. In other words, suffering doesn't cause reactions in people; it exposes their inner character.

Those few people who held on to hope regardless of circumstance or outcome revealed that life only has meaning if there is a hope that even suffering and death cannot destroy. After assessing and observing this unique group of people, *Frankl concluded that one thing they all shared was the feeling they each held while in the camp suffering— they believed that someone was looking down on them from heaven, a friend, spouse, parent, or God—and there was something beyond them, beyond this very life, that gave them hope.* Their hope wasn't based on regaining a future job title, money, health, friends, a person, possession, or any "stuff," but rather on a *living hope*—a hope that won't die if none of those things come through. Frankl makes the point that while we cannot avoid suffering, we can choose how to cope with it, find meaning in it, and move forward.[65]

> *"Life is never made unbearable by circumstances,*
> *but only by lack of meaning and purpose."*
>
> —Victor E. Frankl

So, as one who suffers because another suffers, having a living hope, even if our loved one still suffers, seems to be the ultimate tool of the heart. How can we find meaning in a life whose hope may not result in what we are hoping for? Without a spiritual, imperishable hope, our soul can be crushed as we are hardwired for hope—not a dead religious hope in a far-off future, but a present, active, and living hope that sustains us in the here and now, *as well* as the bonus hope into eternity.

What does this "living hope" look like according to the Bible?

Blessed be the God and Father of our Lord Jesus Christ! According to his great mercy, **he has caused us to be born again to a living hope** through the resurrection of Jesus Christ from the dead, to an inheritance that is imperishable, undefiled, and unfading, kept in heaven for you, who by God's power are being guarded through faith for a salvation ready to be revealed in the last time. **In this you rejoice, though now for a little while, if necessary, you have been grieved by various trials,** so that the tested genuineness of your faith—more precious than gold that perishes though it is tested by fire—may be found to result in praise and glory and honor at the revelation of Jesus Christ. Though you have not seen him, **you love him**. Though you do not now see him, you believe in him and **rejoice with joy** that is inexpressible and filled with glory, obtaining the outcome of your faith, the salvation of your souls. (1 Peter 1:3–9 (ESV), emphases mine)

What is fascinating is that this passage in 1 Peter speaks of someone going through suffering and grieving in trials *at the same time* that they are to be rejoicing and full of joy. How is it possible for joy and suffering to be present at the same time? Here is how I am unpacking this.

The deeper we have empathy and love for others, the more we suffer and feel another's pain. If you are a parent, you get this. When our kids suffer, we suffer even more because our love for them runs so deep. As a mother, I always resonated with this quote from so many, including Dr. Phil, "You are only as happy as your saddest child."[66] To suffer intensely on another's behalf is an indication that we are also filled with strong, empathetic love. So, while we are experiencing deep suffering, we are also allowing our hearts to love deeply. They are related and intertwined. To love deeply is also to have a connection to God, as "God is love" (1 John 4:8). Therefore, since God created us in His image and He is love, we are experiencing Him—a union with God—when we love others enough to suffer with them.

Think about how the Father God must have experienced secondhand suffering as He watched His own Son be whipped, beaten, and brutally nailed to a cross to suffer a slow, agonizing death for no crime whatsoever. If we, as mere humans made in the image of God, weep and mourn and feel deep despair when our kids (or loved ones) suffer, how much more grief would a personal, loving God have whose love runs deeper than ours ever could? I believe God the Father empathizes with us in secondhand suffering, and because He and Jesus are One, He also willingly suffered Himself. As a parent would say,

"This hurts me more than you." I believe when we suffer as His kids, He suffers with us.

So, with all this talk of suffering, what does "living hope" really look like as the answer to healing from secondhand suffering? To me, a living hope looks like an intimate relationship with the eternal God of the Universe made known in the Person of Jesus and empowered by the Holy Spirit living inside us by being "born again." Okay . . . that was a long sentence! For the full effect, re-read it slowly. The Bible says we are "born again *into* a living hope" (1 Peter 1:3–4, emphasis mine). This new birth in us (by a relationship with the Person of Jesus) makes it possible to have joy and sorrow coexist. Instead of sorrow hardening us, it softens us when we have this living hope. According to the late pastor and author Timothy Keller, "We are always happier and sadder than everyone because we have a big, full heart towards God and others. A living hope makes us sadder and happier at the same time!" And he drives it home when he explains: "Our living hope is not a future mansion, but Him. A Prince. A Husband. A Shepherd. A Brother. A Lover. A King with open arms . . . offering approval and honor."[67]

So, while there are many wise tools for the heart to help each of us deal with the pain of not being able to fix a loved one's suffering or even reverse a suffering that led to the untimely death of a loved one, there is one hope that is sustainable. But it is not a tool; it is the living hope of Jesus.

When we think of Jesus as a religion or theology, we miss it. We miss Him. To get to know this living hope, often, we must travel the road where the intersection of suffering and joy meet. It is a road less traveled and a narrow path, but one that is open to all. When the road is traveled with the One who loves us more than any other, life is more enjoyable, more meaningful, and leads to the ultimate destination. It's about intimacy with the only One who can heal our soul—a two-way relationship with a God who loves us, sees us, understands our pain, and suffers with us. He fills our soul and spirit in ways that allow us to endure hard things with Him by our side as our Comforter, Sustainer, Lover, and Restorer, as well as the ultimate "Righter of Wrongs." Jesus couldn't stand religion, rules, and hypocrisy—He was all about bringing wholeness to those who are broken when we are willing to lay down all our tools and allow Him to be the ultimate tool for our hearts.

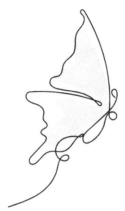

SPIRITUAL REFLECTIONS

Walking in Intimacy with the Bridegroom

"I found Him whom my soul loves."

—SONG OF SONGS 3:4 (ESV)

Have you ever had a dream that is so powerful it awakens you, and you experience heightened sensations in a way that makes you feel it was real? I had a dream like that one night, and while it technically was a dream, I believe I met Jesus for real. I saw Him standing on some rocks in a creek with running water, surrounded by trees, and He turned His face toward me and stared into my eyes with the most loving and kind eyes I had ever seen. It felt as though His eyes penetrated through my whole being, and I was captivated by a love I had never felt before. I remember feeling deeply in love with Him —a different kind of love than anything I had ever felt in this life. It was so intense, deeply sweet, and passionate. I now understood what people had described to me as "intimacy with Jesus." I felt seen, known, and adored. I prayed the feeling would never leave. I will never forget it. It took me one step further on the path of moving my connection to God from my head to my heart.

Some people learn the easy way. Others take more time and a few bumps on the head. Looking back at my spiritual journey, I seem to fall in the latter category. While I know better than to say I "have arrived," I believe some obstacles have been knocked down to make a clear path forward. I continue on this journey, except now I know I am not alone—I am seen, loved, and more peaceful than restless.

Many labels are given to Jesus in the Bible, but my favorite is "Bridegroom." And we (His people) are called "The Bride of Christ." Why the marriage analogy? God often uses realities in our world as illustrations of spiritual truths. Marriage, if done as intended, is a symbolic yet imperfect representation of God's desire to be intimately in union with Him, both now and for eternity. I'm walking with my Bridegroom, Jesus, with an intimacy that is fresh and freeing. It's personal. Marinating in this hidden treasure has been powerful in unlocking the prison of my heart, as it has opened my eyes to what it means to have a two-way relationship with Jesus, my living hope.

Probably the best way to describe my spiritual transformation in this journey as a secondhand sufferer is a poetic metaphor found in the

Bible, the book of Song of Solomon (also known as Song of Songs). At face value, this is a story about King Solomon and his bride and their pursuit of each other and their relationship. Yet, many scholars and authors from the past and present see the eight chapters as a metaphor for the Bride of Christ (us) and the Bridegroom (Jesus). (Another view is that it is a metaphor for God and Israel.) I believe all three are valid and serve different purposes. For me, this book's impact was seeing it through the lens of we as individuals being the Bride (a.k.a. Shulamite Maiden) and Jesus as the Bridegroom. The language is highly symbolic and dripping with beauty and depth when viewed in this light. In the same way that Jesus spoke in parables often to ensure only those who had their hearts in the right place would understand them (those with "ears to hear"), I see Song of Songs similarly. The deeper truths about our spiritual journey lie waiting for those who dare to mine the gold and explore the poetic writing in layers going well beneath the surface.

My friend and Bible teacher Kristen Cummins summarized Song of Songs with this sentence:

> It is a love song and progressive journey that awakens the bride to the divine love of her bridegroom and in doing so, it equips her to overcome all the self-oriented aspects of her heart, transforming her into a lovesick and mature bride focused on partnering with Him and His purposes in the world.[68]

I could see my journey parallel this bride's journey. It seems that *suffering is a key to unlocking true intimacy with Jesus*. To identify with Him fully and thus experience a peace that heals our deepest hurts, we are to *share* in His sufferings. In chapter 4, verse 6 in The Passion Translation, the woman (bride) says to the groom (Jesus):

*I've made up my mind, until the darkness disappears, and the dawn has fully come, in spite of shadows and fears, I will go to the mountaintop with you—**the mountaintop of suffering love** and the hill of burning incense. Yes, I will be your bride.*

This bride is ready to go wherever her Bridegroom takes her, even if it means suffering, because she desires not to be away from His presence. Her love and being with Him, even if enduring suffering, is better than being without Him and staying safe. Rising to a mountain top level represents going higher and deeper in her relationship with Him. Mountains represent obstacles and/or trials to be overcome. This bride, by chapter four, is ready to do this alongside her bridegroom.

This profound metaphor illustrates that our relationship with Jesus is not just one way, about us getting something from Him. Rather, it reveals an amazing insight into the heart of God, that He enjoys us and the "fruits" and "fragrances" of our lives when we genuinely love Him and allow our maturity (from time with Him) to overflow into living out His purposes. Interestingly, His enjoyment of us includes a list of many spices and fragrances (Song of Solomon 4:10–15). Each is symbolic but includes things like saffron, cinnamon, and spikenard, but one that stood out to me is myrrh, like tears from a tree. Myrrh is one of the spices that the wise men brought to baby Jesus in Bethlehem. As a reminder, the three gifts brought were Gold (symbolic of a King), Frankincense (an incense symbolic of Deity), and Myrrh (an embalming oil symbolic of death/suffering/mourning).

Throughout this passionate book, we read about the fragrance of suffering love. Suffering, whether firsthand or second, is something that can indirectly unlock our hardened hearts to greater intimacy with our living hope. Our healing is released when we are in a true love relationship with Jesus. This is not a religion. Our key to freedom from the crippling pain of secondhand suffering is found in a Person, a companion in life like no other. Someone who walks with us through life in a mutually adoring and loving relationship, one that results in life having meaning, purpose, and a healed identity because we know who we are and whose we are. This Bridegroom walks through our suffering with us, finding redemption and healing for our souls in mysterious ways, but not always in the ways we want at first. It is through the testing, the trials, and the fires we walk through in this life that we learn the value of our living hope—one that won't perish, is present with us, and is not a dead religion or philosophy.

> *"I am not a theologian or a scholar, but I am very aware of the fact that pain is necessary to all of us. In my own life, I think I can honestly say that out of the deepest pain has come the strongest conviction of the presence of God and the love of God."*
>
> —ELISABETH ELLIOT

Some religions pretend there is no real suffering or pain in this life, and it is only an illusion. Others say it is the reason not to believe in God. And others say it is because God is a judgmental, angry God. But our Bridegroom suffered for us, so we don't have to in the ultimate sense. And He understands what it feels like to suffer on earth, especially for others ("Jesus wept" over the death of Lazarus), and promises to walk with us no matter how difficult. He carries us in our suffering in this life, offering not only comfort but possible healing, enduring, and unconditional love, and hope for the Day when all things will be made right again.

One more takeaway from Song of Songs is that there are "little foxes" that get in the way of our relationship with God. For me, no doubt, my constant struggle with my brother's lot in life has been just one of these foxes for me. My brother is not the problem. It has been my restless mind that has listened to a voice that whispers lies in my ear that I need to stay stuck, constantly questioning God. The Bridegroom instructs the bride:

> *"You must catch the troubling foxes,*
> *those sly little foxes that hinder our relationship.*
> *For they raid our budding vineyard of love*
> *to ruin what I've planted within you.*
> *Will you catch them and remove them for me?*
> *We will do it together."*
>
> —Song of Solomon 2:15 (TPT)

We all have these obstacles (or foxes) that get in our way from a vibrant relationship with our Bridegroom and our personal vineyard (symbolic for our heart). Identifying which little fox is holding me back from God has been a part of my process. You have heard of many of them as I have chronicled them in my narrative, insights, and spiritual growth path. I've learned that if I don't take them down as I find them, my vineyard becomes overgrown with weeds, and any fruit or spice growing in it is taken away. Then, no one benefits from any mature fragrance or fruit from my life—not others and not Jesus. In other words, if these obstacles in our life are not dealt with, over time, we may no longer be serving the meaning and purpose we were designed for, and we will miss out on the intimacy we are created for with a Bridegroom who is desperately in love with us and longs for our affection as well.

I believe suffering—especially on behalf of those we love—is an invitation to connect to the heart of God at the deepest levels. In America, I don't think we don't do suffering well. Instead, we spend our lives numbing ourselves to not feel pain. This can work for a while, until we encounter a trial or someone we are close to suffers and then we can no longer ignore it. I propose there is a part of God that we can only experience when we walk with others in the midst of their adversity and suffering. God shows up in a unique way when we are willing to step in and sit with others in that place. In an odd way, this experience to feel secondhand suffering for another person, carries an unexpected blessing that is difficult to define, but understandable when we allow ourselves to fully experience it.

Imagine the amount of secondhand suffering our God experiences every day, watching the way His creation behaves with deep heartache. Because He loves us so much, He must weep daily as He grieves what could have been for us, this side of heaven. In fact, when the Father God watched His Son be whipped thirty-nine times, almost to death, and saw Him carry that cross to hang and then suffer a horrible death willingly, He experienced the ultimate case of secondhand suffering. Because of this, God identifies with us in our similar sufferings, and we can, in a small way, identify with His. In Jesus's case, He conquered death three days later with a full bodily resurrection, along with an offer of forgiveness and eternal life to anyone who wants it. There was purpose in His suffering. Jesus is the only one who overcame suffering.

Sometimes, we can't see the purpose in our suffering or the suffering of our loved ones. This mystery makes it tough. But while we may not see the purpose, and maybe there isn't one that makes sense in the actual suffering, we can remember that good can still stem from it—a powerful statement of hope:

> *"And we know that all things work together for good*
> *to those who love God, to those who are the called*
> *according to His purpose."*
> —ROMANS 8:28 (NKJV)

Life is messy and hard. I don't believe we ever "arrive" this side of heaven. The journey *is* the destination. While I don't necessarily like them, I am getting more comfortable with the conundrums, the mysteries, the heartaches, and the delayed happy endings. But not because they are getting any better or there is any less pain. Rather, being on a journey through this life with a living hope—Jesus, the Bridegroom—gives me strength, power, and a source of joy and hope amid the gritty day-to-day ups and downs of life.

At this stage in my life, I've walked a few long miles with God, from an ignorant little girl believing God is somewhere up there but unreachable to a good person trying to impress others with my goodness. From an agnostic with a lot of doubt to a curious but uptight seeker demanding answers. I've been a prideful "Bible Answer Girl" and an emotionally angry sufferer who needed to lay down my brain and pick up my heart. Now, I'm someone who walks with my heavenly Bridegroom, personally fueled by supernatural capacity, increased joy, and a living hope for today, not just for tomorrow. But that is not to imply it is a "happily ever after." I'm still in the thick of it. My guess is you are as well—with or without "living hope."

Without being Kevin's sister, I'm not sure what my life would be like today. Kevin has made me a more compassionate person, a deeper thinker, a fighter—for others and for what is right—a more authentic person with little tolerance for fake or shallow, and someone who never stops pursuing truth and tenaciously never lets go of hope. For me, there is only one thing that is sustainable throughout life, something well beyond religion, rules, or behaviorism, and that is an intimate connection with the living God.

While I have shared my progressive spiritual transformation, I realize you are on your own journey, and it probably looks very different than mine. Interestingly, I have found that the people who are the most passionate in their faith and overflowing with love are those who have been affected by some kind of suffering and humbled by a situation. I believe we are closest to God when we hit a point of surrender, a time when you reach the end of your rope when nothing is going right, when either you are suffering, or someone you love is suffering, and you can't fix it on your own.

I surmise that when we enter the deep space of empathetic pain and sit in it for longer than a minute, we are invited to enter a sacred realm akin to a Holy of Holies, of sorts—a place where we can tangibly sense the presence of God, His holiness, and His comforting love for us. Here, our hearts connect with His, and His Spirit intertwines with ours. In this space, our deepest cries mix with our purest form of love for another, and we find ourselves able to live in the space between heaven and earth, where the paradox of sadness and joy can coexist. How is this possible? With the guidance of God's Spirit within us, we can embrace this authentic tension. However, if we are only living in the natural world, without God's presence and love, it is likely not possible to tolerate these competing emotions for long.

When our hearts become tender and raw, and we come to the end of ourselves in humility and vulnerability, that is when we are most hungry for a supernatural presence, and we cry out for help to God—known or unknown. It is then that He often answers our cries. There really is no better salve for suffering than to know that you are loved with an everlasting love, you are seen by an all-powerful God, and you are not alone—Jesus is with you on life's adventure each step of the way if you choose.

And, instead of the Romper Room lady with the magic mirror who never saw me, I am satisfied with the Bridegroom's compassionate eyes staring into mine without the need for any stage prop mirror. He sees me. And He even knows my name. And He sees you as well. We are not invisible, nor are we alone. There is still hope. And it is worth the pursuit.

TOOLS FOR THE HEART

Lay down all the tools and surrender to God. Cling to Him who wants to walk with you through the heartbreak and allow the process of suffering to bring you to a place of deep intimacy and healing with your Creator, who loves you more than anyone on earth ever can. He is the living hope who never leaves you, and He always sees you. Find the joy and rest through, not despite, the suffering.

Questions to Ponder:

1. Do you dream? Have you ever had a dream about someone that seemed so real you believe it was a supernatural experience? What do you believe about the significance of dreams in your life?
2. If you were to describe where you are in your own spiritual journey, what phrase would you use? What "little fox" is blocking you from progressing in your spiritual transformation?
3. As you think about people's different responses to suffering, as observed by Victor Frankl in the death camps during the Holocaust, which one do you believe you would have if you had to endure that nightmare today? *(1. brutal and cruel; 2. give up all hope; 3. hang on to hope to get life restored as before; 4. inner strength kind of hope, knowing will probably still die)*
4. How does the concept of living at peace within the fusion of suffering and hope resonate with you? Do you believe it is possible? What is your hope—and living hope—based on?
5. Of all the "tools" for secondhand suffering mentioned in this memoir, which have been the most helpful to you in the past or present? And if you were writing a book on your story, what would your bag of tools look like? Have they been effective?
6. Have you experienced the unique depths of intimacy with God as a result of sitting with someone in their suffering and feeling their pain instead of blocking it?

Practical Steps:

- For perspective and wonderful insights into the intersection of hope and suffering, read *Man's Search for Meaning* by Viktor E. Frankl.
- Sit back and soak in the beauty of the song by Phil Wickham called *Living Hope* and meditate on the moving lyrics of the song *Quiet Places* by Jamie Platt.

- Read Song of Songs in the Bible and follow along with additional insights from one of these commentary books to enjoy and expand your understanding of the Bridegroom and Bride's intended relationship.

  ◊ *Song of Songs: Unveiling the Mystery of Passionate Intimacy with Christ* by Watchman Nee

  ◊ *The Divine Romance: 365 Days Meditating on the Song of Songs* (a devotional) by Brian Simmons and Gretchen Rodriguez

  ◊ *Song of Solomon* by C. H. Spurgeon

Final Reflections

When I began this book many years ago, it started out as simply a book about my life with my brother and some lessons I've learned. However, over the last ten years, my kids all flew the nest to other states, my mother died, friends suffered and died, my brother went through several potentially life-ending sicknesses, I re-entered the workforce, my oldest daughter got married and moved across the country, and the entire world stopped when we entered the twilight zone for several years after 2020 which were filled with suffocating lockdowns, nightmarish division among families, friends, and neighbors, and political unrest and several wars. When my brother came down with COVID and was sent to a hospital, I fought for his life by taking my advocacy skills to new heights with multiple doctors, moving up the ranks to the Chief Medical Officer, to obtain life-saving proven treatment which was being withheld from him during these confusing times. Additionally, due to overreaching governmental agencies, our family was denied the ability to see Kevin for over fourteen months.

For anyone who lived through those years with loved ones in a government-controlled institution, you know what I am talking about. My own secondhand suffering exceeded my endurance capacity during that time as nothing made sense, and my brother was forced to live through some of the worst suffering ever as he was alone, surrounded by scared (but kind) caregivers in hazmat suits without the ability to see smiles for three-plus years (and ticking). Many of you witnessed your loved ones not getting the medical care needed, your elderly not being allowed to have advocates and family with them in the hospitals, and a whole lot of upside-down protocols that ripped at people's hearts. Not to mention, too many people suffered and died alone. It seemed during those years that the whole world was not only suffering but experiencing the most intense secondhand suffering we've ever seen globally.

One of the consequences of all the lockdowns and Kevin not having family look in on him for his health was that he ended up having to go into hospice for serious pneumonia, where he required more oxygen than his institution was allowed to give for their license. In the months that followed, I battled day and night to get Kevin's health back in order as I continually tried to convince his team of Hospice nurses and doctors that my brother was not dying (he wasn't) so he could get off hospice to receive the services he needed. I was finally successful, and my brother and I grew closer than ever as we saw each other often. And from these battles for his life, his compassionate doctor was open to my plea for additional immune support care and to this day, we have added many additional therapies which are helping Kevin stay out of hospitals and remain as healthy as possible. There continue to be battles—some that are mere consequences of Kevin's body atrophying from lack of regular use physically and mentally and others that stem from the complexities that come from needing 24/7 care in a community facility.

Sadly, the public health government guidelines have continued to affect the disabled and elderly in our state years after the 2020 "new normal" began. Even after the official emergency ended, I'm still advocating for my brother's right to not be isolated when he is healthy, among other rights as outlined by the ADA (Americans for Disabilities Act). What I've learned is so many of these guidelines are up for interpretation as they are not laws; they are suggestions. However, when your loved one lives in an institution whose authority and very existence comes from government agencies like the state Department of Health, there is an understandable reluctance for these institutions or group homes to challenge these guidelines because if they don't comply, their funding and licenses could be at stake (which would hurt the vulnerable people who need to be cared for in these homes). This is one of the many reasons why everyone needs an advocate.

One final story illustrates a moment when I thought I was going to lose my brother. After Kevin returned from the hospital for G-tube-induced aspiration pneumonia, I was called to be with him in the middle of the night as I was told he might not make it. After driving on the empty freeway at 3:00 a.m. while crying my eyes out to God, I asked Him to spare his life, but also I surrendered his life to God if his time on earth was truly ending. Upon arriving at Kevin's bedside, it was dark as they tried to get him to sleep. I held his hand and played some soft worship music, prepared for the worst. Feeling exhausted and hoping he was asleep after several hours, I clicked on my phone light to make sure he was sleeping so I could tiptoe away to get some sleep myself. To my surprise, Kevin was staring right at me with wide open glimmering eyes and a big giggle/smile/smirk on his face, which loudly spoke, *"Sister, I'm not dying yet."* He made me laugh as I realized he was laughing at all of us around his side, thinking he was on his deathbed. The joy of the Lord is my brother's strength. Another small miracle!

The two trains running parallel in my life, but at different speeds, have been lessons learned from growing up with a quadriplegic brother and personal spiritual growth. As this memoir progressed, it became difficult to separate them. For most of my life, I have only seen the messy, knotted, and random side of my life's tapestry. Feeling someone else's pain, fighting for them, and dealing with grief, guilt, and anger on a chronic basis is not pretty. Yet every once in a while, I try to turn over the tapestry to see the art that has formed due to these messy tied knots of diverse challenges and how they are being woven together for good—for me and hopefully for you through these writings.

I've come to believe that when we press into the depths of our pain that we cannot fix and hit a wall, there really is no place else to go except face to face with God. Unless we choose despair, which is a dead end. It is when we hit that wall that we have a choice—by crying out to God in surrender, we may discover the wall can become a door that opens for us to go places only possible with the God of the Universe as our escort. Places like new mindsets, fresh energy, solutions we had not thought of before, small and large miracles, a new perspective, and a supernatural joy that becomes our strength.

More than anything, the door leads us to a new heart, one that:

. . . lives content within the tension of unmet
expectations and inner peace.

. . . surrenders control when there is nothing left to do
but cry out to an almighty God.

. . . finds new perspectives when feeling disappointment.

. . . believes in one's inner voice and becomes a voice for others.

. . . decides to no longer waste energy with unhealthy emotions like guilt and fear.

. . . accepts blessings without guilt because they are non-transferable and meant to be enjoyed.

. . . discerns which voices to listen to and tunes out the rest.

. . . allows oneself to feel deep love and pain for another and find a deep connection to the heart of God as a result.

. . . is open and vulnerable.

. . . admits a need for people and seeks out and engages in real community.

. . . is humble enough to pray to God.

. . . pursues truth and discovers hidden treasures.

. . . walks through the pain to the other side, finding silver linings along the way.

. . . is honest with oneself and others, laying down any pretense.

. . . seeks one's purpose out of pain.

. . . doesn't stuff anger or resentment but faces it head on, eventually discovering a path to inner joy.

. . . reframes timeworn cliches and grows them into deeper nuggets of wisdom to live by.

. . . embraces the powerful motif of "search and find" and learns to enjoy the wonder of the pursuit.

. . . sits with others in their pain, increasing one's capacity to love.

. . . learns the joy of receiving as well as giving.

. . . is no longer afraid to conquer some giants to live in one's destiny.

. . . is brave enough to live outside the cage of conformity and seek the all-powerful Spirit of God.

. . . cares enough about oneself to get healthy by transforming one's mind with right thinking.

. . . finds God, only to realize He has been there all along.

. . . is hungry for emotional and spiritual wholeness and goes after it.

. . . can still bloom at the point where the greatest pain and the greatest joy coexist.

. . . recognizes one's greatest hope is not only "someday" but also now.

So, when we hit those insurmountable walls and come to the end of ourselves, consider that God can transform the wall into a doorway. Much like Lucy's journey in The Lion, the Witch and the Wardrobe, where she stumbles upon a wardrobe against a wall and enters a supernatural kingdom where Aslan lives and engages with her, let's remain vigilant to look for walls that become doors that grant us passage to a hidden world of possibilities as we engage with a surrendered heart and an ongoing hope for a breakthrough. The walls exist. But in the invisible realm, so do the doors. So, when we feel stuck, we must press through the seemingly impenetrable wall that can transform into a door with our steps of faith and perseverance. The adventure through, not around, the hardship is a path to growth and unexpected peace. The journey begins and ends with the heart.

While I still, and will continue to, experience secondhand suffering for not only my brother but others, I have learned to find the hidden gems, the silver linings, the pearls that come from abrasive trials, the smiles from a hurting body . . . and even the small miracles. The fact that my brother, who is locked in a body that traps him from experiencing life as most of us know it, can still smile and laugh and find joy in the small stuff of life is my reminder that there is more to suffering than meets the surface. *Suffering itself is a tool that can open our hearts and minds to deeper realms of truth and intimacy with ourselves, others, and, if we choose, our Creator.*

For the "Kevins" in your life, I pray that they will be catalysts for you also to ask, question, wrestle, seek, learn, grow, and find ultimate comfort, hope, and joy—and some small miracles thrown in—amid that ever-persistent ache in your soul. It is in this pursuit that I believe you will discover the depths of intimacy with the Creator that surpasses understanding. Whether or not we see a miracle for our loved one, we will benefit from stilling our souls and resting to know that God is with us, He truly loves us, He sees us, He hears us, and ultimately, He will make all things right again, whether on earth or in heaven. A friend asked me recently if I believe in big miracles of healing for people like my brother and your loved ones. The short answer is that I do. I believe God still heals people today; however, I also know sometimes full-blown healing doesn't come in our lifetime. For now, I am grateful for the numerous smaller miracles I have seen and for starting to see the gold being mined in my life out of my perseverance as my brother's sister and advocate.

> "But He knows the way that I take;
> when He has tried me, I shall come out as gold."
>
> —Job 23:10

Perhaps, through your own secondhand suffering, you may stumble onto your God-given purpose that flows out of your pain as your heart and mind find healing and hope this side of heaven. I pray you discover beauty out of ashes, joy out of sorrow, purpose out of hardship, doorways out of walls, and a revived heart full of hope for today and all your tomorrows.

> "When you can't get a miracle, you can still
> be a miracle for someone else."
>
> —Nick Vujicic

About The Author

Camille Block was raised in a suburb outside of Los Angeles, across the canyon from beautiful Malibu, where her father worked as a college professor of business at Pepperdine University. At three and a half years old, Camille's comfortable life took a dramatic turn with the birth of her brother—a healthy baby who lost oxygen at birth, causing a lifelong disability for him and a character-forming emotional imprint on her.

Camille progressed through her "normal" life with a dull, empathetic ache in her soul for her brother, who was living a very different life than she. Setting out to slay the religious pat answers of well-meaning people and challenge the vacuous worldly musings that left her unsatisfied, she has spent her life on a journey diving beneath the surface, seeking an antidote for her invisible suffering spurred on by her brother's plight.

Finding a voice for her brother, Camille has also uncovered her voice for many other silent sufferers. *Hope for Secondhand Suffering: Tools for the Heart When You Can't Fix Your Loved One's Pain* is a memoir and spiritual journey of a sister who wrestles honestly with universal cries of the heart, such as the question of why, along with grief, justice, faith, God, and hope. She comes alongside readers, step by step, offering personal anecdotes, honest insights, practical tips, and her own spiritual reflections to help others facing similar struggles.

Through the publication of **Hope for Secondhand Suffering,** Camille seeks to help silent sufferers feel seen, heard, and known—equipping them to find their unique purpose, as she continues to find hers.

Previous publications include Camille's debut article in Grown & Flown, My Daughter is Now a Wife, and This Goodbye is the Hardest, and several articles written for the LinkedIn business community related to career transitions.

1. Holding a Bachelor of Arts degree in social science with a business management minor from Pepperdine University, Camille has had a full career in business, marriage, and motherhood. As empty nesters with adult children – Madeline (married to Ingram), Abigail and Oliver – she is married to her husband Jonathan of 34+ years and runs her own small business as a career coach. She also dedicates significant time to advocating for her special needs brother and in her free time, enjoys exploring new hobbies like gardening and beekeeping.

Introduction

1. "Secondhand Smoke," Google.com, Oxford American College Dictionary, January 8, 2024.

Chapter One

2. Olivia Guy-Evans MSc, reviewed by Saul Mcleod, PhD, "Motor Cortex: Function and Location," SimplePsychology.com, September 21, 2023, https://www.simplypsychology.org/motor-cortex.html.
3. "Cerebral Palsy," Centers for Disease Control and Prevention, October 6, 2023, http://www.cdc.gov/ncbddd/cp/facts.html.
4. Ibid.
5. "Cognitive dissonance," Merriam-Webster's Dictionary, https://www.merriam-webster.com/dictionary/cognitive%20dissonance.
6. Reinhold Neibuhr, 1892–1971, "Lords-Prayer-Words.com: Traditional and Contemporary Prayers," https://www.lords-prayer-words.com/famous_prayers/god_grant_me_the_serenity.html.
7. Karl Marx, Goodreads.com, https://www.goodreads.com/quotes/7962423-religion-is-the-opiate-of-the-masses.

Chapter Two

8. Dan Silvestri, "Lessons from *Blink: The Power of Thinking Without Thinking* by Malcolm Gladwell," a book review published in The Startup, August 2, 2018, Medium.com, https://medium.com/swlh/lessons-from-blink-the-power-of-thinking-without-thinking-by-malcolm-gladwell-ac03aa343eee.
9. https://quotefancy.com/quote/1420107/W-Eugene-Smith-I-try-to-take-what-voice-I-have-and-I-give-it-to-those-who-don-t-have-one.
10. "Advocate," Merriam-Webster Dictionary, https://www.merriam-webster.com/dictionary/advocate.
11. A.J. Turner, "Are You Putting God in a Box?" New Spring Church, https://newspring.cc/articles/are-you-putting-god-in-a-box.

Chapter Three

12. Melonie Janet Mangum, *Until I See: Peaceful Paths to Parenting Children with Special Needs* (CreateSpace, December 1, 2015), 61–62.
13. Jeanne Safer, Ph.D., *The Normal One: Life with a Difficult or Damaged Sibling* (New York City: Bantam Dell Publishing, 2002), 204.
14. American Psychiatric Association. *Diagnostic and Statistical Manual of Mental Disorders.* 5th ed. Washington D.C.: 2013.
15. Kate Strohm, *Being the Other One: Growing Up with a Brother or Sister Who Has Special Needs* (Boston, MA: Shambhala Publications, 2002), 12–13.

16. Dallas Willard, *Hearing God: Developing a Conversational Relationship with God* (Downers Grove, IL: InterVarsity Press, 2012), 230–31.
17. Hidden Manna Ministry, *Prayer Boot Camp: Preparation for the Battle of Your Life* (Laurel Park, WV: Whitestone Publishing, 2011), 61.
18. Catherine Ducharme, "Getting Out of Our Own Way," Fluency.com, March 15, 2021, https://www.fluencyleadership.com/2021/03/15/getting-out-of-our-own-way/.
19. Olan Stubbs, "The Devil Cannot Condemn You: How to Kill Accusations with Conviction," DesiringGod.com, May 10, 2018, https://www.desiringgod.org/articles/the-devil-cannot-condemn-you.

Chapter Four

20. "Empathy," Merriam-Webster.com, https://www.merriam-webster.com/dictionary/empathy.
21. "What does the Bible say about empathy?" Gotquestions.org, https://www.gotquestions.org/Bible-empathy.html.
22. "Can you teach people to have empathy?" BBC.com, June 29, 2015, https://www.bbc.com/news/magazine-33287727.
23. Bruna Martinuzzi, "What's Empathy Got to Do With It?" 2009, MindTools.com, https://www.mindtools.com/ax2le82/whats-empathy-got-to-do-with-it.
24. Dr. Antonio Damasio, *Descartes Error: Emotion, Reason, and the Human Brain* (New York City, NY: Penguin Books, 2005*),* Bruna Martinuzzi, "What's Empathy Got to Do With It?" 2009, MindTools.com, https://www.mindtools.com/ax2le82/whats-empathy-got-to-do-with-it.
25. Daniel Goleman, *Emotional Intelligence: Why It Can Matter More Than IQ* (New York City, NY: Bantam Books, 2005), "The Meaning of Emotional Intelligence," Last Eight Percent powered by IHHP.com, https://www.ihhp.com/meaning-of-emotional-intelligence/.
26. Daniel Goleman, *Working with Emotional Intelligence* (New York City, NY: Bantam Books, 2000), "The Meaning of Emotional Intelligence," Last Eight Percent powered by IHHP.com, https://www.ihhp.com/meaning-of-emotional-intelligence/.

Chapter Five

27. Tracy Brower, Ph.D., "How To Build Community and Why It Matters So Much," Forbes, Oct 25, 2020, https://www.forbes.com/sites/tracybrower/2020/10/25/how-to-build-community-and-why-it-matters-so-much/?sh=54e35f3d751b.
28. Words and music by Kevin Ray Lawson. Copyright 1995. Cedarstone Music BMI (admin Music Services Inc.). Lyrics printed by permission. All rights reserved.

Chapter Six

29. "The Road Not Taken," Robert Frost Selected Poems, Fall River Press, 2011, 25.

30. Czarina Ong, "Evangelist Beth Moore Says True Peace Comes in Situations That Are Completely Surrendered to Christ," Christiantoday. com, June 4, 2016, https://www.christiantoday.com/article/evangelist-beth-moore-says-true-peace-comes-in-situations-that-are-completely-surrendered-to-christ/87492.htm.

Chapter Seven

31. Brad Cummings, producer of the major motion picture, "The Shack" (Lionsgate 2017).

32. Ibid.

Chapter Eight

33. *Andrew Boyd, Daily Afflictions: The Agony of Being Connected to Everything in the Universe* https://www.goodreads.com/work/quotes/503504-daily-afflictions-the-agony-of-being-connected-to-everything-in-the-uni .

34. Emmy Griffiths, "Ashton Kutcher Becomes Emotional Talking About His Twin Brother," HelloMagazine.com, April 10, 2017, https://www.hellomagazine.com/celebrities/2017041038029/ashton-kutcher-becomes-emotional-talking-about-his-twin-brother/.

35. Walter Wangerin Jr., *Reliving the Passion: Meditations on the Suffering, Death, and the Resurrection of Jesus as Recorded in Mark,* https://www.goodreads.com/work/quotes/137824-reliving-the-passion.

36. Jean-Dominique Bauby, "My Mind Takes a Flight: extract from The Diving Bell and the Butterfly," The Guardian, January 27, 2008, published by Harper Perennial, https://www.theguardian.com/film/2008/jan/27/features.review4.

37. Jean-Dominique Bauby, "My Mind Takes a Flight: extract from The Diving Bell and the Butterfly," The Guardian, January 27, 2008, published by Harper Perennial, https://www.theguardian.com/film/2008/jan/27/features.review4.

38. Elisabeth Kübler-Ross, Goodreads.com, https://www.goodreads.com/quotes/202404-the-most-beautiful-people-we-have-known-are-those-who.

39. Fred Rogers, *The World According to Mr. Rogers: Important Things to Remember* (New York, NY: Hachette Books, 2003); https://www.goodreads.com/quotes/319182-part-of-the-problem-with-the-word-disabilities-is-that.

40. "Nick Vujicic in China: What Kind of Joy Do You Have?" https://www.

youtube.com/watch?v=s5WlD0PMYt0.

41. Joni Erickson Tada, *A Place of Healing: Wrestling with the Mysteries of Suffering, Pain, and God's Sovereignty* (Colorado Springs: David C. Cook, 2010); https://bibleportal.com/author/joni-eareckson-tada/book/a-place-of-healing-wrestling-with-the-mysteries-of-suffering-pain-and-god-s-sovereignty.

42. Elizabeth Elliott, *Something Is Never for Nothing* (Nashville: B&H Publishing, 2019); https://www.goodreads.com/work/quotes/62941041-suffering-is-never-for-nothing.

Chapter Ten

43. Tristen Inagaki, Ph.D., University of Pittsburgh and Naomi Eisenberger, Ph.D., University of California, Los Angeles, *"The Neurobiology of Giving Versus Receiving Support: The Role of Stress-Related and Social Reward-Related Neural Activity," Psychosomatic Medicine: Journal of Biobehavioral Medicine (February 2016).*

44. Christopher Bergland, "3 Specific Ways That Helping Others Benefits Your Brain," The Athlete's Way, February 21, 2016, https://www.psychologytoday.com/blog/the-athletes-way/201602/3-specific-ways-helping-others-benefits-your-brain.

45. Britt Mooney, "What Is the Land of Milk and Honey?" Christianity.com, July 10, 2023, https://www.christianity.com/wiki/bible/what-is-the-land-of-milk-and-honey.html.

46. "Sozo," Strong's Concordance G4982, Knowing Jesus, https://bible.knowing-jesus.com/strongs/G4982.

47. Reggie Mercado, *The Wildlife: Our Supernatural Journey with Jesus* (2020), 45–46.

Chapter Eleven

48. Maya Angelou, "Caged Bird," *The Complete Collected Poems* (New York City: Random House Publishing, 1994).

49. Reggie Mercado, *The Wildlife: Our Supernatural Journey with Jesus*, 97.

50. "Mindfulness," Dictionary.com, https://www.dictionary.com/browse/mindfulness.

51. Kendra Cherry, MSEd, "What Is Neuroplasticity?" VeryWellMind.com, November 8, 2022, https://www.verywellmind.com/what-is-brain-plasticity-2794886.

52. Ibid.

53. Dr. Caroline Leaf, "You Are Not a Victim of Your Biology!" DrLeaf.com, October 3, 2018, https://drleaf.com/blogs/news/you-are-not-a-victim-of-your-biology.

54. Ibid.

55. Daniel J. Siegel, M.D., "How You Can Change Your Brain," Psychalive.org, https://www.psychalive.org/how-you-can-change-your-brain/.
56. Ibid.
57. Daniel J. Siegel, M.D., *Aware: The Science and Practice of Presence* (New York: TarcherPerigree, 2018).
58. Daniel J. Siegel, M.D., "How You Can Change Your Brain," Psychalive.org, https://www.psychalive.org/how-you-can-change-your-brain/.

Chapter Twelve
59. Heaven by Randy Alcorn, pages 250–51, https://www.amazon.com/ Heaven-Randy-Alcorn/dp/0842379428/ref=sr_1_2?crid=TIRU7V1CY0ZI& keywords=heaven+by+randy+alcorn&qid=1698982111&sprefix=heaven +by+rand%2Caps%2C196&sr=8-2.
60. See 2 Corinthians 1:22, 5:5; Ephesians 1:14; 2 Timothy 1:14.
61. Rebecca Springer, *Within Heaven's Gates* (New Kensington, PA: Whitaker House, 1984), 59.
62. Written by: MATTHEW WEST, BERNIE HERMS, RANDY PHILLIPS Lyrics © Universal Music Publishing Group, Kobalt Music Publishing Ltd., Warner Chappell Music, Inc. Lyrics Licensed & Provided by LyricFind Sung by Danny Gokey.
63. Eric Carle, *The Very Hungry Caterpillar* (New York: Penguin Random House, 1987).
64. Norbert Juma, "215 Butterfly Quotes Honoring Your Own Metamorphosis," Everydaypower.com, April 8, 2023, https:// everydaypower.com/butterfly-quotes/.

Chapter Thirteen
65. Victor E. Frankl, *Man's Search for Meaning* (Boston, MA: Beacon Hill, 2006).
66. Phil McGraw, "A mother is only as happy as her saddest child," AZquotes. com, https://www.azquotes.com/quote/1418022.
67. "Living Hope," Timothy Keller Sermon Jam, YouTube.com, July 6, 2019.
68. For more information about Kristen, visit kristencummins.com.

Printed in the USA
CPSIA information can be obtained
at www.ICGtesting.com
JSHW011700120724
66112JS00007B/22